POSTCOLONIAL
ECONOMIES

About the editors

Jane Pollard is a Senior Lecturer in the Centre for Urban and Regional Development Studies at Newcastle University. Her research interests embrace geographies of money and finance and their intersection with regional economic development. She is a co-editor of *Knowledge, Space, Economy* (2000) and has published extensively in, among other journals, *Antipode*, *Journal of Economic Geography*, *Environment and Planning A*, *Geoforum* and *Transactions of the Institute of British Geographers*.

Cheryl McEwan is Reader in the Geography Department at Durham University. Her research interests lie at the intersections between development, cultural and political geographies and draw primarily on postcolonial and feminist theories. She is author of *Postcolonialism and Development* (2009) and *Geography, Gender and Imperialism* (2000), co-editor of *Postcolonial Geographies* (2002), and has published extensively in such journals as *Society and Space*, *Political Geography*, *Transactions of the Institute of British Geographers*, *Cultural Geographies* and *Geoforum*.

Alex Hughes is a Senior Lecturer in Geography at Newcastle University. Her research interests include cultural political economy, global commodity chains and networks, transnational retailers and corporate responsibility, and ethical trade and business responsibility. She is a co-editor of *Geographies of Commodity Chains* (2004) and has published in a range of journals, including *Environment and Planning A*, *Journal of Economic Geography*, *Transactions of the Institute of British Geographers* and *Geoforum*.

POSTCOLONIAL ECONOMIES

Edited by

Jane Pollard, Cheryl McEwan and Alex Hughes

Zed Books

LONDON & NEW YORK

Postcolonial Economies was first published in 2011 by
Zed Books Ltd, 7 Cynthia Street, London N1 9JF, UK
and Room 400, 175 Fifth Avenue, New York, NY 10010, USA

www.zedbooks.co.uk

Editorial Copyright © Jane Pollard, Cheryl McEwan and
Alex Hughes 2011
Copyright in this collection © Zed Books 2011

The rights of Jane Pollard, Cheryl McEwan and Alex Hughes to be
identified as the editors of this work have been asserted by them in
accordance with the Copyright, Designs and Patents Act, 1988

Typeset by Pindar NZ Ltd
Index: Rohan Bolton, Rohan.Indexing@gmail.com
Cover designed by Rogue Four Design
Front cover image © Sebastian Forsyth/Alamy
Printed and bound in Great Britain by CPI
Antony Rowe, Chippenham and Eastbourne

Distributed in the USA exclusively by Palgrave Macmillan, a division of
St Martin's Press, LLC, 175 Fifth Avenue, New York, NY 10010, USA

A catalogue record for this book is available from the British Library
Library of Congress Cataloging in Publication Data available

ISBN 978 1 84813 405 8 hb
ISBN 978 1 84813 404 1 pb

Contents

Contents

Acknowledgements

This book has its roots in an ESRC seminar series and we owe a debt of gratitude to several groups of people. First, we would like to thank our co-organisers of the seminar series, Uma Kothari, Nina Laurie and Alison Stenning. Second, thanks are due to all our participants who helped produce such a stimulating series of seminars and ongoing conversations: Sarah Bracking, Gavin Brown, Dipesh Chakrabarty, S. Charusheela, Katharine Gibson, Olivia Harris, Nitasha Kaul, Wendy Larner, Nina Laurie, Roger Lee, Cathy McIlwaine, Timothy Mitchell, Ruth Pearson, Meena Poudel, Saraswati Raju, Diane Richardson, Tomo Suzuki, Christine Sylvester and Rorden Wilkinson. Finally, thanks go to all the support staff at Manchester, Durham and Newcastle (and most especially Sue Robson) who helped to organise the seminars and made sure they ran smoothly.

Introduction: postcolonial economies

Jane Pollard, Cheryl McEwan and Alex Hughes

Introduction

Postcolonial approaches to understanding economies are of increasing academic and political significance as questions about the nature of neoliberalism, globalisation, transnational flows of capital and workers and the making and re-making of territorial borders assume centre stage in debates about contemporary economies and policy. Despite the growing academic and political urgency in understanding how 'other' cultures encounter 'the West', economics-oriented and political-economic approaches within social sciences (e.g. Development Economics, Economic Geography and the discipline of Economics itself) have been relatively slow to engage with the ideas and challenges posed by postcolonial critiques. In turn, postcolonial approaches have been criticised for their marginalisation of 'the economic' and for not engaging with existing economic analyses of poverty and wealth creation. This book aims to break new ground in providing a space for nascent debates about postcolonialism and its treatment of 'the economic' and brings together scholars in a range of disciplines that include Development Studies, Economics, Geography, History, Law and Women's Studies.

The chapters that follow take 'postcolonial' to refer to a political, anti-colonial sensibility and a suite of theoretical approaches that seek to disrupt and contest hegemonic Western ways of knowing, writing and seeing the world. Timothy Mitchell observed (2002: 3) that the idea of 'economy' has remained curiously unexplored by social scientists in contrast with other categories like class, gender, nation and culture. Yet, there is now a growing interest in the genealogy of the discipline of Economics (McCloskey 1998; Mitchell 1998, 2002; Mirowski 2002; Zein-Elabdin and Charusheela 2004). More recently, the US–UK centred subprime crisis, which morphed into an international sovereign debt crisis, has provided more fuel for (long-standing) critiques of the preferences of orthodox Economics for ever more sophisticated modelling of perfect, efficient, frictionless market systems as opposed to analysis intent on understanding the messy geographical unevenness of capitalism and the variegated material, social and political consequences of this most recent crisis. Heterodox scholars are now starting to explore how postcolonial theory may inform Keynesian, institutionalist, feminist and Marxian economic traditions (Kayatekin 2009) and, while much has been made of the mutual antipathy between postcolonial approaches and economic theory, these chapters illustrate some of the empirical, theoretical and political work underway by scholars – in a variety of contexts – looking for productive possibilities at the intersections of the postcolonial and the economic.

The book has its origin in an Economic and Social Research Council (ESRC)-funded seminar series on Postcolonial Economies, which ran from January 2006 to October 2007.[1] The seminar series stimulated interdisciplinary debate and knowledge sharing around postcolonial critiques of 'the economic' by facilitating discussion of the genealogies and geographies of economic knowledges in academic and policy debates, of how, and on what terms, postcolonial approaches and economic theory might enrich each other, and of what postcolonial economic understandings might look like in terms of policy and pedagogy. The book is designed to make two main contributions. First, the volume brings together, for the first time, dispersed social science researchers who are

---

1 The seminar was organised by Alex Hughes, Uma Kothari, Nina Laurie, Cheryl McEwan, Jane Pollard and Alison Stenning.

building cross-disciplinary dialogue about postcolonialism and its treatment of 'the economic' as a means to explore the uneven material and social realities of capitalism. Second, the chapters that follow seek to critique and enrich contemporary efforts to re-think economy, which tend to be rooted, empirically and theoretically, in Western-centred conceptions of what constitutes 'diverse' or 'alternative' economic practices (Gibson-Graham 1996, 2006).

The volume is designed to open up dialogue and debate between scholars writing from different disciplinary and theoretical positions, rather than to posit a coherent theoretical benchmarking statement about what postcolonial treatments of the economic should look like. Thus, the chapters signal some of the heterogeneity of postcolonial approaches, reflecting their growth in tandem with other 'isms' that have, in different ways, sought to re-vision economies (Pollard *et al.* 2009). The chapters focus on a range of social science understandings of 'the economic' that engage in broad terms with postcolonial critiques and are often influenced by post-structuralist and other heterodox approaches to economy. For all their diversity, however, these chapters have a number of elements in common as they re-think 'the economic'.

First, in different ways, the chapters contribute to theorising 'the economic' as plural, contested, and above all, situated. These chapters are all conscious of the whereness, the historical geographies of their knowledges and, specifically, the relationship between the production of Western knowledge and the exercise of Western power that often marginalises geographic, linguistic and cultural 'others'. In addition to challenging such representations and acknowledging that the 'mainstream' of economic theorising emerges from the experiences of 'successful' or 'deindustrialised' Anglo-American regions (and the geographic and institutional context of such theory is rarely specified or critiqued, see Yeung and Lin 2003), these chapters also start to work through some of the implications of their situatedness and to explore how such a recognition might encourage scholars to think in new ways about their discipline in general, and research on the economy in particular. In different ways, the chapters challenge existing intellectual and disciplinary practices that separate social scientists researching economic issues in 'the Global South' and post-socialist contexts from those researching similar issues in 'Western' capitalist economies.

Second, the chapters advance debates about the interplay between culture and economy. 'Cultural economy' is a term used to reflect how culture (concerning identities and life-worlds) and economy (concerning resource production, allocation and distribution) are intertwined. It refers to 'the processes of social and cultural relations that go to make up what we conventionally term the economic' (Amin and Thrift 2003: xviii), paying particular attention to process and practice, and to the embeddedness of social and cultural practices in particular sites. The chapters in this book not only challenge the ontological separation of culture and economy and move away from a super-structural notion of culture (as others have done), but also respond to the call made by Amin and Thrift (2003: xxi) to explore '. . . indigenous knowledges, non-Western moral orders . . . and alternative modernities' in the dynamics of cultural economy, by foregrounding the relevance of postcolonial approaches and understandings of economy from the Global South.

Third, in advancing this agenda, a number of these chapters also confront some of the methodological challenges posed by postcolonial approaches that seek to find ways of moving beyond universalising economic knowledges. In so doing, they encourage us to reconsider the analytical resources we use to conduct research on the economy. Some of the chapters incorporate ways of knowing the economy that include biography, autobiography, literature and other personal/inter-personal accounts and that contrast with aggregate, quantitative data and a priori categories. They use such techniques to explore how a whole range of economic entities and movements – markets, intermediaries, biopolitical governance, legal interpretations and workers – are produced in specific forms and contexts.

Engagements: postcolonial theory and economic theory

Interrogating the relationship between postcolonial theory and economic theory is, of course, nothing new. However, this relationship is often presented as one of mutual antipathy, tension and/or neglect. In dismissing the universalist assumptions of political economy, postcolonial theory has been accused of ignoring the material ways in which colonial power relations persist (Ahmad 1992; Dirlik 1994, Hardt and Negri 2000) and neglecting urgent life-or-death questions (San Juan 1998). Some of the fiercest criticism has been reserved for the ironic way in which an alleged neglect of economy by postcolonial theory has solidified a fundamental schism between Western theorising and the practical needs of impoverished people globally (McEwan 2003). It is also accused as offering 'no means for challenging the economic system' (Sayer 2001: 688). As one critic put it:

> The sanctioned occlusions in postcolonial criticism are a debilitating loss to thinking about colonialism and late imperialism. This dismissal of politics and economics which these omissions reflect is a scandal.
>
> (Parry 2002: 78)

Much of this criticism has, of course, arisen from a debate between postcolonial and Marxist theorists. This is also quite ironic because without Marxism some of the most influential ideas that postcolonial theory has produced, from Fanon to Spivak, would be much poorer (McEwan 2003). Yet some Marxist scholars accuse postcolonial theory of being complicit with capitalism. However, as Ismail (2005: xxxiv) argues, this kind of thinking 'criticises an idea not on its own terms but by talking about economics, of class'. In other words, postcolonial theory as it emerged in the 1980s did not set out to theorise economics or class and should not, therefore, be criticised for failing to do so. Ismail characterises such criticism as a defensive reaction from a conservative, dogmatic left whose empiricist, historicist understandings of the social and the economic were, and are, threatened in a fundamental way by postcolonialism's attack on the epistemological dominance of Western theory. And even within Marxism, there has been criticism of what has been seen as a personalised quarrel, rather than an intellectual one. Lazarus (1993, 1999), for example, while being critical of postcolonial approaches to the issue of nationalism, performs an intellectual engagement with its theories and dismisses what he sees as an anti-intellectual rejection by other Marxist thinkers.

According to Parry (2002), what Marxist critics such as Ahmad, Dirlik and San Juan actually achieve is a much more rigorous engagement of postcolonialism with the legacy of Marxism. However, while it has not been the express intention of all that is now referred to as postcolonial theory to engage directly with Marxism on questions of economy, to suggest that postcolonial theorists neglect economy and, in particular, theories of capital is inaccurate. Indeed, several postcolonial theorists, such as Spivak, Said and Chakrabarty, have consistently argued for a postcolonial criticism that is worldly and attuned to both discursive and material concerns. As Rattansi (1997: 497) argues:

> [I]t is simply untrue to say that global capitalism has been ignored in postcolonial research, although . . . what postcolonial studies has been about is finding non-reductionist ways of relating global capitalism to the cultural politics of colonialism.

A great deal of postcolonial theory has been engaged with exploring the constitutive relation between imperialism, colonialism and global capitalism (see, for example, Spivak 1987; Said, 1993; Chatterjee 1996; Miyoshi 1997). Much of Spivak's work has been concerned with exploring connections between the micro-spaces of knowledge production and the macro-spaces of the global economy/international division of labour, and several of her most influential writings have engaged directly with Marxism (Spivak 1985, 1990, 2000). Her reflections on the question of value, for example, attempt to reveal the perceived disconnect between economic and cultural questions and to stress the dialectical link between the two. Similarly, Chakrabarty (2000) interrogates the consequences of theorising from within the epistemic space of capital. He contrasts writing within the space of History 1, which reproduces the universal history and logic of capital (2000: 63–4), with revealing the presence of History 2s. The latter are the multiple possibilities that exist under and/or in proximity to the logic of capital, but 'do not belong to the "life process" of capital' (2000: 64). This allows Chakrabarty to theorise the human bearer of labour as something other than the use value of capitalism (Gidwani 2008: 217). Another example is provided by Ashcroft's (2001) analysis of the impact of tropical sugar production for

Caribbean societies and cultures, in which he demonstrates the link between the material and the discursive in processes of postcolonial transformation.

Chakrabarty's critique of the ways in which particular, Western conceptions of economy become universalised is also instructive of the ways in which the significance of culture is erased in certain contexts and emphasised in others. This is evident, for example, in understanding how neoliberalism remains hegemonic within global economic governance, crowding out alternative models of economic development despite the fact that these have often been more successful than neoliberal models in other parts of the world. The strongly Confucian model (based on a notion of human morality and good deeds) adopted in South Korea, for example, saw it become one of the rapidly industrialising Asian 'tigers' during the 1960s. The United Nations Development Programme (1996) held up South Korea as one of the few countries to have developed in an equitable manner, maintaining the most equitable income distribution of any economy in the world. However, while the model might be of interest to economists, it is accorded little relevance beyond the South East Asian context since it is seen as fundamentally rooted in Korean culture. Thus, while neoliberalism travels because it is depicted as universal, despite being rooted in Western cultural values, the Korean model remains a localised, particularised model for success. The universalising of particular, Western models of economic development perpetuates the notion that there is little to learn from Korea, or alternatives elsewhere, because its economic progress is inherently tied into its cultural values. Provincialising Europe (Chakrabarty 2000) thus becomes an important political project in challenging the hegemony of Western economical theorising by revealing its cultural rootedness and opening up space for alternative notions of economy.

These examples illustrate that the alleged neglect by postcolonial theorists of economy is exaggerated, as is the failure of postcolonial theory to engage with critiques of capitalism. As Yeoh (2001: 462–3; Hall 1996; Slater 1998) suggests, the task of interrogating the relationship between postcolonialism and global capitalism is a crucial one that 'requires a more critical and simultaneous engagement with both registers'. This is not to argue, however, that postcolonial theory and its treatment of economic issues are uncontested, fully developed or unproblematised in the former colonial world. There has long been a fractious relationship, for example, between postcolonial studies and Latin American studies. Leftist theorists in Latin America claim that postcolonial studies is old news, yet the postcolonial theory that emerged with Subaltern Studies and Edward Said in the 1980s ignores this and equates 'postcoloniality' with West or South Asia. In other words, postcolonial theory is situated, but often refuses to recognise itself as such. As the work of Enrique Dussel, Fernando Coronil and Arturo Escobar, among others, testifies, there is a long history of theorising back from Latin American contexts, specifically in relation to dependency theory, unequal development, disarticulation, post-development; in essence, the critique of colonialism and capitalist development in general. Many would claim that this produced something akin to postcolonial theory *avant la lettre* in Latin America. Indeed, it could be argued that Latin America has at various historical junctures been part of a global network of anti-capitalist and anti-colonial theorising (see Young's (2001) arguments on the Tricontinental, for example), which goes unacknowledged by many contemporary postcolonial theorists. It is, therefore, important to recognise Latin American economic theory as part of postcolonial responses to hegemonic theorising and to translate its lessons by conceptualising postcoloniality as a problem of political economy.

A further criticism that might be made of the engagement between postcolonialism and economic theory is that the scattered speculations have not coalesced into a coherent body of critique. As Zein-Elabdin and Charusheela (2004) argue, 'theorizing the economy continues to be a point of weakness in much postcolonial scholarship'. They suggest, echoing Spivak that the structure of disciplinarity that currently governs the production of academic knowledge is the biggest obstacle to an engagement of postcolonial and economic discourses. In addition, they also suggest that there has been a silence or reluctance within postcolonial scholarship to open up and deconstruct given economic categories such as 'capital' or the 'international division of labour', preferring instead to fall back on dependency frameworks or world systems theories.

Even Spivak, for example, while deconstructing certain economic concepts (see Castree, 1997 on Spivak's critique of value theory), fails to deconstruct the concept of the international division of labour. Thus the impressive creativity and sophistication in the area of cultural analysis that postcolonial critique demonstrates has still not permeated its treatment of economy; 'terms such as underdevelopment and neo-colonialism are in current usage even as their theoretical origins implicate them in a teleology and determinism highly incongruous with postcolonial critiques of modernity' (Zein-Elabdin and Charusheela 2004: 5). However, more recently, there have been some significant advances in this area of critique.

One particularly fertile area of recent engagement between postcolonial approaches and broader questions of economy, which in some cases does work towards rethinking the constitution of capitalism, has been what might be described as postcolonial critique of economic development. Kapoor (2008), for example, explores what a postcolonial politics might look like in the context of global development (see also McEwan 2009). Part of Kapoor's analysis is to challenge the amnesia about (neo)colonialism within development and to question its 'deep-seated loyalties to scientific progress and universal economic prescriptions' (2008: xv). Another example is Gidwani's (2008) attempt to rethink the constitution of capitalism through an analysis of the politics of work in central Gujarat, India. Through a focus on the entrepreneurial, land-owning Patel caste, Gidwani interrogates concepts of value, development and capitalism to demonstrate how political economy might be liberated from Eurocentrism. Gidwani, drawing on Marxist, post-Marxist and postcolonial theory, is explicit in raising questions about what a postcolonial critique of Marx and capitalism might deliver in terms of rethinking capitalism. Finally, Wainwright (2008) brings together postcolonialism and political economy in his analysis of southern Belize to question how capitalism reproduces inequality in the name of development and how it is that the deepening of capitalist socialist relations comes to be taken as development. Such engagements between economy and postcolonialism give life to the fact that postcolonial studies has not, and should not, concede the space of materiality – the provisioning of livelihoods, tangible constraints on life, relations of production and distribution – to economics. As Gidwani (2008: 217) argues, what postcolonial theory offers to a rethinking of economy is an acute sensitivity 'to contingency and conjuncture in processes of change'; it is 'conscious of capital's hegemonising operations, yet unwilling to reduce history to its logic'; and it is 'skeptical of capital's ability to assimilate all forms of life that oppose its aspirations'.

Postcolonial economies

This volume is intended as part of an emerging conversation between social science treatments of 'the economic' and postcoloni-alism, which, as we have seen, has begun to interrogate the politics of knowledge production about 'the economy'. Underpinning this engagement is a desire to postcolonialise or, in Dipesh Chakrabarty's words, to provincialise dominant social science approaches to the economic. In turn, this desire is driven by a political imperative that works against a divisive geopolitics of knowledge by requiring an engagement with ideas from across disciplines and from those 'other' places to which economic theory is often blind. The latter still unconsciously universalises the western parochial, and thus 'non-western' economies are seen in terms of 'a lack, an absence, an incompleteness that translates into an "inadequacy"' (Chakrabarty 2000: 32) or, at best, something reduced to 'varieties of capitalism' (Pollard *et al.* 2009). The chapters in this book counter such visions in a number of ways, for example by advancing theorisations of economy, or by recognising the multiplicity of worlds that may or may not see themselves as economic in these terms. The latter may include alternative, 'non-Western' or indigenous forms of economic theory and knowledge such as those discussed in the chapters by Dipesh Chakrabarty, Eiman Zein-Elabdin and Roger Lee (see also Howitt and Suchet-Pearson 2006). They may also include alternative economic spaces such as those articulated in the chapters by Nitasha Kaul, Hilary Lim and Cathy McIlwaine, as well as the ordinary economies of everyday life discussed in the chapters by Christine Sylvester and Patricia Noxolo (see also Lee 2006).

The chapters of this book attempt to bring postcolonialism into dialogue with social science approaches to economy and advocate mutual engagement rather than rejection. Rejection is untenable for, as Roger Lee has argued, the singularity of economy is the need to enable social and material reproduction, in other words, to be 'life-sustaining' (Lee 2006). Lee concedes, of course, that sustaining life is not simply a question of material success, but also of the performance of other values. Thus, rather than abandoning Western economic models, the authors in this book are responding to the challenge, as articulated by Gayatri Spivak (1988: 57), to 'produce a reading which is politically more useful, rather than a reading that would simply throw away an extremely powerful analysis because it can be given a certain kind of reading'. As such, we hope that they help to open up an agenda for further productive dialogue. These chapters also demonstrate that recognising more complex and multi-directional flows of economic knowledge and policy require that postcolonial approaches towards the economic are not confined to an engagement with the more obviously postcolonial worlds of diasporic communities and the Global South. Rather, they are starting to work towards a position that 'northern theory' be more conscious of its own perspectives and more open to embracing different perspectives through which to view economic practices (see also, for example, Connell 2007). As some of the chapters here have attempted, it is as important to turn these perspectives on the North to disruptive effect as it is to break the silences from the margins (see also Pollard and Samers 2007).

What this points towards (see the chapters by Wendy Larner and Patricia Noxolo, in particular), and worthy of further attention, is an examination of how and where economic practices and theories travel (Larner and Laurie 2010). Moreover, more consideration needs to be given to the ways in which dominant modes of practice and theory become 'domesticated', or internalised and reproduced at a variety of spatial scales (Smith and Rochovská 2007; Stenning *et al.* 2010) within projects, policies and target groups. Such concerns, we argue, should be fertile terrain for postcolonial approaches to the economic. As Pollard *et al.* (2009) suggest, the growing body of work that explores the development industry through institutional and embodied ethnographies is a good illustration of this approach, often drawing inspiration from work that sees economic policies as technocratic projects (Mitchell 2002; Goldman 2005). Yet, although there has been work on, for example, how neoliberalism travels (Peck 2004), much of this has explored the circulation of knowledges within advanced economies and the movement of such knowledges out from the West. Less work has drawn attention to the travels of economic policy made elsewhere and not enough analysis of how neoliberalism travels has acknowledged the ways in which indigenous actors have responded to and remade economic policy.

As Pollard *et al.* (2009: 139) argued, postcolonial approaches can 'reveal the ways in which parallel policy-making circuits have long operated simultaneously but separately, structuring the geographies of learning along clearly defined North-South lines'. Assumptions about the production and circulation of economic knowledge create blindness to the possibilities of knowledge sharing about contemporaneous experiences of successful economic strategies in the Global South, which is often tantamount to a refusal to learn from experiences elsewhere (see Laurie 2007 on workfare policies). The chapters of this book emphasise some of the ruptures and happenstance of economies in order to illustrates how particular forms of representation take shape and travel. As Pollard *et al.* (2009) argue, there is political importance to the consideration of difference in these kinds of approach; this is not an emphasis on difference for its own sake, but to counter 'the discursive erasure threatened by neoliberal theory' (Gibson-Graham 2008: 8) and other hegemonic forms of economic knowledge production. Further readings of the economic through an engagement with postcolonial theory might inspire more detailed analyses of subalterities, not only those produced through the iniquities of capitalism, but of other forms of oppression such as patriarchy, neo-colonialism and racism (McCall 2005).

Structure of the book

Section 1: theorising the economic

The first section of the book comprises four chapters which in different ways adopt postcolonial approaches both to challenge traditional notions of economy associated with the discipline of Economics and Marxian political economy and to posit alternative, hybrid and more grounded conceptualisations of value, exchange and distribution. Dipesh Chakrabarty provides an introductory note to this section, outlining a set of challenges that postcolonial criticism presents to understandings of economy in general, and economic history in particular. He draws on the work of Kenneth Pomeranz (2000) in *The Great Divergence: China, Europe, and the Making of the Modern World Economy* to question the Eurocentric/ Western nature of abstract political-economic categories such as land, labour and capital. He suggests that these categories are simultaneously analytical and historically and geographi- cally situated, and that this dual nature of categories should be acknowledged. He highlights also the importance of philology and the appreciation of cross-cultural differences in the words, and meanings of the words, used to define these political-economic categories. And finally, he proposes a more explicit recognition of the abstract and particular position(s) of academic knowledge in the process of pursuing a postcolonial approach to questions of political economy.

Eiman Zein-Elabdin addresses directly the limited engagement to date between the discipline of Economics and postcolonial theory. While Economics marginalises questions of culture, the converse is shown to be the case for postcolonial theorisation through which economic and material circumstances of people are downplayed in literary and philosophical accounts that privilege the role of identities in cultural formations of power and resist- ance. She acknowledges that while postcolonial theory could fruitfully be brought to bear on both orthodox and heterodox economics, it is unsurprisingly in the latter sub-disciplinary area that it has had some influence. However, this inter-disciplinary conversation is limited and has potential to go much further in radically re-theorising economy. The conceptualisation of the culture–economy relationship is argued to be a key part of this challenge. Zein-Elabdin advances this argument by exploring the potentiality of what she terms some 'economic moments' in exist- ing, influential postcolonial critique. These moments (implicit, as well as explicit) are captured in selected postcolonial works – Said's

(1979) Orientalism, Spivak's (1985) questioning of the notion of value and Bhabha's (1985, 1994) concept of hybridity. Each is shown to offer a foundation upon which to construct alternative readings of economy, which challenge the ontological separation of culture and economy and instead help us to re-imagine their integration in grounded practices.

Roger Lee's chapter continues the challenge posed in this section to the separation of culture and economy in prevailing economic theories. Like Dipesh Chakrabarty, he argues that economies and their theorisation are always intertwined with, and shaped by, social and cultural meanings and life-worlds. The materialities of economy, he explains, are themselves moulded by social relations, including those connected with colonialism and postcolonialism. The diversity of economies, therefore, is a notion advanced in this chapter. Moreover, the spatiality – incorporating both territoriality and relationality – of diverse economies is highlighted. Drawing on arguments made by Gibson-Graham (2006), Lee suggests that 'weak theory', which avoids universalising tendencies, holds potential both for theorising and for practising postcolonial economic spaces. This is suggested to be important for the construction of a critical postcolonial economic geography.

Wendy Larner also prompts a conversation between postcolonial approaches and understandings of economy through a focus on the sub-discipline of economic geography and its traditional conceptual register. She adopts an autobiographical approach in order to critique accepted genealogies of economic geography dominated by Anglo-American geographers and modes of theorisation. Postcolonialism is understood here as a politics of method for challenging hegemonic discourses and for capturing more multiple and situated accounts of economy than those that have tended to dominate the literature. Through her rich account of becoming a geographer in New Zealand through the 1980s and subsequently working in the UK, she emphasises the complex ways in which knowledge of the economy travels in practice. Documenting her experiences and understandings of the neo-liberalisation of economy and society in New Zealand, and asserting the particularities of this process, she argues for a recognition that all economic geographies are always multiple and positioned and that such complexity and particularity should not be ironed out by the theoretical frameworks used by geographers to understand the economy.

Section 2: postcolonial understandings of the economic

The three chapters in this section all bring postcolonial concepts and approaches to bear on understanding a range of economic spaces. In so doing, they illustrate the radical ways in which postcolonial theory can alter imaginings of materiality and economy. Nitasha Kaul places the spotlight on a particular kind of economic space – the bazaar – in order to present a set of alternative conceptualisations of market and exchange than those dominant in orthodox Economics. She captures the 'lived experiences' of a particular bazaar, Janpath in New Delhi. As in the preceding chapters, this account also challenges the notion that culture and economy operate as separate spheres. In a similar vein to Larner, Kaul suggests that such spaces are multiple and 'contested'.

Hilary Lim provides a critical take on the complex postcolonial geographies bound up in the grounding of two Islamic financial institutions – *hawala* (an informal and trust-based facility for transferring funds) and the *waqf* (a form of charitable bequest through land) – in the legal landscape of Britain. Following the work of de Sousa Santos (1987), a cartographic metaphor is applied to this case in order to illuminate the nuanced ways in which these forms of Islamic finance are either accepted into the 'centre' of British law or cast to its periphery. The chapter provides an interesting counter-argument to the notion of a legal trust as a European economic concept that was subsequently exported around the world, tracing its origins instead to medieval Islamic traders. The chapter also suggests that both *hawala* and the *waqf* offer some alternative and more inclusive ways of delivering economic empowerment and that their reception by British law needs to be interrogated in order to understand this potential.

Cathy McIlwaine picks up the theme of lived experiences, introduced in previous chapters, and addresses their importance for academic accounts of economic spaces. Her focus is on the particular lived experiences of migrants to London from Colombia, Ecuador and Bolivia. Through the use of qualitative research, incorporating interviews and focus groups with these migrants, she seeks to understand their various survival strategies. Biographical accounts are therefore privileged as a source of knowledge concerning transnational migration. Advocating an approach that blends a postcolonial position with materialist interpretation, she illuminates how migrants' everyday lives are shaped by the interplay of cultural identification and a range of economic concerns such as work and its material consequences.

Section 3: postcolonial economies: policy and practice

Christine Sylvester opens up this section, which provides a postcolonial critique of dominant and problematic development policies and illuminates lived postcolonial experiences and practices. Sylvester argues for the importance of taking seriously postcolonial readings of individual people's thinking and what she terms 'thought in motion' at times of crisis. This move is juxtaposed against policies and practices of development about 'life in the aggregate'. Understandings of biopolitics are woven through three postcolonial narratives of thought in motion to make the argument. These narratives are constructed through engagement with three different novels, each representing people making everyday livelihood decisions in situations of 'bare life' (Agamben 1998): in the context of genocide in Rwanda during 1994, in the Biafra War in Nigeria in the1960s, and in contemporary Zimbabwe. The postcolonial readings and arguments concerning individual people's thinking at times of crisis address material issues through stories prioritising the decision-making of individuals. In so doing, the chapter sets postcolonial readings and the challenges faced and decisions taken by individuals against the power of economists, economic models and dominant/orthodox notions of economy. Whereas the latter erase the richness of human agency and experience in response to economic and other crises through their drive to produce 'development aggregates', which then often fail to produce adequate responses to these crises, Sylvester argues that development should also be seen through the eyes of local people who are making daily livelihood decisions in situations of conflict, despair, uncertainty, ambivalence, hope and resistance. She advocates the reading of postcolonial stories as part of development theory, training and practice in the field as a means of understanding the thoughts and actions of subject to development interventions.

Patricia Noxolo's chapter completes this section on policies and practices of postcolonial economies by addressing the politics of the increasingly popular movement of development volunteering. With reference to field research conducted with returned UK volunteers, this chapter challenges positive views of development volunteering by arguing that it is in practice productive of cultural and economic difference. Noxolo continues the analytical theme of the culture-economy dynamic by addressing the complex moral economies of development volunteering. Two contrasting kinds of moral economy – gifting and professionalism – are shown to be part of the relationships of postcolonial responsibility bound up in transnational development volunteering. And it is the tension between these two forms of moral economy that are argued to be productive of differences between volunteers and host communities.

References

Agamben, G. (1998) *Homo Sacer: Sovereign power and bare life*, D. Heller-Roazen (trans.), Stanford University Press, Stanford.

Ahmad, A. (1992) *In Theory: Classes, nations, literatures*, Verso, London.

Amin, A. and Thrift, N. (eds) (2003) *The Blackwell Cultural Economy Reader*, Blackwell, London.

Ashcroft, B. (2001) *On Postcolonial Futures: Transformations of colonial culture*, Continuum, London.

Bhabha, H. (1985) 'Signs taken for wonders: Questions of ambivalence and authority under a tree outside Delhi, May 1817', *Critical Inquiry*, 12(1): 144–65.

— (1994) *The Location of Culture*, Routledge, London.

Castree, N. (1997) 'Invisible Leviathan: Speculations on Marx, Spivak, and the question of value', *Rethinking Marxism*, 9(2): 45–78.

Connell, R. (2007) *Southern Theory*, Polity, Cambridge.

Chakrabarty, D. (2000) *Provincialising Europe: Postcolonial thought and historical difference*, Princeton University Press, Princeton.

Chatterjee, P. (1996) *Nationalist Thought and the Colonial World*, Zed Books, London.

de Sousa Santos, B. (1987) 'Law: A map of misreading: towards a postmodern conception of law', *Journal of Law and Society*, 14: 279–302.

Dirlik, A. (1994) 'The postcolonial aura: Third World criticism in the age of global capitalism', *Critical Inquiry*, winter: 329–56.

Gibson-Graham, J. K. (1996) *The End of Capitalism (As We Knew It): A feminist critique of political economy*, Blackwell, Oxford.

— (2006) *A Postcapitalist Politics*, University of Minnesota Press, Minneapolis.

— (2008) 'Diverse economies: Performative practices for "other worlds"', *Progress in Human Geography*, available at: http://phg.sagepub.com/cgi/rapidpdf/0309132508090821v1.

Gidwani, V. (2008) *Capital Interrupted: Agrarian development and the politics of work in India*, University of Minnesota Press, Minneapolis.

Goldman, M. (2005) *Imperial Nature: The World Bank and struggles for social justice in the age of globalization*, Yale University Press, New Haven.

Hall, S. (1996) 'What was "the post-colonial"? Thinking at the limit', in I. Chambers and L. Curti (eds), *The Postcolonial Question: Common skies, divided horizons*, Routledge, London, pp. 242–60.

Hardt, M. and Negri, A. (2000) *Empire*, Harvard University Press, Cambridge, MA.

Howitt, R. and Suchet-Pearson, S. (2006) Rethinking the building blocks: ontological pluralism and the idea of 'management', *Geografiska Annaler B*, 88: 323–35.

Ismail, Q. (2005) *Abiding by Sri Lanka*, University of Minnesota Press, Minneapolis.

Kapoor, I. (2008) *The Postcolonial Politics of Development*, Routledge, London.

Kayatekin, S. (2009) 'Between political economy and postcolonial theory: First encounters', *Cambridge Journal of Economics*, 33(6): 1113–18.

Larner, W. and Laurie, N. (2010) 'Travelling technocrats, embodied knowledges: Globalising privatisation in telecoms and water, *Geoforum*, 41(2): 218–26.

Laurie, N. (2007) 'Workfare and the partial geographies of technocratic learning', paper presented at the Annual conference of the Association of American Geographers, San Francisco.

Lazarus, N. (1993) 'Postcolonialism and the dilemma of nationalism: Aijaz Ahmad's critique of Third Worldism', *Diaspora*, 2(3): 373–400.

— (1999) *Nationalism and Cultural Practice in the Postcolonial World*, Cambridge University Press, Cambridge.

Lee, R. (2006) 'The ordinary economy: Tangled up in values and geography', *Transactions of the Institute of British Geographers*, 31(4): 413–32.

McCall, L. (2005) 'The complexity of intersectionality', *Signs: Journal of Women and Culture and Society*, 30: 1771–802.

McCloskey, D. N. (1998) *The Rhetoric of Economics*, University of Wisconsin Press, Madison.

McEwan, C. (2003) 'Material geographies and postcolonialism', *Singapore Journal of Tropical Geography*, 24(3): 340–55.

— (2009) *Postcolonialism and Development*, Routledge, London.

Mirowski, P. (2002) *Machine Dreams: Economics becomes a cyborg science*, Cambridge University Press, Cambridge.

Mitchell, T. (1998) 'Fixing the economy', *Cultural Studies*, 12(1): 82–101.

— (2002) *Rule of Experts: Egypt, technopolitics, modernity*, University of California Press, London.

Miyoshi, M. (1997) 'Sites of resistance in the global economy', in K. Ansell-Pearson, B. Parry and J. Squires (eds), *Cultural Readings of Imperialism: Edward Said and the Gravity of History*, Lawrence and Wishart, London.

Parry, B. (2002) 'Directions and dead ends in postcolonial studies', in D. T. Goldberg and A. Quayson (eds), *Relocating Postcolonialism*, Blackwell, Oxford, 66–81.

Peck, J. (2004) 'Geography and public policy: constructions of neoliberalism', *Progress in Human Geography*, 28: 392–405.

Pollard, J. S., Laurie, N., McEwan, C. and Stenning, A. (2009) 'Economic geography under postcolonial scrutiny', *Transactions of the Institute of British Geographers*, 34(2): 137–42.

Pollard, J. S. and Samers, M. (2007) 'Islamic banking and finance and postcolonial political economy: Decentring economic geography', *Transactions of the Institute of British Geographers*, 32(3): 313–30.

Pomeranz, K. (2000) *The Great Divergence: China, Europe, and the making of the modern world economy*, Princeton University Press, Princeton, NJ.

Rattansi, A. (1997) 'Postcolonialism and its discontents', *Economy and Society*, 26(4), 480–500.

Said, E. (1979) *Orientalism*, Vintage, New York.

— (1993) *Culture and Imperialism*, Chatto and Windus, London.

San Juan, E. (1998) *Beyond Postcolonial Theory*, Palgrave, London.

Sayer, A. (2001) 'For a critical cultural political economy', *Antipode*, 33: 687–708.

Slater, D. (1998) 'Post-colonial questions for global times', *Review of International Political Economy*, 5: 647–78.

Smith, A. and Rochovská, A. (2007) 'Domesticating neo-liberalism: Everyday lives and the geographies of post-socialist transformations', *Geoforum*, 38(6): 1163-78.

Spivak, G. (1985) 'Scattered speculations on the question of value', *Diacritics*, 15(4): 73–93.

— (1987) *In Other Worlds: Essays in Cultural Politics*, Methuen: London.

— (1988) 'Can the subaltern speak?', in C. Nelson and L. Grossberg (eds) *Marxism and Interpretation of Culture*, University of Illinois Press, Chicago.

— (1990) *The Post-Colonial Critic: Interviews, strategies, dialogues*, S. Harasym (ed.), Routledge, New York.

— (2000) 'Other things are never equal: A speech', *Rethinking Marxism*, 12(4): 37–45.

Stenning, A., Smith, A., Rochovská, A. and Światek, D. (2010) *Domesticating Neo-Liberalism: Spaces of economic practice and social reproduction in post-socialist cities*, Blackwell, Oxford.

Wainwright, J. (2008) *Decolonizing Development*, Blackwell, Oxford.

Yeoh, B. S. A. (2001) 'Postcolonial Cities', *Progress in Human Geography*, 25(3): 456–68.

Yeung, H. and Lin, G. C. (2003) 'Theorizing economic geographies of Asia', *Economic Geography*, 79(2): 107–28.

Young, R. (2001) *Postcolonialism: an historical introduction*, Blackwell, Oxford.

Zein-Elabdin, E. O. and Charusheela, S. (eds) (2004) *Postcolonialism Meets Economics*, Routledge, London.

Section 1

Theorising the economic

1

Can political economy be postcolonial? A note

Dipesh Chakrabarty

I

Postcolonial criticism of the 1980s and 1990s arose from the left field – there is no right-wing postcolonial theorist to my knowledge – and was therefore often subject to a particular kind of criticism from Marxist or other left-leaning intellectuals who complained that postcolonial thinking emphasised textual criticism at the expense of political-economic analysis. The charge was never entirely true – Gayatri Spivak, for instance, always remained interested in questions to do with 'international division of labour' and in many other issues of development.[1] Katherine Gibson and Julie Graham, writing under the name J. K. Gibson-Graham, have produced economic analyses incorporating postmodern/postcolonial insights (Gibson-Graham *et al.* 2001; Gibson-Graham 2006; Gibson-Graham and Roelvink 2010). Recently, Vinay Gidwani (2008) has also made significant new contributions to this body of literature.

I claim no expertise in economics or political economy. But since my early training as a historian in India took place in the 1970s when a certain kind of Marxist political economy ruled

---

1 Her famous essay 'Can the Subaltern Speak?' (Spivak 2010) demonstrates the truth of this proposition.

the day and when economic history had the pride of place in all
discussions of colonial rule, I too began my career subscribing
to the opinion – common among Marxists those days – that
economic facts constituted a kind of limit for human freedom,
that the economy was the 'base', and the everything else about
any social structure followed from it. There were, of course,
quite sophisticated debates around about the extent to which
economic factors were determining of other factors in history,
discussions about what Engels may have meant in his famous
1890 letter in which he spoke of the economy being determining only 'in the last instance', and many speculations about how
one would recognise 'the last instance' if one ever ran into it.
But however sophisticated the discussions may have been, they
were all about saving the primacy of the economic in historical
explanations. Much of our historiographical revolt in the series
Subaltern Studies was against this primacy given to the economic in
radical historians' explanations of rebellions by subaltern classes.
With Mao as our inspiration, we rejected what we saw as the
'economism' of the usual Marxist explanations and gave primacy
to the political instead. Peasant insurgencies, we argued, always
began by destroying the usual social and material symbols of
domination possessed by the oppressive classes and these acts were
about how power worked in Indian rural society (Guha 1983).
Capitalist and colonial rule in India, we further argued, worked by
acting on these levers of power in Indian society.[2] This rejection
of 'economism' was also reflected in the interest many *Subaltern
Studies* scholars developed in post-structuralism and deconstruc-
tion. In my book *Provincializing Europe*, I tried to advance the
proposition that the question of transition to capitalism in any
setting was a question of translation as well, of a group of people
being able to translate their life-worlds into the categories of
capitalism (Chakrabarty 2000, 2007).

Our turn towards the political and the cultural/textual gave rise
to the general criticism among historians of India that *Subaltern
Studies* neglected economic history. I don't know if we did. But

---

2 Some of these arguments are rehearsed in Chakrabarty (2002); see also Chatterjee
   (2010).

it is true that while we wrote much on historico-philosophical problems of modernity and capitalism, we never did much to revitalise economic history as such. The 'new' economic history that developed in India in the 1990s, thereafter adopted, implicitly or explicitly, rational choice frameworks for analysis.[3] This delivered the subject from the shibboleths and tyrannies of a stultified nationalist-Marxism that dominated before but the price of the liberation was the debunking of Leftist historiography in general.

I have since wondered about what it might mean to incorporate insights from postcolonial criticism into the writing of economic history. Unfortunately, I do not consider myself best suited for the task. But reading Kenneth Pomeranz's widely acclaimed book *The Great Divergence: China, Europe, and the Making of the Modern World Economy* (2000) afforded me an opportunity to think about the problem and in this short essay I want to share with the reader some of my preliminary thoughts.

II

At the outset let me acknowledge how much I learnt from Kenneth Pomeranz's superb and revolutionary book, *The Great Divergence* (hereafter *TGD*). Pomeranz's scholarship is extraordinary, his intellect truly vigorous, his judgements astute and brave, and his heart – if one may speak of such things in an academic context – is absolutely in the right place insofar as the project of 'de-centring Europe' is concerned. This book deserves every bit of the praise that has been heaped on it. There is one more characteristic of Pomeranz's scholarship that I appreciated on reading both this book and his reply to his critics in a debate that followed in the pages of *The Journal of Asian Studies*. Even where he has the better of his opponents in terms of facts and arguments, Pomeranz is remarkably gracious and generous in his response to opposition. This is not a small merit in the academic world I know.

Much of Pomeranz's argument in *TGD* I find at least provocative and challenging even when my agreement with the book is

---

3 One of the most prominent Indian historians of this school is Tirthankar Roy.

not total. The overall project seems entirely laudable. Studies of transition to capitalism in various parts of the world often become Eurocentric through the deployment, conscious or unconscious, of the assumption that patterns of economic growth in Western Europe provide some kind of a unique model by which to judge the performance of other economies and societies. Pomeranz challenges this tendency of thought. He does so by seeking to demonstrate empirically that up until the eighteenth century there was very little to distinguish between the economic and institutional features of Western European societies and some areas of Asian world: Japan, the Yangzi delta in China and the Gujarat region of Western India. This attempt at empirical demonstration is no mean feat involving, as it did, research on many different literatures and sites at once. As the subsequent debates have shown, Pomeranz is able to hold his ground in the face of criticism by scholars who are specialists on areas where Pomeranz does not claim expertise. As a student of South Asian history, I can only admire the care with which Pomeranz sifts the sands of the economic history of the subcontinent in the Mughal and 'early modern' period. The book demonstrates in an exemplary manner the power of 'historical facts' in reversing habits of thought.

Pomeranz also mounts a challenge to those practitioners of history who see the present as the culmination of a process of historical becoming. Scholars have often written long and continuous histories of industrialisation in Europe reinforcing the commonplace idea that gradual and unique transformations over a long period prepared (Western) European societies and economies for the industrial and capitalist domination of the world that they were to enjoy from the nineteenth century on. Pomeranz throws the developmental narrative into disarray by highlighting the largely contingent nature of the discovery of fossil fuel (coal) and the forced opening up of the New World. These, in his view, were the two contingent factors that enabled Europe to remove the bottleneck of 'land constraint' that choked the possibilities for industrialisation in non-European societies that were otherwise on a par with Europe until about the eighteenth century.

Pomeranz thus succeeds in two of his aims: de-centre Europe and challenge historicism (or at least a certain popular version of it). By showing that industrial Europe becomes itself by dint of factors external to its geography or any perceptible, immanent logic to its historical evolution, Pomeranz avoids the problems of immanentist, internalist accounts of European becoming. These are definitely the three major methodological achievements of the book apart from the many substantial contributions it makes in its own field of early-modern economic history (these I am not able to evaluate critically though I find them thought-provoking to say the least). These gains are the dividends yielded by Pomeranz's consciously chosen method of writing comparative, connected histories.

Pomeranz begins the book with a somewhat polemical swipe at some unnamed, 'current "postmodern" scholars'. These scholars, he writes, 'make it impossible to even to approach many of the most important questions in history (and in contemporary life)' by 'abandoning cross-cultural comparison altogether and focusing almost exclusively on exposing the contingency, particularity, and perhaps unknowability of historical moments' (*TGD*, 8). I have no intention of defending these scholars who after all go unnamed in Pomeranz's book. Besides, I also value comparisons. Even more than that, I think comparison is unavoidable in social sciences. Some scholars explicitly set out to compare. Others don't. But our conceptions and theories, to the extent that they are social measures as well, provide scales and yardsticks whose use-value lies in their enabling us to compare. I have no quarrels therefore with comparative methods as such. But comparisons and the questions of unknowability or indeterminacy in history may not be as mutually exclusive as the quotation from Pomeranz suggests.

The problem of comparison is about the scale or the measure that helps us to compare. I want to use this opportunity to think about this question of the measuring scale as it comes up in Pomeranz's work. What I say is not as such a criticism of Pomeranz. I am not asking for a different book from Pomeranz. He has written the book he wanted to write and he has done so superbly. I have no significant criticisms to offer on his own terms. This is more a reflection on these terms themselves with a view to exploring what we all may collectively learn from thinking about the comparative method as it is employed in this book. What

I have to say may also connect back with Pomeranz's polemic with 'postmodernism' (the scare-quotes are, advisedly, his).

My point of entry is a couple of moments in the text where Pomeranz discusses some of his own preferences in social theory and that particularly in areas where he explicitly negotiates some anthropological theory. Pomeranz begins the book by acknowledging that most available comparisons between 'West and the rest' are biased in favour of the West. But it is preferable, he writes, 'to confront biased comparisons by trying to produce better ones' (*TGD*, 8). What is important is to view 'both sides of the comparison as "deviations" when seen through the expectations of the other, rather than leaving one as always the norm'. This, he adds, 'will be much of his procedure' in *TGD* (*TGD*, 8). Later, Pomeranz takes to task, rightly I think, texts that create a dichotomy:

> between societies in which "commodities" and "markets" determine social relations, and exchange is conceived as the individualistic pursuit of gain, on the one hand, and those in which social relations regulate the economy, status governs consumption, and people are concerned with reciprocity, on the other. When these dichotomies are applied to history, the result tends to be a division between a Europe that became "materialist" first and the rest of the planet, which because it has not yet crossed the divide, had to have "commodities," "materialism," and "economic man" introduced from the outside.
>
> (*TGD*, 128)

Instead he prefers, after Arjun Appadurai, the idea of 'a continuum that runs from "fashion systems" on the one hand to "coupon" or "license" systems on the other'. 'This formulation', writes Pomeranz, 'avoids placing societies in one camp or another . . . and so makes it clear that we have both "economy" and "culture" in all societies' (*TGD*, 129).

Pomeranz thus carefully avoids having to rank societies on any evolutionary scale culminating in the coming of capitalism. But the idea of a culture/economy continuum is not unproblematic. We may have 'economy' and 'culture' in all societies but they may be present in different degrees (otherwise the continuum will become a point). The *homo economicus* may have been present from the beginning of human history but it seems reasonable to suggest that some societies value it more actively as a way of being than others. More importantly, surely not all societies – at least up until the eighteenth and early nineteenth centuries – explicitly made this conscious analytical distinction between 'culture' and 'economy'. Nor did all societies create abstract objects of intellectual investigation such as 'economy' and 'culture'. In fact, it could be safely said, that only societies with more 'economy' created intellectual tools for studying something called the 'economy'. I obviously have in mind the history of Political Economy, an academic subject without which an exercise such as Pomeranz's would be unthinkable.

The question is, are these knowledge protocols or abstract categories such as 'land', 'labour' and 'capital' still European/ Western or Eurocentric in any sense since we all use them now and since they seem applicable to all societies? Or does their use, however unavoidable, also devolve on us the responsibility of remembering their histories as part of the politics of knowledge today? Or are they just analytical/descriptive categories giving us access to social realities that we would otherwise miss? In Pomeranz's text, categories like 'free' and 'unfree' labour or 'land' work as simple analytical and descriptive terms, shorn of whatever philosophical or theological associations these words may have had even as late as the seventeenth century.

That the categories of political economy are peculiarly European in origin seems less questionable. Also, it is well known that at their origin these categories were often possessed of certain moral and/or theological import (not surprising if one remembers that economics emerges from moral philosophy in the eighteenth century).[4] And since such import could never be completely rational, we would be justified in saying that these categories contained a certain degree of prejudice – that is to say, a certain element of that which was particular, prejudicial, and not universal – built into them even as they emerged as academic, analytical categories. Consider, for instance, the question of price of commodities.

---

4 Amartya Sen has made this point time and again, reminding economists of the continuing relationship between economics and ethics (Sen 1987).

Analytically, price is the point where the supply and demand curves meet on paper. Historically, however, as Michael Perelman has shown in his book *The Invention of Capitalism*, classical political economic thought was in part an intellectual war on the habits of the poor. Adam Smith's teacher Frances Hutcheson had this to say on the issue of price in his *System of Moral Philosophy* (1755): 'If people have not acquired the habit of industry, the cheapness of all the necessities of life encourages sloth. The best remedy is to raise the demand for all necessities. . . . Sloth should be punished by temporary servitude at least' (Perelman 2000: 16).

Now, do we need to know about Hutcheson and his contemporaries in using categories like price or labour today? Books on physics – as distinct from those on history of science – seldom teach the history of thought in the physical sciences. So why should the practitioners of political economy be concerned about the murky origins of their analytical categories? Has not the dross of all particularistic thought been drained away as they have morphed as effective analytical tools? Here, I think the answer is both yes and no. To the extent that political economy (or social science categories) can speak the language of mathematics, that is to say, to the extent that it does not speak prose, political economy can indeed claim to have become something like the universal languages of the physical and mathematical sciences. But I think that the social sciences also shares in the fate of the other sciences – such as the biological or medical ones – which are mired in the prose (and hence the prejudices) of the world. Here, origins do matter because they are never completely transcended. Prose brings with it the history of its own idiomaticity and that is always a matter of a particular rather than universal history.

Take the category of 'labour efficiency'. By definition, efficiency is measured by the ratio of output over input (of labour). However, as any labour historian of colonial Asia would know, records in nineteenth-century South and South East Asia – well after classical political economy had evolved as a recognised intellectual endeavour – demonstrate tellingly how themes of race were indissolubly implicated in this category. The Europeans in devising local, regional or global schemes of migration of labour always asked themselves: 'Do the Chinese make better workers than the Indians, or the Indians better than the Malays?'[5] In other words, colonial or even contemporary discussions of an issue such as 'labour efficiency' could easily slide into its opposite, that of sloth or laziness. This issue seldom enters academic analyses in a straightforward way today as there cannot be an objective, analytical category of 'laziness' shorn of all suggestions of interest, power and domination. The prejudicial aspect of the category 'labour efficiency' now has unnamed, shadowy, spectral presence – built into the recommendations of the International Monetary Fund (IMF) and the World Bank, I imagine. Origins let us invoke this spectre and see the category 'efficiency' for what it is – both an analytical tool as well as a piece of technology of power.

A better example yet is the category 'land' and let me conclude this section with a brief discussion of it. The indigenous people of Australia in the eighteenth and for a large part of the nineteenth century constituted societies that, in Pomeranz's terms, probably had more 'culture' than 'economy'. 'Land' was critical to their ways of being, but a sentence such as this one would not have been translatable into their languages as a reified, objectified and abstract category of 'land' simply would not have made sense to them. Yet European colonisation proceeded on the basis of an imagination that took the political-economic category of 'land' for granted. Eventually, the Aborigines had to deal with this category as they learned to make 'land' claims over time. In the push and pull of politics in everyday life in Australia, 'land' has become a hybridised category – the courts routinely listen to both political-economic understandings and 'Aboriginal' understandings (now mediated by anthropologists and historians). Soon, I hope, we will have political economists of Aboriginal origin making perfectly legible and effective political claims or writing economic analyses on behalf of their people. But that does not deny the fact this is a contested category. It is both a tool of disinterested analysis and at the same time a tool of ideological and material domination if not also of epistemic violence.

---

5 The classic book on this theme is Alatas (1977).

III

If, then, the categories of political economy or social science analysis are in varying degrees both analytical and prejudicial in their content, it follows that incorporating this insight into their treatment in classrooms would entail, at least, three steps that will need to be taken simultaneously:

(a) acknowledging this dual nature of our analytical categories;
(b) raising, and wherever possible, dealing with the problems of categorial translation as part of the narrative of transition to capitalism, and
(c) returning to questions of analysis and knowledge.

In bringing this note to a close, let me briefly explain these steps using Pomeranz's book only as an example (i.e. without the implication that Pomeranz himself should have taken these steps). Taking the first step – point (a) in our schema above – would mean accepting that words that feature in both ordinary language and analytical prose are always caught up in the strife-ridden nature of the world that exists outside the classroom. In distilling them out of their worldly uses and in giving them special or specialised meanings in our disciplines, we cut off or disable many of their usual semantic connections. Thus, we 'forget' that 'price' is part of class struggle when we represent it simply as a point on a two-dimensional graph. The process is not always successful. Sometimes the clamour of our conflicts in everyday world enters the classroom and students or colleagues refuse to accept the disinterested quality our disciplines attribute to these words. Nurtured in an academic way, this may very well give rise of critiques of disciplines from inside themselves (as indeed happened with Anthropology in the 1970s and 1980s). Another way to handle this problem may be to include, in a Foucault-like manner, intellectual and social histories of our analytical categories – this would require some philological expertise – into our discussion of these words in the classroom. But this has to be done carefully, without reducing the analytical categories to their strife-torn lives in our daily worlds or expunging such pasts altogether. This exercise calls for the achievement of a delicate balance and that may be a difficult task. But the difficulty does not invalidate my point.

The second point is an extension of the first but now set in a cross-cultural context. For instance, one could ask of Pomeranz's book: What were the different words in Chinese, Japanese and Gujarati sources that Pomeranz implicitly translates as 'land?' Do these words look to horizons of meaning that the English word never looked to? In translating them back into the word 'land' – with very specific etymological meanings – with the unthought assumption that the meanings that fall through the cracks of this translation do not matter? This, incidentally, was often the structure of British colonial glossaries in India that assimilated many Indian expressions to only one English word. Or should economists or comparative economic historians be, ideally, multi-lingual philologists too? Of course, this is an extreme demand, unreasonable to expect of any one scholar. But I am speaking of ideals here. And I am also making the point that it is through such implicit rough translations of categories that we make our way into the world that global capital makes. A postcolonial political economy will try to make such translational processes visible.

My third point relates to an idea of defending academic knowledge as a special way of knowing. I am not a relativist. And I do not believe that all knowledge-systems or ways of knowing the world are equally open to *reasonable* criticism. For example, knowledge-claims that are based on the position 'We have the experience, so we know and you don't' are not open to such criticism. The disciplines we teach in universities have their blind-spots no doubt but they all, in their own ways, teach us certain methods for argumentation and for the marshalling of evidence in support of our arguments. Whether such evidence be archival, textual, literary, filmic does not matter for my point, we all have ideas about what constitutes the relevant archive for the discipline at issue. We argue in everyday life too and present 'evidence' but the rules for such disputation are different. Often the rules are implicit than explicit and may include all kinds of social claims to privilege, ranging from 'we have the experience, so we know' to 'I am old and/or rich, so I must be granted authority' and so on. The classroom or the seminar represents an abstract Kantian space that is also abstracted

from society. Once we know this, we also know that it is absurd
to ask of society that it behaves like a classroom and solve all its
conflicts on the basis of procedures and protocols of argumentation developed for the classroom or the seminar only (*reasonable*
argumentation, the furnishing of acceptable proofs, etc.). By the
same token, we cannot expect the classroom to become like society
where all issues are decided through actual participation in strife.
Here I am defending the status of 'knowledge' as knowledge. This
does not mean, as I have said before, that social strife does not
enter the classroom or the seminar from time to time. Of course,
it does, for the abstraction of the classroom is never complete.
But we need to understand the classroom for what it ideally is: an
abstract place for the pursuit of knowledge that actually becomes
'knowledge' only because it seeks to abstract itself from the everyday world. That is what the disciplinary aspects of a discipline are:
procedures for abstracting data from our life and then so arranging
this abstract data – conscious models to narrations – that the world
can become an object of our study. If, in the name of politics, we do
not teach ourselves (or our students) these procedures, we maim
our own – or their – analytical abilities. That, to my mind, would
be a regrettable consequence.

   A postcolonial approach to political economy will, therefore,
entail taking all these three steps at once.

References

Alatas, S. H. (1977) *The Myth of the Lazy Native: A study of the image of the
   Malays, Filipinos and Javanese from the 16th to the 20th century and its function
   in the ideology of Colonial Capitalism*, Routledge, London.
Chakrabarty, D. (2002) 'A small history of subaltern studies' in *Habitations
   of Modernity: Essays in the wake of Subaltern Studies*, University of Chicago
   Press, Chicago.
— (2000, 2007), *Provincializing Europe: Postcolonial thought and historical
   difference*, Princeton University Press, Princeton, NJ.
Chatterjee, P. (2010) 'Reflections on "Can the Subaltern Speak"' in
   R. C. Morris (ed.), *Can the Subaltern Speak? Reflections on the history of an
   idea*, Columbia University Press, New York, pp. 81–6.
Gibson-Graham, J. K. (2006) *A Postcapitalist Politics*, University of Minnesota
   Press, Minneapolis.

Gibson-Graham, J. K. and Gerda Roelvink (2010) 'An economic ethics for the Anthropocene', *Antipode: A Radical Journal of Geography*, vol. 41, Supplement 1, 320–46.

Gibson-Graham, J. K., Resnick, S. and Wolff, R. D. (eds) (2001) *Re/presenting Class: Essays in postmodern Marxism*, Duke University Press, Durham, NC.

Gidwani, V. (2008) *Capital, Interrupted: Agrarian development and the politics of work in India*, University of Minnesota Press, Minneapolis.

Guha, R. (1983) *Elementary Aspects of Peasant Insurgency in Colonial India*, Oxford University Press, New Delhi.

Perelman, M. (2000) *The Invention of Capitalism: Classical political economy and the secret history of primitive accumulation*, Duke University Press, Durham.

Pomeranz, K. (2000) *The Great Divergence: China, Europe, and the making of the modern world economy*, Princeton University Press, Princeton, NJ.

Sen, A. (1987) *On Ethics and Economics*, Basil Blackwell, Oxford.

Spivak, G. (2010) 'Can the subaltern speak?' in R. C. Morris (ed.), *Can the Subaltern Speak? Reflections on the history of an idea*, Columbia University Press, New York, pp. 21–78.

2

Postcolonial theory and economics: orthodox and heterodox

Eiman O. Zein-Elabdin

It is highly premature to attempt an evaluation of the possible impact of postcolonial discourse on a discipline as broad and politically entrenched as Economics. In this chapter, rather than impacts, I examine the entry of postcolonial critique into the disciplinary boundaries of Economics. Although the first systematic effort towards bridging the gap between these two fields is recent (Zein-Elabdin and Charusheela 2004), this had been preceded by a decade long awareness among some economists (e.g. Olson 1994; Grapard 1995). Today several volumes reflect varied degrees of familiarity and engagement with postcolonial arguments or authors (Cullenberg *et al.* 2001; Barker and Kuiper 2003; Ferber and Nelson 2003; Bergeron 2004), and the term postcolonialism is now codified in the institutional classifications of economic research fields.[1] This visibility may not signal more than a fashion-

---

1 These classifications are regularly published by the American Economic Association in the *Journal of Economic Literature*. Since 2006, the term postcolonialism, together with colonialism and imperialism, has appeared under the category of international relations and international political economy, itself a sub-category of international economics. These classifications are also adopted in the description and advertisement of academic jobs in economics.

able accommodation, but it is nonetheless significant and opens up space for substantive interventions.

In the past twenty-five years, Economics has experienced a great deal of rethinking and innovation, partly the result of the influence of feminist and postmodernist critiques and partly the cultural distances reduced by accelerated globalisation (McCloskey 1985; Resnick and Wolff 1987; Amariglio *et al.* 1996; Garnett 1999; Ferber and Nelson 2003; Hodgson 2007). Yet, the bi-polarism of a dominant regime or orthodoxy (neo-classical economics) and a body of critical theories (heterodoxy) remains, even as each pole becomes internally more differentiated. Neoclassical economics, the choice theoretic model in which atomistic 'rational' decisions culminate in supremacy of 'the market' as a medium of resource allocation, underwrites a great deal of policy making and dominates the public perception of Economics as a 'science'. On the other hand, the term heterodoxy, while somewhat ambiguous and in contention, serves to distinguish a diverse group of philosophies – most notably Marxian, institutionalist, post Keynesian and feminist – from the neoclassical approach.[2]

Thus far, postcolonial arguments have found a space primarily within heterodox scholarship. Feminists have led the way in this regard (Olson 1994; Grapard 1995; Barker and Kuiper 2003; Charusheela and Zein-Elabdin 2003), with others following gradually (Cullenberg *et al.* 2001; Zein-Elabdin 2001; Bergeron 2004; Danby 2004; Kayatekin 2004). In these different contributions, postcolonial theory has been mostly adopted to deconstruct the cultural hegemony of Economics, but its insights are increasingly being utilised in the search for new ways to theorise 'the economic' (Zein-Elabdin and Charusheela 2004).

---

2 See Lee (2008) for an outline of heterodox economics. Debates abound as to whether the orthodox/heterodox distinction pertains to theory and method or to policy issues; and, of course, not every piece of economic literature neatly complies with this topography. For instance, the Austrian school, which insists on extreme individuality but questions the restrictive nature of mathematical formalism in neoclassical economics, is part orthodox, part heterodox. Ecological economics and neoclassical feminism also complicate the picture. See Foldvary (1996) and Garnett (1999) for a cross section of heterodox economic analyses, and Hodgson (2007) for a discussion of the changing face of the mainstream.

In this chapter, I would like to argue that the possibility of a distinct postcolonial economic approach depends on transcending the superstructural conception of culture found throughout social science and humanities discourse, a conception still common despite abundant denunciations of reductionism and economism. By superstructural I do not only mean the classical Marxian argument from 'base' to 'superstructure', but any generic form of theoretical separation of 'culture' and 'economy'. In this sense, the Weberian reversal of causality from culture to economy is also superstructural. Both are deeply rooted in the ideal/material substance dualism of Enlightenment philosophy, which establishes the disciplinary division of labour between Economics and Cultural Studies.[3] Theorising economic postcoloniality requires dropping this binary conception of the relationship between 'culture' and 'economy'. Indeed, if culture is understood as a processual social frame of reference giving rise to different sensibilities and practices, including 'economic' ones, it is difficult to even speak of such a 'relationship'. Instead, I will tentatively use the expression *culture-economy link* to describe that which gets lost in debates over economic/cultural or material/symbolic, and is therefore never articulated as a positivity, but only a negative of 'the economic'. It is akin to Homi Bhabha's 'Third Space of enunciation' (1994: 37), which refuses encapsulation between idealist and materialist philosophies in the realm of cultural meaning and difference.

Postcolonial discourse makes culture its key analytical category, so much so that it has been repeatedly admonished for neglecting questions of economic (or material) nature – as distinct from what is understood to be purely cultural preoccupations. There is some truth to this argument (Zein-Elabdin and Charusheela 2004).[4] However, the common lamentations of postcolonial

---

3 A full treatment of this subject and its massive literature in philosophy and anthropology is beyond the scope of this chapter, and must therefore be left for another occasion.

4 Our critique of postcolonial discourse was directed at its compliance with the structure of disciplinarity which results in 'a tendency to give economists a free rein on the question of material life' (p. 5) rather than at an absence of economic concerns in postcolonial critique.

theory's evasion of 'political economy' seem to rest on a shared implicit understanding of 'the cultural' as a separate ontological and, therefore, analytical space from 'the economic'. Such an understanding in part reflects the influence of Marxism, which appears to be the only economic tradition of relevance for both its adherents and opponents in postcolonial studies.[5] Accordingly, I would also argue that to fully explore and articulate a non-binary analysis of culture-economy, postcolonial discourse must engage with the full breadth of contemporary economic thought, both heterodox and orthodox, without conceding epistemic authority on the 'material' to the discipline of Economics.

In the next section I briefly revisit the 'materialist' charge against postcolonial theory – namely, its lack of attention to questions of economy – in order to illustrate the commonality of a superstructural idea of culture, and implications for a new theorising of 'the economic'. I then identify what may be described as 'economic moments' in some of E. Said, G. Spivak and H. Bhabha's work to suggest that, despite general perceptions in the critical literature, these theorists – as it is manifested in major works – have laid solid ground for a profound revision of both economy (the substantive sphere where economic processes of all types take place) and Economics (the discipline/theory, which purports to explicate these processes).[6] In the following two sections I outline postcolonial critique's current status within Economics, and discuss what I see as necessary steps for theorising the space of economic postcoloniality.

---

5 Bartolovich and Lazarus (2002) argue that there is an ignorance of Marxism in postcolonial studies and a reflexive tendency by Marxists to summarily dismiss postcolonial critique. See Moore-Gilbert (1997) on the embattled status of Marxism within postcolonial theory. At any rate, I do not wish to homogenise Marxian thought, especially given the substantial theoretical revisions it has undergone in recent history. See Resnick and Wolff (1987), Amariglio *et al.* (1996), Gibson-Graham (1996) for notable examples.

6 Of course focusing on these three authors is not meant to exclude other key contributions to the field, e.g. Chakrabarty (1992) and other Subaltern Studies texts, but the work of these three, especially Said and Bhabha, has been most criticised for avoiding economic concerns.

Materialist critiques of postcolonial theory

Postcolonial theory has often been taken to task for lack of attention to the economic plight of the subaltern. In this section I focus on a few classic interventions, which have come to define the general perception of an economic deficiency in the field. I name all such critiques materialist, regardless of their specific political point of view, in order to allow an examination of their unifying character vis-à-vis other criticisms of postcolonial theory. Furthermore, since in Economics the term material is not associated exclusively with a Marxian perspective, this also serves to broaden postcolonial discussions of economic questions. There is much value in the materialist interventions; my intention is not to diminish their richness but only to show that their superstructural conceptions of culture have precluded the recognition of significant economic themes and implications in postcolonial theory.

The crux of the materialist argument is that 'postcolonial thought seems more concerned with issues of culture and representation by Westerners, and with questions of personal identity, authenticity and autonomy confronting diasporic academics from decolonized nations residing in the West, than with material-structural issues of economic power which are arguably of greater relevance to the mass of ordinary people living in formerly colonized nations' (Charusheela 2004: 40–1, also see Hall 1996). Without rehashing the details of this argument, one may note that its different versions share two major features. First, they either expressly draw on Marxian philosophy (Ahmad 1992, 1995; Dirlik 1997; San Juan 1999; Parry 2004) or are critically informed by it (McClintock 1994; Hall 1996). Second, although in these interventions a transparent concept of culture is rarely articulated, what generally comes across reflects a theoretical separation between a realm of ideas and meaning, and one of political economy or material phenomena. This is the shared superstructural understanding underlying the customary division of labour between the fields of Economics and Cultural Studies.

The sharpest attacks on postcolonial theory have denounced it for anti-Marxism (Ahmad 1992) and 'rejection of capitalism as a "foundational category"' (Dirlik 1997: 505). Although these interventions are by now old and have been repeatedly addressed, they are still invoked, often without much critical scrutiny (San Juan 1999; Parry 2004). The materialist voices are right to call for more attention to actual economic and political conditions. Unfortunately, instead of careful analysis of these conditions, the result has been hollow generalisations about political economy. Frequent use of the terms capital and capitalism became the metaphor for economic treatment or at least evidence of preoccupation with material problems.[7] General references to a 'dependent periphery' (San Juan 1999: 11) seem to exhaust the conditions of the global majority. The problem, of course, lies not in espousing Marxism in itself, but in the conflation of economic analysis at large with a capitalism-centered approach such that, for these critics, the rejection of capitalism as a foundational category entails the end of all economic thought or even imagination of a different sociality.

Those who did not proclaim a Marxian belonging, nonetheless, drew on its analytical vocabulary to a similar effect. For instance, concerned with a 'crisis' in theories of history and progress, McClintock (1994) argued that postcolonial discourse obscured international power regimes and concomitant failures of economic development. Though seemingly critical of 'both capitalist and communist' narratives, her analysis is scarcely distinguishable from any Marxist critic who deploys as self-evident the terminology of 'capital' (pp. 298, 301), 'finance capital' (p. 296), 'surplus extraction' (p. 300), the 'industrial working class' (p. 301) and 'capitalist development' (p. 302). Hall (1996) has very aptly responded to Dirlik's (1997) attack, and at the same time acknowledged the absence of a self-critical reflection on the relationship between 'postcolonialism and global capitalism' (p. 257) and the 'disavowal' of the economic (p. 258) in the field. He rebuked 'Western Marxism' (p. 250) for minimising the colonial episode within its European historiography. Yet, Hall also largely accepted Dirlik's package of

---

7 Ahmad's (1992) complaint about lack of theoretical rigour and historical accuracy in Said's work was followed by a theoretically liberal and historically unpunctuated use of the term 'capital': finance, transnational, advanced, imperialist, corporate and cultural. Similarly, Dirlik's (1997) more detailed account of global economic/social dynamics was peppered with the terms capital, capitalism and global capitalism (old and new) with little explanation.

'global capitalism'. His objection to 'deterministic economism' (p. 258) did not keep him from repeating the rubric of 'dependent development' (p. 248), itself a corollary of the historicist framework of postwar Marxian-derived scholarship.

Beneath this set of materialist critiques lies a superstructural concept of culture. For Ahmad (1992: 8) '"culture" generally and the literary/aesthetic realm in particular are situated at great remove from the economy and are therefore, among all the superstructures, the most easily available for idealization and theoretical slippage'. Dirlik's (1997) depiction of postcolonial discourse itself as an ideological progeny of global capitalism reflects not only a superstructural but – as Hall (1996) noted – also a highly reductionist stand. This is echoed in San Juan's rendering of postcolonial theory as a result of 'post-Fordist capitalism' (1999: 8), which, by reducing political economy to textual analysis, elides questions of power and resource inequality. While Parry (2004) does not go so far, she distinguishes between culture and discourse, on the one hand, and histories, on the other such that 'discourses of representation should not be confused with material realities' (p. 19). In McClintock's (1994) case, the superstructural treatment of culture can be detected in its equation with the space of ideas and artistic production in an even more restrictive fashion.[8]

What I am arguing here is not that one can never invoke the term culture to indicate the specific realm of ideas, creativity or meaning. The problem arises when such usage subordinates it to 'material' considerations thought to operate separately from and take precedence over 'cultural' ones. This understanding results in failure to conceptualise a link of culture-economy in any social context beside a capitalist one, and from any theoretical position other than Marxian metaphysics. This problem has been behind the common inability in the literature to grasp significant economic dimensions in the work of leading postcolonial theorists.

---

8 According to McClintock postcolonial discourse occludes 'international disparities in cultural power, electronic technology and media information' (p. 297). Her idea of culture or cultural power – as separate from electronic technology and media – is not entirely clear, but she gives as evidence of these disparities statistical data on newspapers circulation, film production, television sets, radios and spending on scientific research and development in Africa compared to the US and Asia.

Economic moments in postcolonial theory

Postcolonial theory coheres in three broad problematics: rejection of cultural domination, reclaiming subaltern agency and understanding postcoloniality as a hybrid contemporary condition. Although different in approach, scope and political grounding, the articulation of these problematics in Said (1979, 1993), Spivak (1985, 1990) and Bhabha's (1983, 1985, 1994) work presents a continuous project with profound economic applicability and implications. The following outline is selective, but I think sufficient to illustrate the point.

From the very beginning Said was aware of the significance of economics as he wondered '[h]ow did philology, lexicography, history, biology, political and *economic theory*, novel-writing, and lyric poetry come to the service of Orientalism's broadly imperialist view of the world?' (1979: 15) [emphasis added].[9] This is a highly explicit economic moment, which could have made the discussion of economy more integral to postcolonial discourse than it has been so far. Unfortunately, despite the centrality of culture to his critique of orientalism, it appears that Said himself employed a concept of culture that distanced the realm of economy. In other words, although he rejected Marxian doctrine, his definition of culture shared its superstructuralism. This emerges from the statement: 'it [culture] means all those practices, like the arts of description, communication, and representation that have relative autonomy from the economic' (Said 1993: xii). This understanding may or may not explain Said's exclusion of classical political economy texts from orientalist discourse, but – as the previous section showed – it cast a long shadow over the field's approach to culture, including that of his critics.

Spivak picked up the question regarding the role of economics by consistently keeping an eye on the 'economic text' and the

---

9 More precisely, he alluded to development economics as a theatre for orientalist imaginations: 'there emerged a complex Orient suitable for study in the academy, for display in the museum, for reconstruction in the colonial office, . . . for instances of economic and sociological theories of development' (1979: 7). Escobar (1995) followed up on this observation by exposing developmentalism as a contemporary economic parallel to orientalism.

concept of 'value' (1985, 1990). She warned against 'dismissing considerations of the economic as "reductionism"' (1985: 82), and directly engaged in conversation with professional economists (2000). The economic bits of her contributions are ensconced within a high level of generality, which I think is substantively necessary for revealing the continuity of European modernist discourse across different disciplines. This counter-disciplinary approach is exemplified in her article 'Scattered Speculations on the Question of Value' in which she makes a head-on attempt to reveal 'the role of the economic text in the determination of Value' (1985: 92). This is another manifest, even stronger, economic moment in postcolonial discourse as she wishes to scrutinise the foundational theme of economics (value) by once again asking 'what is it?' (p. 75), and to show that the attempt to produce a unified value form generates universalities such as 'humanity' and 'development'.[10]

Though ultimately she does not answer the question of what is value in this article, this is beside the point. By simply drawing attention to the pervasive 'complicity between cultural and economic value-systems', and that the 'binary opposition between the economic and the cultural is so deeply entrenched' (p. 83), she opens up a whole research agenda for challenging the authoritative/authoritarian discourse of Economics. Far from reducing issues of political economy to textual analysis, this is a crucial step towards re-theorising 'the economic'. The persistent concern with the question of value is also behind Spivak's quarrel with the project of 'gender and development,' which she argues merely facilitates the entry of South poor women into 'global capital' (2000: 39). Her attempts to retain Marx, while simultaneously questioning the ideal/material dichotomy, have not been immune to the kind of generalisations about capitalism noted earlier; but

---

10 The article responds to writers, in particular J. Goux, who posit an analogy in the origins of value between money and sex. For her, the analogy misses Marx's materialist concept of value. She argues, when examining Marx's chain of value (Value → Money → Capital), these writers focus on 'the developmental narrative entailed by the emergence of the Money-form as the general representer of Value' (p. 77). In contrast, she suggests, this chain is an indeterminate and discontinuous process rather than linear or evolutionary.

this should in no way eclipse the major contribution in drawing attention to the common economy/culture dualism.

Economic moments in Bhabha's work are not so evident, and some may find it incredulous to speak of any traces of economic material in his writings for which he sustained severe charges of obscurantism and complicity with 'global capitalism' (Dirlik 1997). Yet, Bhabha's work offers extremely rich grounds for dislodging the discursive hegemony of Economics. Escobar (1995) has already shown that the twentieth century postwar project of international development has all the theoretical prerequisites of Bhabha's (1983) concept of colonial discourse.[11] Development inscribes difference between two groups (developed and under/less-developed economies); designates an analytical 'space for subject peoples' where their 'problems' are examined based on 'stylized facts' produced by economists; and justifies policy intervention in the lives of those 'degenerate types' – the poor, malnourished or illiterate. More importantly, Bhabha's ideas are helpful for unraveling binary conceptions of culture and economy, and thereby beginning to comprehend the space of economic postcoloniality.

Although not as visible as Said's hints at economic orientalism, or Spivak's efforts to decode value, many of Bhabha's statements, such as 'the postcolonial perspective ... departs from the traditions of the sociology of underdevelopment or "dependency" theory' (1994: 173), are instantly translatable in economic terms.[12] In this sense, his most crucial economic moment is embodied in the statement: '[i]t is from this hybrid location of cultural value ...

---

11 Bhabha's colonial discourse 'turns on the recognition and disavowal of racial/ cultural/historical differences', creates 'a space for a "subject peoples" through the production of knowledges', and construes 'the colonized as a population of degenerate types on the basis of racial origin, in order to justify conquest and to establish systems of administration and instruction' (1994: 70).

12 Other postcolonial critics have thoughtfully examined the dependency perspective. Susan Bergeron (2004) notes, though still Eurocentric, dependency theory was sound in its critique of mainstream development economics. Unfortunately, dependency's most enduring legacy is that it inscribed the impression that 'peripheral' economies are dependent on the 'centre'. The persistent language of 'economic marginalization' (Dirlik 2000: 9) maintains this impression. In this regard, rather than dependent or marginal, it is more accurate to think of 'underdeveloped' countries as subaltern, namely, they are discursively constructed as dependent, and silenced by the development discourse.

that the postcolonial intellectual attempts to elaborate a historical and literary project' (ibid.). The notion of hybridity has been mocked as mindless cosmopolitanism (Dirlik 1997) or a symptom of 'a crisis of late imperial culture' (San Juan 1999: 15), but such characterisations miss its subversive nature and its potential as a theoretical framework for generating more convincing depictions of postcoloniality. In Bhabha's work (1985, 1994) hybridity holds great potential for what may be a distinct postcolonial economic approach because theoretically this 'hybrid location of cultural value' also contains the type of 'in-between' economic relations and processes found in situations of multiple cultural intersections, producing a continuum of different lifeways. In other words, hybridity promises a theoretical entry point to what may be characterised as postcolonial economies (Zein-Elabdin 2009). I will return to this concept in the final section.

In short, pioneering postcolonial theorists did not always speak to economic themes directly or in the familiar language of 'poverty', 'the market', 'class' or 'capitalism'. However, their theoretical contributions have challenged the epistemic and philosophical underpinnings of these terms themselves together with other taken-for-granted tropes of economic discourse. These, seemingly disparate, moments suggest a continuous intervention, with both a deconstructive task (interrogating the dominant status of Economics) and a reconstructive one (drawing the parameters of economic postcoloniality). The following section outlines the extent to which postcolonial contributions have crossed the disciplinary boundaries of Economics.

Postcolonial critique in economics

Postcolonial inroads into Economics may be traced in both direct and indirect ways. The direct presence surfaces in references to literature and authors, while the latter may be inferred from the general openness of the discipline to the role of culture and cross-cultural encounters. So far, the direct presence of postcolonial critique is felt only within heterodox scholarship, overt familiarity with it is largely absent from the pages of neoclassical literature. On the other hand, the general aura of cultural studies is evident in the heightened profile of culture in all of Economics, both orthodox and heterodox. This interest in 'the cultural' opens up spaces for more postcolonial engagement.

The orthodoxy

To date, apart from the addition of postcolonialism to the list of professional economic research fields there is hardly any mention of postcoloniality – as a concept or contemporary condition rather than a purely historical marker – in neoclassical literature. Two of the only three articles, that I could find, with some reference to postcolonial studies happen to be invited contributions to heterodox texts. The articles register two different reactions: one is defensive of markets and capitalism, the economic heritage of European modernity; the second is sympathetic but struggles with how to reconcile postcolonial and economic approaches.

The first reaction is represented by D. McCloskey, whose influential book on rhetoric (1985) highlighted the role of language in the crafting of neoclassical economic theory. As a historian, however, McCloskey has no patience for postcolonial critique.[13] For all her self-proclaimed postmodernism, McCloskey (2000: 32) takes the positivist position that 'the numbers justify a narrative of Progress'. A somewhat similar position is echoed in J. Bhagwati's explanation of hostility towards globalisation. Bhagwati, a prominent figure in international economics, blames contemporary intellectuals such as Said and Bourdieu for an 'anti-capitalist' sentiment among opponents of globalisation. According to him, this sentiment is fed by the argument that the supporters of capitalism 'are engaged, as Edward Said (2001) claims, in a "dominant discourse [whose goal] is to fashion the merciless logic of corporate profit-making and political power into a normal state of affairs"' (Bhagwati 2005: 81).[14] What is highly significant is that

---

13 McCloskey dismissively complains – 'Gayatri and other postcolonialists seem to take the very sensible point of the subaltern school of historians that the colonial experience was identity-making for *the colonized* and turn it into an all-purpose influence *on the colonizers*. I know, I know: the Other, the Orient, and so forth' (p. 33).

14 It is not clear how much of Said's work Bhagwati has read as he only cites this article.

this essay is part of a publication by the United Nations World Institute for Development Economics Research (UNU 2005) in which a band of influential economists discuss globalisation, and international inequality, among other issues of 'development'. The only evidence of awareness of postcolonial critique in the volume is Bhagwati's oblique reference to Said.

Not all neoclassical economists are as oblivious or hostile. Cecilia Conrad (2004) expresses the dilemma for postcolonial sympathisers among orthodox economists – '[f]or most of us, reading an essay with postcolonial in its title is akin to reading a foreign language like French or Spanish. Some words seem familiar, but we are not confident in their meaning. Furthermore, postcolonial theorists seem intent on undermining our confidence in the words we think we do understand' (p. 271). For Conrad, the main barrier is methodological; neoclassical economists rely heavily on deductive reason while postcolonial critics are at best skeptical of it. She illustrates the difficulty with respect to 'race'. From postcolonial theory she takes the lesson that racial categories are 'fluid and malleable' (p. 272), and goes on to explore the implications of this observation for economic modelling. Her conclusion is that when it comes to historical examinations of race, postcolonial critique does not alter the results; the record is too overwhelming. However, it complicates analyses of contemporary contexts where race and racial discrimination are less transparent. This has considerable repercussions since much public policy – whether in education, housing or health care – is based on model-derived quantitative studies.

Taken alone, these three anomalous articles would underestimate the indirect impact of postcolonial discourse as part of the general twentieth century philosophical challenges to European modernity. Economics has not escaped this critical tide as registered in increasing openness of its dominant paradigm, even if only at the level of rhetoric, to the cultural dimensions of economy. For a long time neoclassical theory has treated culture, *aka* 'tastes and preferences,' as a given exogenous variable. Indeed, this is the fault line in the discipline – heterodox approaches accord some weight to cultural, historical factors in examining patterns of provisioning, relations of production and distribution, and wealth accumulation. In contrast, orthodox economics presumes a universal rationality embodied in the model of *economic man* – that 'homogeneous globule of desire' with 'neither antecedent nor consequent', which Thorstein Veblen (1898: 389) ridiculed more than a century ago.[15] Still, the neoclassical school maintained this deeply superstructural analytical framework, where the 'economic' stands entirely outside of 'culture'. This has somewhat changed in recent decades. The emergence of cultural economics, experimental and behavioural economics, among various other explorations (UNU 2005; Hodgson 2007), marks considerable dissatisfaction with the long-standing neoclassical treatment of culture.

To be sure, the apparent global defeat of socialism has made the idea of the individuated rational agent – however much revised – and its reflection in 'self-regulating' markets more dominant especially at the policy level. Many of these recent explorations wish to rehabilitate the theoretical core of neoclassicism. Nevertheless, the on-going struggle with 'culture' in economic orthodoxy opens up space for interventions.

Heterodoxy

References to and adaptations of different aspects of postcolonial critique have appeared in the work of feminist, institutionalist, post-development, postmodernist, post Keynesian and Marxian economists. This is not to say that most heterodox economists are familiar with postcolonial theory. However, key contributions such as Said's on the European construction of Othering and Mohanty's analysis of 'third world' feminism are widely enough seen in the literature that my present discussion does not exhaust all texts containing references to them. Needless to say, various strands of heterodoxy are not mutually exclusive; postcolonial work in Economics draws on more than one heterodox tradition.

Feminists early on saw the applicability of orientalism to the context of Economics. Paulette Olson (1994: 77) drew on 'the

---

15 Veblen pioneered the institutionalist tradition at the end of the nineteenth century when he applied ideas from the then new field of anthropology to economics.

postcolonial critique of western humanism' in order to extend the boundaries of the institutionalist school and raise institutionalists' awareness of 'racist, sexist and classist biases' in mainstream economics. Ulla Grapard (1995) directly linked orientalism to the androcentric bias in neoclassical theory by suggesting that '[t]he socially constructed binary opposition that earlier Orientalists argue separates the Orient from the European world – the different human characteristics ascribed to the Oriental and the European, and the hierarchical ordering of cultural values – constitute a process of differentiation and "Othering" that in our culture also pertain to gender categories' (p. 50). More recently, Jennifer Olmsted (2004) criticised orientalism among some feminist economists' own attitudes towards women in Muslim societies.

But feminist economics has gone beyond the mere exposure of orientalism. Drucilla Barker and Edith Kuiper (2003) state that a feminist philosophy of economics 'takes seriously the questions and challenges posed by a recognition of the social nature of science, as well as by postmodernism and postcolonialism' (p. 15). To underscore this statement, all three papers in their book section entitled 'rethinking categories' are written from postcolonial perspectives. S. Charusheela takes on the category 'paid labor', generally valorized in feminist scholarship as the key to women's autonomy and bargaining power. Her 'counter-history' reveals that, for 'ethnic-minority, immigrant, and non-Western women' (2003: 290), this category has operated mainly through 'dispossession and exploitation'. While S. Charusheela challenges the privileging of paid labour, Cynthia Wood cautions against marginalising its obverse, 'unpaid labor', and questions its uncritical extension to all women's work worldwide, arguing that a postcolonial economic reading must rethink both paid and unpaid labour, and recognise 'the importance of nonmarket work' (2003: 311).[16]

---

16 My paper in the same volume (Zein-Elabdin 2003) complicates the category of feminist economics itself in light of the common subaltern position that women share within neoclassical theory with men from formerly colonised, non-industrial cultures. For another feminist economic collection with postcolonial presence, see Ferber and Nelson (2003).

Other heterodox literature similarly invokes postcolonial critique. Judith Mehta (1999: 38–41) calls on Said's contributions (1979, 1993) in exposing 'cultural Otherness' to rightly argue 'we must find other ways of looking' in order to 'reappropriate the s/Subject'. Cullenberg *et al.* (2001: 47) point out that '[p]ostcolonial theory has become an important literature over the last twenty years and shares in many ways the concerns of some postmodernists, feminists, and Marxists'. In particular, they note hybridity as an important concept for recognising cultural integration and the mutual constitutedness of postcoloniality. Their discussion of the non-essentialist nature of subalternity and the complexity of resistance shows substantial appreciation of, and more than a passing familiarity with, postcolonial theory.

Another strand of heterodox literature is concerned with interrogating 'development' philosophy, substance and methods. Going further than contending with the dominant discourse of modernisation and progress, these texts incorporate postcolonial ideas in rethinking economic concepts. S. Charusheela (2001) points out the dilemma of feminist developmentalist scholarship between ethnocentrism and relativism in trying to conceptualise women's agency in the 'third world'. From different angles, Susan Bergeron (2004) and Colin Danby (2004) deconstruct the 'national economy' as a focal unit of analysis for the dualistic framework of development economics. I have relied on Chakrabarty's (1992) incisive treatment of the modern European claim on History to show the historicist convergence of Marxian and neoclassical development economics (Zein-Elabdin 2001), and on Spivak's (1990) strategy of catachresis to open up the idea of development to different cultural perspectives (Zein-Elabdin 2004). That the United Nations World Institute for Development Economics Research panel of economists (UNU 2005) was largely unaware of postcolonial critique reveals the daunting task that remains for shaking up developmentalism in economics.

On the whole, heterodox authors have taken up the task of deconstructing the power of economics. Although heterodoxy has been more hospitable to postcolonial critique, it is consistent with a complex, properly postcolonial conception of culture to avoid both uncritical embrace of heterodoxy and habitual dismissal of orthodoxy. The reconstructive goal of offering alternative understandings of contemporary 'economic' phenomena requires much more. Achieving this goal depends on the ability to transform current imagination of the absent culture-economy link.

The terrain of economic postcoloniality

If postcolonial critique is to inform a theorising of economic postcoloniality, it must reexamine and articulate differently what I have called a *culture-economy link*. I will not attempt to fully elucidate this idea here, only to point out that at least some of its elements are present within the broad parameters of the postcolonial economic moments introduced earlier, which suggest departure from the binary separation between the economic and the cultural (Spivak 1985) and from theories of underdevelopment and dependency, in order to recognise the hybrid location of postcoloniality (Bhabha 1994). In the following I elaborate on two crucial steps towards theorising culture-economy: reappraisal of the status of Marxian doctrine in discussions of postcoloniality, and building non-binary conceptions of culture.

As I have argued, the debate about lack of economic substance within postcolonial studies has been framed around the stance towards Marxian philosophy, but understanding postcoloniality on its own terms cannot be accomplished with an *a priori* centring of capitalism – or any other foundational economic concept such as 'the market'. First, there is the matter of Marxism's historicism and implication in the imperial project of European modernity as has been amply demonstrated by postcolonial critics (Chakrabarty 1992), and granted among critical Marxian scholars (Bartolovich and Lazarus 2002). Centring capitalism offers a theoretical framework, which, as S. Charusheela (2004: 49) has pointed out, 'disallows the non-capitalist from entering the terrain except as the obverse of capitalist-modernity's self-narrative'. The historical complicity of Marxism need not be a factor if the theory fully captured present realities, but worldwide a vast universe of communities lies beyond the theoretical framework of a capitalist economy even with bold revisions.[17] Examples of these include national as well as transnational economies, scattered farmers, pastoral clans, refugee settlements and entire war and humanitarian relief economies. By Dirlik's own account, 'four-fifths of the global population . . . are simply marginalized', they exist outside the 'pathways of transnational capital' (1997: 518–19). If this is true, where does a capitalism-centred framework leave those populations? Postcolonial analysis must work through a careful delineation of the concrete processes and sensibilities that underlie and sustain these 'margins'.

Second, despite substantial revisions, culture remains a negative of class in much Marxian literature. In the attempt to transcend determinist and economistic treatment, postmodern Marxists have defined culture as 'processes of the production and circulation of meaning' not necessarily 'the effect of a base-superstructure model' (Amariglio *et al.* 1988: 487). Resnick and Wolff (1987: 169) conceptualise advertising as 'a major cultural process' occurring within the capitalist enterprise. Yet, the problem remains as class continues to be 'the guiding thread from and with which a particularly Marxist knowledge is constructed' (Amariglio *et al.* 1988: 488). The residue of a superstructural separation between culture and economy is readily seen in that '[t]he specific forms in which art, music, literature, and history exist are the combined *result* of forms of economic processes (including the class processes), . . .' (ibid.) [emphasis added]. Yet, if one takes seriously the idea of overdetermination, the basis for these revisions, it is as arbitrary to begin from class as it is to begin from culture. As Mehta (1999: 38) realised, we must find other ways of looking, namely, outside the grid of capitalist/non-capitalist-developed/ underdeveloped.

Looking differently means striving to apprehend the hybrid location of economic postcoloniality. I have used the term *postcolonial*

---

17 Different mutations of contemporary capitalist economies have mandated significant revisions in Marxian scholarship, most notably the work of S. Resnick and R. Wolff (1987), who enlist the concept of overdetermination to offer a contemporary theory of the capitalist enterprise. Their distinction between varieties of class positions (e.g. fundamental and subsumed) goes towards more accommodation of the widening circle of capital ownership and control.

economy (Zein-Elabdin 2009) in the context of contemporary Africa to describe a continuum of relations and mechanisms for provisioning and accumulation, shaped in a confluence of encounters from the remotest locale to what is considered most cosmopolitan and global, and threading different technologies, institutions and lifeways. Such an economy is not only culturally embedded – like all economies – but unfolds in an environment of change (positive or negative), uncertainty and ambivalence. The threading of different rationalities, habits and institutions produces unique, complex and unpredictable eco-cultural patterns. The closest theoretical formulation to such hybridity in economics today is the notion of a 'mixed economy', grounded in the dualistic liberal modernist framework of market and state, and in consequence fails to grasp any higher degree of complexity. This outline of a 'postcolonial economy' is still a broad and tentative framework, but it invites further thought.

Looking differently also entails investigating the culture-economy nexus away from the superstructural separation between 'the economic sphere' and 'the realms of culture and knowledge' (Dirlik 2000: 16). In other words, it means exiting the Marx/Weber, material/ideal philosophical binarism. Culture is neither a mere constraint on an already formed individual rationality, i.e., a negative of 'the economic' in neoclassical theory, nor an isolable realm of meaning, a negative of class in much of Marxian literature. Culture may be seen as a process in and by which economic meaning as well as rationality themselves get articulated and lived out; in this sense, meaning is always present inside the concepts and acts of 'choice', 'labour', 'production' and 'class', or other economic terms. Culture-economy then must be thought of in the same instant as an organic, not mechanistic or hierarchical, whole that ties together the meaning and the tangibility of action.

In explaining this culture-economy link, it is helpful to draw on Bhabha's description of a 'Third Space' in the production of meaning and cultural difference, a moment between presentation and enunciation (1994: 36). In his words, '[t]he pact of interpretation is never simply an act of communication between the I and the You designated in the statement' (ibid.). This may appear far removed from the present context, but indeed it is not because he offers this idea in rejection of ideal/material dualism.[18] It is not necessary to enter into the intricate sense of his usage of this space concept, or to adopt his emphasis on temporality, to appreciate its relevance and potential for the issue at hand. The mere idea of a 'third' or 'in-between' space is highly suggestive of refusal to be encapsulated by either idealist or materialist philosophies, and therefore permits the imagination of a non-binary concept of culture. The culture-economy link that I envision here is similar in its 'thirdness', i.e. not allowing a theoretical dualistic separation between 'the economic' and 'the cultural' whether at the level of individual consciousness and subjectivity or social relations and institutions. Articulating this 'third space' of culture-economy is the biggest challenge for efforts to understand and theorise economic postcoloniality.

Emergent postcolonial scholarship in economics approaches this challenge, with the help of several theoretical perspectives. For example, Serap Kayatekin (2004) joins Marxian class and Bhabha's ambivalence to produce a thick historical analysis of sharecropping relations in the US. She describes her project as an effort to fill 'a much-needed gap in the Marxist economics literature on the relationship between culture and economy' (p. 236). Danby (2004: 254) is critical of the common culture/economy 'split'. Proposing a 'social ontology which does not compartmentalize economy from other aspects of the social world', he combines a post-Keynesian approach with the literature on transnational migrancy to improve current understanding of global financial flows. His work shows that these flows necessarily go through transnational families and kin networks, in ways that may or may not encompass capitalist processes; it is thus far more illuminating than the culture-free language of 'pathways of

---

18 Bhabha argues '[i]t is often taken for granted in materialist and idealist problematics that the value of culture as an object of study, and the value of any analytic activity that is considered cultural, lie in a capacity to produce a cross-referential, generalisable unity that signifies a progression or evolution of ideas-in-time' (p. 36–7). Gibson-Graham (1996: 90) use this idea of a third space to 'identify a range of economic practices that are not subsumed to capital flows', i.e. economic but not capitalist practices. This, however, is a narrower meaning than what I have in mind here.

transnational capital'. In previous work, I have drawn attention to some of the intimate culture-economy intersections, which anyone with interest in understanding contemporary Africa must examine (Zein-Elabdin 2003, 2009); and suggested that institutional theory (Veblen 1898), despite some limitations, is well suited for this effort because of its non-teleological philosophy and paradigmatic emphasis on culture.

This emerging scholarship is still very preliminary, yet indicates that contesting capitalism as a central analytical category need not signal an end to economic thought. The postcolonial method employed in these three studies not only rejects the theoretical dichotomy between the material and the cultural, but it is also decidedly pluralist and syncretic, and accordingly allows for multiple readings and answers. As such, it does not embrace or reject off hand or in total any particular approach or theoretical framework (Zein-Elabdin and Charusheela 2004). It does demand that in rethinking the economic concept of labour, for instance, one must interrogate both neoclassical (paid and unpaid) and Marxian (necessary and social) conceptions. A postcolonial theorising cannot afford to take either one at face 'value'.

Conclusion

In this chapter, I made a twofold argument that in order for postcolonial discourse to make constructive and lasting contributions to revising understandings of contemporary 'economic' phenomena, it must transcend the superstructural conceptions of culture currently found in social science and humanities literature; and must engage with the full range of available economic philosophies instead of almost exclusively and habitually relying on the Marxian tradition. This in no way calls for wholesale rejection of Marxian wisdom, it merely exercises or honours the hybrid character of postcoloniality itself.

The dominance of a superstructural concept of culture has led to a general perception that postcolonial theory is purely cultural or discursive and accordingly lacks economic substance. But even a partial look shows that pioneering theorists have laid solid ground to mount a profound critique of economics and contribute to redrawing its subject matter. Their work realises the deeply entrenched binary opposition between the economic and the cultural (Spivak 1985) in current discourse, and offers highly relevant entryways for understanding the hybrid state of economic postcoloniality (Bhabha 1994). In particular, the postcolonial economic moments identified in this chapter – economic orientalism, cultural-economic value and economic hybridity – offer a promising beginning for further probing and research.

Currently, postcolonial perspectives are largely confined to heterodox scholarship where they continue to deconstruct economic discourse as an integral part of modern European cultural hegemony. The reconstructive work of theorising *culture-economy* – though much more challenging – is also under way. This work necessarily calls for fruitful collaborations between postcolonial critics located inside and outside Economics. The potential of such collaboration for making a substantial impact on current thinking will depend on the ability to further transform the concept of culture. This cannot be achieved without reflecting on the breadth of the discipline of Economics – orthodox and heterodox. That is to say, decentring 'the market', on the one hand, and 'capital', on the other, as the two finite and competing ways of conceiving the past, present and future.

References

Ahmad, A. (1992) *In Theory: Classes, nations, literatures*, Verso, London.
— (1995) 'The politics of literary postcoloniality', *Race and Class*, 36(3): 1–20.
Amariglio, J. L., Resnick, S. A. and Wolff, R. D. (1988) 'Class, power, and culture', in C. Nelson and L. Grossberg (eds), *Marxism and the Interpretation of Culture*, University of Illinois Press, Urbana.
Amariglio, J. L., Callari, A., Resnick, S. A., Ruccio, D., and Wolff, R. D. (1996) 'Nondeterminist marxism: The birth of a postmodern tradition in economics', in F. Foldvary Jr (ed.), *Beyond Neoclassical Economics: Heterodox approaches to economic theory*, Edward Elgar, Cheltenham, UK.
Barker, D. K. and Kuiper, E. (eds) (2003) *Toward a Feminist Philosophy of Economics*, Routledge, London.
Bartolovich, C. and Lazarus, N. (eds) (2002) *Marxism, Modernity, and Postcolonial Studies*, Cambridge University Press, Cambridge.

Bergeron, S. (2004) *Fragments of Development: Nation, gender and the space of modernity*, University of Michigan Press, Ann Arbor, MI.

Bhabha, H. K. (1983) 'The other question: Stereotype, discrimination and the discourse of colonialism', *Screen*, 24(6): 18–36.

— (1985) 'Signs taken for wonders: Questions of ambivalence and authority under a tree outside Delhi, May 1817', *Critical Inquiry*, 12(1): 144–65.

— (1994) *The Location of Culture*, Routledge, London.

Bhagwati, J. N. (2005) 'Globalization and appropriate governance', in *Wider Perspectives on Global Development*, United Nations University, New York, the World Institute for Development Economics Research, and Palgrave Macmillan.

Chakrabarty, D. (1992) 'Postcoloniality and the artifice of history: Who speaks for "Indian" pasts?', *Representations*, 37(winter): 1–26.

Charusheela, S. (2001) 'Women's choices and the ethnocentrism/relativism dilemma', in S. Cullenberg *et al.* (eds), *Postmodernism, Economics and Knowledge*, Routledge, London.

— (2003) 'Empowering work? Bargaining models reconsidered', in D. K. Barker and E. Kuiper (eds), *Toward a Feminist Philosophy of Economics*, Routledge, London, pp. 287–303.

— (2004) 'Postcolonial thought, postmodernism, and economics: Questions of ontology and ethics', in E. Zein-Elabdin and S. Charusheela (eds), *Postcolonialism Meets Economics*, Routledge, London.

Charusheela, S. and Zein-Elabdin, E. (2003) 'Feminism, postcolonial thought, and economics', in M. A. Ferber and J. A. Nelson (eds), *Feminist Economics Today: Beyond economic man*, University of Chicago Press, Chicago, IL.

Conrad, C. A. (2004) 'Econometrics and postcolonial theory: A comment on the fluidity of race', in E. Zein-Elabdin and S. Charusheela (eds), Routledge, London, pp. 271–4.

Cullenberg, S., Amariglio, J. and Ruccio, D. F. (eds) (2001) *Postmodernism, Economics and Knowledge*, Routledge, London.

Danby, C. (2004) 'Contested states, transnational subjects: Toward a post Keynesianism without modernity', in E. Zein-Elabdin and S. Charusheela (eds), *Postcolonialism Meets Economics*, Routledge, London, pp. 113–29.

Dirlik, A. (1997) 'The postcolonial aura: Third World criticism in the age of global capitalism', in A. McClintock, A. Mufti and E. Shohat (eds), *Dangerous Liaisons: Gender, nation, and postcolonial perspectives*, University of Minnesota, Minneapolis, MN.

— (2000) 'Globalization as the end and the beginning of history: The contradictory implications of a new paradigm', *Rethinking Marxism*, 12(4): 4–22.

Escobar, A. (1995) *Encountering Development: The making and unmaking of the Third World*, Princeton University Press, Princeton, NJ.

Ferber, M. A. and Nelson, J. A. (eds) (2003) *Feminist Economics Today: Beyond economic man*, University of Chicago Press, Chicago, IL.

Foldvary, F. E. Jr (ed.) (1996) *Beyond Neoclassical Economics: Heterodox approaches to economic theory*, Edward Elgar, Cheltenham, UK.

Garnett, R. (ed.) (1999) *What Do Economists Know? New economics of knowledge*, Routledge, London.

Grapard, U. (1995) 'Robinson Crusoe: The quintessential economic man?', *Feminist Economics*, 1(1): 33–52.

Hall, S. (1996), 'When was the "Post-Colonial"? Thinking at the limit', in I. Chambers and L. Curti (eds), *The Post-Colonial Question: Common skies, divided horizons*, Routledge, New York.

Hodgson, G. M. (2007) 'Evolutionary and institutional economics as the new mainstream?', *Evolutionary and Institutional Economics Review*, 4(1): 7–25.

Kayatekin, S. K. (2004) 'Hegemony, ambivalence, and class subjectivity: Southern planters in sharecropping relations in the post-bellum United States', in E. O. Zein-Elabdin and S. Charusheela (eds), *Postcolonialism Meets Economics*, Routledge, London, 2nd edition, pp. 235–52.

Lee, F. S. (2008) 'Heterodox economics', in S. N. Durlaf and L. E. Blume (eds), *The New Palgrave Dictionary of Economics*, 2nd edition, Palgrave Macmillan, Basingstoke.

McClintock, A. (1994) 'The angel of progress: Pitfalls of the term "Post-colonialism"', in P. Williams and L. Chrisman (eds), *Colonial Discourse, Post-Colonial Theory: A reader*, Columbia University, New York.

McCloskey, D. N. (1985) *The Rhetoric of Economics*, University of Wisconsin, Madison, WI.

— (2000) 'Postmodern market feminism: A conversation with Gayatri Chakravorty Spivak', *Rethinking Marxism*, 12(4): 27–36.

Mehta, J. (1999) 'Look at me look at you', in R. F. Garnett Jr (ed.), *What do Economists Know? New economics of knowledge*, Routledge, London.

Moore-Gilbert, B. (1997) *Postcolonial Theory: Contexts, practices, politics*, Verso, London.

Olmsted, J. C. (2004) 'Orientalism and economic methods: (Re)reading feminist economic discussions of Islam', in E. O. Zein-Elabdin and S. Charusheela (eds), *Postcolonialism Meets Economics*, Routledge, London.

Olson, P. (1994) 'Feminism and science reconsidered: Insights from the margins', in J. Peterson and D. Brown (eds), *The Economic Status of Women under Capitalism: Institutional economics and feminist theory*, Edward Elgar, Aldershot.

Parry, B. (2004) *Postcolonial Studies: A materialist critique*, Routledge, London.

Resnick, S. A. and Wolff, R. D. (1987) *Knowledge and Class: A Marxian critique of political economy*, University of Chicago Press, Chicago, IL.

Said, E. W. (1979) *Orientalism*, Vintage Books, New York.

— (1993) *Culture and Imperialism*, Vintage Books, New York.

— (2001) 'The public role of writers and intellectuals', *The Nation*, 17 September 2001.

San Juan Jr, E. (1999) *Beyond Postcolonial Theory*, St. Martin's Press, New York.

Spivak, G. C. (1985) 'Scattered speculations on the question of value', *Diacritics*, 15(4): 73–93.

— (1990) 'Poststructuralism, marginality, postcoloniality and value', in P. Collier and H. Geyer-Ryan (eds), *Literary Theory Today*, Cornell University Press, Ithaca, NY.

— (2000) 'Other things are never equal: A speech', *Rethinking Marxism*, 12(4): 37–45.

United Nations University (2005) *Wider Perspectives on Global Development*, United Nations University, New York.

Veblen, T. (1898) 'Why is economics not an evolutionary science?', *Quarterly Journal of Economics*, 12(July): 373–97.

Wood, C. (2003) 'Economic marginalia: Postcolonial readings of unpaid domestic labor and development', in D. Barker and E. Kuiper (eds), *Toward a Feminist Philosophy of Economics*, Routledge, London.

Zein-Elabdin, E. O. (2001) 'Contours of a non-modernist discourse: The contested space of history and development', *Review of Radical Political Economics*, 33(3): 255–63.

— (2003) 'The difficulty of a feminist economics', in D. Barker and E. Kuiper (eds), *Toward a Feminist Philosophy of Economics*, Routledge, London.

— (2004) 'Articulating the postcolonial (with economics in mind)', in E. O. Zein-Elabdin and S. Charusheela (eds), *Postcolonialism Meets Economics*, Routledge, London.

— (2009) 'Economics, postcolonial theory and the problem of culture: Institutional analysis and hybridity', *Cambridge Journal of Economics*, 33: 1153–67.

Zein-Elabdin, E. O. and S. Charusheela (eds) (2004) *Postcolonialism Meets Economics*, Routledge, London.

3

Acts of theory and violence: can the worlds of economic geographies be left intact?

Roger Lee

The act of enframing is a work of force as much as reason and the two should not be seen as opposites but examined together.
Timothy Mitchell (2002: 296)

L'Occident possède une arrogance géographique. Il veut annexer, colonizer.
Chenva Tieu (2010: 2)

One of the (many) difficulties of thinking critically about, let alone practising, economic activity are the various abstractions of the notion of economies. This is made more difficult if, as is conventional, economies are reduced to their singular – economy. Are there such things/practices/relations that may sensibly be labeled as economies? Can these economies be in some way autonomous? Can they exist distinct from social, cultural and environmental life? If not, what is the point of Economics which so reifies economy and, conventionally, a singular notion of economy at that? Are economies singular? Is it, in other words, possible to frame them within certain singular imperatives (of, for example, efficiency) or purposes (the allocation of scarce resources to alternative uses; the production, circulation and consumption of the material means of social life)? Are certain modes of economic action (such as perfect knowledge, rational expectations, the abstraction of economy from social life) merely normal, to be expected and assumed? Or are economies multifaceted, having a range of social and environmental characteristics? And are they diverse? Can they take on a variety of forms and relations? In which case, what are their purposes and through what diverse forms of social relations do they come to be understood and practised? And can economies be infinitely diverse? Are all forms of economies possible? Or are there limits on material, social and environmental sustainability and effectiveness of economies? If so, how do these limits come to be understood and practised?

And this is not all. Whether separate or autonomous or not, economies (or what are labeled as economies) cannot but take place. They are temporal and spatial entities grounded in space and time. They are, in other words, economic geographies. What does this imply not only about the co-constitution of geographies and economies but the co-constitution of space and time and the influential role of economic activity in these constitutive relations? Further, geographical space is both territorial and relational. It is both domain and performance. Territories shape and constrain, but are themselves transgressed and shaped by, the relational geographies produced by the circuits and flows of value that sustain economic activity. So how might the geographical differentiation of economies and the economic differentiation of geographies – each formative of the other – be incorporated into an understanding of economy?

Beyond all of this, the difficulties of thinking and practising economy are compounded when the adjective postcolonial is used as a descriptor. Whatever the reasons for qualifying economy in this way, the adjective may have the effect of legitimating – even reincarnating – both the colonial and the economic when the critical point is their displacement. How, then, to think and to practise postcolonial economic geographies critically?

This short intervention does not pretend even to begin to answer these questions. All that it can do is to consider (some of) them a little further. The justification being that posing these questions in this piled up way is itself, perhaps, a contribution – if not in this essay, then for those better able to address them.

The postcolonial impulse

Many questions are begged by the notion of postcolonial economic geographies. How, then, might it be possible even to begin to consider them? Central to the meaning of 'postcolonial' is, surely, space – and, therefore, simultaneity. The colonial is about relations across and within spaces – both relational and territorial – rather than relations through time – and hence chronology. Indeed a chronological approach lays stress on the colonial as a defining moment and so defines the post-colonial[1] in terms of that moment. And yet, the postcolonial is about spatial sidelining, decentring and displacement – 'provincializing' to use Dipesh Chakrabarty's (2000) term – of colonising spaces. And such relations necessarily imply contestation and change: the postcolonial as dynamic struggle.

Thus a first condition in addressing the question of postcolonial economic geographies is an acceptance of geographical simultaneity – the co-existence and co-production of multiple geographies and histories, multiple spaces and times that collide, intersect in, and constantly bring their own historical geographies to bear on, the conduct of human life. The postcolonial can never be simply postcolonial but neither can it escape the colonial and post-colonial legacy. These geographies run from the past through the present to the future. They are powerfully formative. Secondly, these multiple space-times are contested – even if only by query – and even if they appear, to all intents and purposes, to be widely accepted. And such contestations may reflect not merely a critique of what is but of what is not and the challenges to belief and lifeworlds of these presences and lacunae. Thirdly, then, geographies are necessarily overdetermined – even, or perhaps especially, when they appear to be singular processes. They are ordinary.

Contestation and overdetermination, no matter how nuanced and subtle they may be in particular practice, are a part of the historical geographies of all social life extending from pasts,

---

1 The usage 'post-colonial' (with hyphen) here (and elsewhere in this essay) is intended to signify the spaces and times of what Derek Gregory (2004) calls 'the colonial present'. 'Postcolonial' refers simultaneously both to the complex state of the imposition of the colonial, its practices and legacies, and to its critique and displacement.

through presents to futures. Such geographies cannot begin to be comprehended without adopting an approach which recognises these complexities of their interpretation. But, at the same time, this is not to argue for an approach in which anything goes. Relations of power are always highly formative. But they are, therefore, always vulnerable. As such it is the politics of power (the power of governmentality and resistances to it, for example) in the emergence of economies/economic geographies that is at question here, not just relations of power themselves.

It is this that I take to be the postcolonial impulse. Whatever else it may be taken to mean, postcolonial implies continuing critique. On the one hand, it implies a continuing querying of, and resistance to, both the formative relations of (the powers of) signification and representation and the material and the discursive consequences of such powerful thoughts and actions. On the other, it implies a continuing reassertion of, and insistence on, such powers and their consequences. Postcolonialism is, therefore, an inherent dialectic of critique and counter critique. It involves the politics of power in a continuous attempt to reinstate resistant others as others against their attempts to become the subjects of history and geography. But at the same time it is also to insist that such others are themselves entities of cultural, social, economic, political and environmental significance in the making of geographies and histories and that, thereby, they require incorporation, suppression and transformation.

Viewing postcolonialism in this way may help to avoid the tendency to assume somehow that the postcolonial merely transcends rather than that it involves a dynamic process of mutually formative reproduction and transformation. It also implies a critique of postcolonialism's other. Attempts to resist the emergence of postcolonial identities point to the power of those identities. It is precisely the significance of these identities that lies behind the complex relations of the postcolonial impulse

(Postcolonial) economic geographies

A distinction is sometimes made in postcolonial thought (and elsewhere) between the discursive power of culture in the production, legitimation and proselytisation of meaning and significance, and the material power of economy in shaping and driving circuits of value. However, if the distinction between the material and the discursive is recognised as being merely a product of an unsustainable mode of binary thinking and the communicative deficiencies of available vocabulary, while the economy is recognised as, in part at least, a cultural artefact, such a distinction is unnecessary. It also gets in the way of a more critical sense of the postcolonial as a dynamic and multidimensional set of relations.

The rest of this chapter focuses on economy/economic geography understood in this inherently integrative sense as necessarily and at one and the same time a set of cultural, material, social, political and environmental relations. Such an explicit concern with economic geography/economy draws implicit attention to the continuing exclusion, or at least minimal treatment, of the category economic from critical thought in social science (see, for example, Mitchell 2002: 3–7; Lee 2010). A treatment of economy which implicitly accepts it as a self-evident category places it, as a concept, beyond critique. Thus an unquestioned acceptance of its meanings and significance is a means of imposing very specific meanings. And yet, economy is an inseparable element of social and cultural life and can take on many meanings and many forms of significance (see, for example, Rankin 2004).

Furthermore, a critical concern for economic geography/ economy also opens up the possibility of making an argument that there is something irreducibly material about the economic that constrains critical attention. That economies must be materially effective is a taken-for-granted – a banality. And yet the environmental relations of economies show how critical are such materialities, the understanding of which still bedevils the formulation of even remotely adequate responses to environmental change. However, the material relations of economic geographies are not god-given; they are socially constructed in the context of sets of social relations (not least those of colonialism and postcolonialism) which are themselves formed out of constant political struggle over the meaning, purposes and control of economic activity. All economies must be materially effective – that is the material imperative. However, beyond the minimum requirements for just social reproduction, not only are there wide quantitative limits on what 'effective' might mean in this context but the relationship between economy as the material consumption, production and circulation of value and the social relations which give meaning and purpose to, and evaluation of, the material is highly diverse (Lee 2006).

These issues within economic geographies are significant as one way in which the incorporation, suppression and transformation of would-be subjects of geography and history may be achieved is through the design, spread and application of apparently universal ways of (economic) thought and the models of social practice that go with them. There are at least three ways in which this universality – and the generalised othering that goes along with it – may take place.

The economy

First, even the very notion of what might be considered to be an economy/economic geography may be shaped by the templates of such universal models. From at least the end of the sixteenth century and the formation and highly organised practices of the English East India Company (Ogborn 2007), notions of calculation, design and authority have been imported into subject economies/economic geographies. In the middle years of the twentieth century, this tendency applied to the specification and definition of what could be taken to be *the* economy. The Anglo-American design of national income accounting was not only imposed upon the world – not least to ascertain what had been acquired by the victors, for example in Japan, at the end of the second world war – but came to be the hegemonic means of economic framing and calculation. Tomo Suzuki (2007) refers to this process as 'accountics'. This is a hybrid of accounting and politics which serves to transport a particular set of economic meanings and calculation from one location to another so enabling compatibilities between territories and, in consequence, requiring local adjustments and obliterating local meanings of economy. This process of colonisation signifies what an economy/economic geography is taken to be: a territorial (normally national) entity defined and measured in terms of intra- and extra-territorial flows of income defined in terms of Western standards and categories.

This presumption of economy/economic geography as a set of macro-economic flows taking place within and between national territories not only privileges a particular conception of economy but a particular conception of national polity and state apparatus highly appropriate for colonising powers (see Mitchell 2002). It is reproduced through the work of a range of institutions (universities, think tanks, experts, [financial] media, governments, central banks, international economic organisations . . .). While pursuing agendas of their own, such institutions may promulgate differentiated versions of this universal notion of economy against which particular economic geographies come to be measured and understood and, thereby, given an identity.

And, of course, the very choice of 'particular economic geographies' is far from innocent in this respect. It reflects economies of particular significance for the promotion of the politics of power – (e.g. central and eastern Europe and the former Soviet Union after 1989; the NICs after the financial crisis of the later 1990s; what are frequently referred to as 'rogue states' – with all the prior judgements entailed in such a phrase – in, for example, explaining away continued inequalities in global income per head; China and India with the apparent shift of global economic power to the East). Equally indicative are the economies ignored either as being insignificant – for example those economies formed and practised outside the mainstream, at least when they do not threaten national fiscal or social security systems – or as being largely unrecognised.

An example of the latter was the naïve fascination with the notion of interconnectivity as a way of getting to grips with the rapid spread of financial crisis during the years at the end of the 2000s. It was as if the notion of economies as relational geographies had hardly occurred to those for whom the crisis switched on the light of recognition and realisation. Certainly, elucidation had been considerably improved in the wake of the crisis. For a time at least, new perspectives on economy were opened up – not least around the need for democratic constraints on the relations of economic and especially financial power. Even the mainstream financial media advocated what heretofore would have been regarded in the mainstream as crazy economics. Such advocacy included the (flawed) incorporation of emotion into economic behaviour but rarely addressed the structural imperatives of capitalism in giving rise to and driving the crisis. The political-economic geographies of relationality remained largely ignored or beyond comprehension.[2] In a way, this is not surprising as the power of these relational geographies in driving colonial and neo-colonial relations and globalisation and in shaping postcolonialism placed them beyond the ideologically acceptable and revealed all too clearly the exploitative and geographically indifferent relations of capitalism.

Capitalism

Thus, and secondly, capitalism – albeit often wilfully and hopelessly inadequately elided with market economies – may take on a universal form. Just as the notion of postcolonialism may serve to legitimise what it sets out to consign to history, so too the critique of capitalism understood as structure also serves to extend and legitimise it – not least in critiques which could see only systemic revolution as solution.[3] The problem here is that capitalism frames the critique and responses to it (Gibson-Graham 1996, 2006). The structural logics of a powerful capitalism dampen or blot out possible alternatives and the discourses of difference to which and from which alternative economies may contribute. In this way, capitalism is universalised rather than provincialised and legitimated. And it is naturalised rather being itself recognised merely as other.

Despite its recognition of the complex relationships between the geographies of an expansive capitalism, a world already full of history and geography and the power geometries to which they give rise, an excellent example of the limitations imposed by such

---

2 A partial exception were the insights of Adair Turner in a series of papers – see, for example, Turner (2009).

3 See, for example, Harvey (2006) for an indication of how such arguments come to be made.

universalisation, is provided by Eric Hobsbawm's (1979: 310) description of the making of the world economy:

> The capitalist world economy has grown up as an international, and increasingly worldwide, system evolving largely as a function of the development of its 'advanced' sector, and in the first instance largely for the benefit of that sector. With certain exceptions, it therefore transformed the remainder of the world, insofar as this was not temporarily left to its own devices as lacking, for the time being, economic interest, into a set of subsidiary and thus dependent economies.

Dynamic circuits of capital push out selectively into the domains (both already capitalist and [today decreasingly] non-capitalist) which surround them. Such expansive and highly uneven capitalist geographies reflect both the possibilities and imperatives of capitalist social relations (Brenner 1986).

In similar fashion, Ernest Mandel (1975) captures some of this range of possibilities and, crucially, those of the contradictions between the dynamic geographies of circuits of capital and those of circuits of value into which they may seek to expand (see Lee 2011). Mandel suggests that the dynamic geographies of capitalist economic development consist of three interrelated moments:

i) ongoing capitalist development in the domain(s) of established capitalist accumulation;
ii) pre-capitalist and partial capitalist development [and, it might be added, non-capitalist development] outside these domain(s) and
iii) struggles between the expansion of i and the resistance of ii.

Thus it is possible to envisage the process of the formation and transformation of the world economic geography in terms of Mandel's three moments and Hobsbawm's globalising capital-centric economic geographies as intersections between dynamic and exteriorised circuits of capital and local circuits of value driven by social relations other than those of capitalism. The point here is less about the accuracy or otherwise of this kind of description of the making of the world economic geography than it is about the unproblematic primacy given to capitalism as the natural expansionary order thereby defining, measuring and assessing all other forms of economic geography against what are simply taken to be the norms of capitalism.

This has at least two damaging effects (damaging, that is to critical understanding). First, the implicit assumption of progress (Livingstone 2007; Barnes 2006) in these accounts ignores the complexity of non-capitalist domains and the largely spurned teaching (not least of complexity, society and ecology) offered therein (Mitchell 2002). Secondly, the significance of the assumption of the unproblematic primacy of capitalism relates not only to interpretations and transformations of the past (with all the powerful political implications that follow) but to practices of the present and the future. For J. K. Gibson-Graham (2008: 615), '. . . the performative effect of these representations was to dampen and discourage non-capitalist initiatives, since power was assumed to be concentrated in capitalism and to be largely absent from other forms of economy'.

Thus Gibson-Graham (2008: 619) asks:

> [W]hat if we were to accept that the goal of theory is not to extend knowledge by confirming what we already know, that the world is a place of domination and oppression? What if we asked theory instead to help us see openings, to provide a space of freedom and possibility?

To see, in other words, diverse economies/economic geographies. Following Eve Sedgwick (2003), Gibson-Graham (2008: 619) advocates the use of 'weak theory' to help achieve this goal. Weak theory 'involves refusing to extend explanation too widely or deeply, refusing to know too much . . . it could never tell us that the world economy will never be transformed by the disorganized proliferation of local projects', thereby opening up a 'differentiated landscape of force, constraint, energy, and freedom . . . and we could open ourselves to the positive energies that are suddenly available'.

An alternative way of thinking about this is to recognise that all theory is too simple to cope with the complex possibilities and constraints of ecological and social impulses in economic life. Indeed strong theory must demand a simplistic view of a complex world.

The weakness of strong theory derives from its exclusivity in its attempt to be comprehensive. The only possible responses are either acceptance of what is inevitably a simplistic representation of complex reality or rejection and confrontation. The strength of weak theory lies in its interpretative openness – recognizing that it can offer only partial understandings of a highly differentiated and always provisional social reality.

(Lee 2006: 429)

And this implies that there must be clear limits on the extent to which (strong) theory can (per)form economy. Overdetermination constantly intervenes. A range of drivers – including, for example, collective commitment to a project, cooperation, ethics, social justice, environmentalism, a range of knowledges beyond the purview of comprehension even by strong theory – shape economies. In other words, this perspective allows a consideration of the ordinariness of economies (Lee 2006) including their material imperatives.

Theory

But before moving on to consider this, a brief reminder of the very well-known limits of normative economic theory (Sheppard 2009). While markets are indispensable to the practice of economic life, they have taken on a super-ontological significance in neo-classical economic theory. Economies are frequently reduced simply to markets as if production, consumption or other modes of economic exchange and integration either do not or should not exist or are self-evidently banal and unproblematic. The economy becomes the market. This tendency was further exacerbated as rational choice theory elevated narrow economic rationality to a form of social rationality. But it did so by adopting the notion of the autonomous, all-knowing and self-interested individual as the subject of the system. In this way it thereby not only denied the possibility of other forms of social relations but assumed that self-interest was the singular driving force and criteria of choice and social/economic assessment guaranteeing harmony, efficiency and effectiveness. And, of course, universality – and the autonomous individual is an especially formative universality, not

least in the context of colonialism – reigns. This is a double form
of centring – a naturally and (by rights) universal self – which is
highly appropriate in the promulgation of colonialism.

And yet, despite its professed concerns for difference and
ecological sensitivity (Sheppard *et al.* 2009), Economic Geography
is not immune from such strong theorising (for recent reviews
see Coe *et al.* 2007; MacKinnon and Cumbers 2007). And, at the
same time, its critical response tends to be additive and eclectic
with little focus. Certainly, it is one thing to recognise the limits
of theory. But it is rather another to put considered alternatives
into place other than as superficially contextualised and apparently
new ideas which are presumed to sweep away the old with neither
a backward glance at the probabilities of path dependence on,
and integration with, the old (see Martin and Sunley 2001) nor
a recognition of the wider context within which such new ideas
take shape.[4] And, more importantly, such interventions are highly
provincial (Chakrabarty 2000), based on Western norms and
concepts with little, if any, recognition either of the limitations of
the ideas, and concepts at work and even less of the relational –
postcolonial – transformations of such ideas within and beyond
the 'provinces' from where they come.

In these and no doubt other ways, the politics of power strives
to deny that what is thereby continuously reinstated as other is,
rather, a facet (at the very least) of self and a powerful ongoing
relation of mutual formation. Having said this, however, I want to
argue that Economic Geography faces a particular set of constraints
on the development of a provincialised body of theory which is
prepared to do the hard work of taking Economics seriously while,
at the same time, recognising the absolute centrality of difference
in the search for ways of sustaining economic life. In this context,
the failure to recognise the parochiality of apparently universal
economic thought and practice and so to develop a postcolonial
Economic Geography is perhaps not so surprising especially in
light of the lack of critical attention given to the significance of the

---

4 Two quite different kinds of argument on this theme which provide critical contex-
tualisations of developments in economic geography within the intellectual frames
in which they arose are offered by Jamie Peck (2005, 2008) and by Ron Martin and
Peter Sunley (Martin 2010; Martin and Sunley 2006).

distinction between the imperatives of the materiality of economic geographies and its socially arbitrated role as a determinant of economic life (see earlier 67–68).[5] Nevertheless, given these material (ecological and social) imperatives of economic geographies, and given that the possibilities of difference are central to a resolution of the contradictions presented by the material depredations of economy on social and environmental life, a postcolonial Economic Geography remains a major lacuna.

Economic geographies and circuits of value

While the ordinariness of economic geographies stresses the spatial and temporal diversity of value, it nevertheless represents an apparent constraint – the irreducible and vital materiality of economic activity – on the notion of postcolonial thought. All economic geographies – however socially and culturally constituted, shaped and signified – must enable effective (in the sense of the adequate consumption, exchange and production of value, i.e. things of worth) circuits of value without which human life is incapable of survival. So the question becomes how much difference (as opposed to universality) is possible in economic geographies?

Economic geographies are the geographies constituted in the struggles of peoples to continue to be able to make a living through the construction of, and participation in, such circuits of value sustainable across space and time. These circuits enable the formation and circulation of value. However, circuits of value cannot be either temporally one-off or spatially non-dimensional. They must be sustainable both geographically and historically. They must, in other words be capable of reproduction and change across space and through time. In this, their institutional and geographical logistics are critical. And circuits of value are, therefore, irreducible: they either happen or they do not.

They are also inherently exploitative. To be effective, circuits of value must be capable of producing at least as much value as is

---

5 Rather, the debate has focused on the relationships between economic and non-economic determinants of economic life. See, for example, Harvey's (2006) response to such issues.

necessary to enable those involved in them to stay alive and to be fit enough to continue to produce value. But for this to happen, a surplus of value is necessary to cope with environmental vicissitudes and other potential interruptions. The total amount and quality of value produced in a place and time must be at least the quantitative and qualitative equal of the value needed to reproduce the circuit of value in that place and at that time. In other words, people engaged in circuits of value must be capable of producing and must be prepared – or be forced – to produce more value than they need for subsistence in a given space and time. Without such exploitation such circuits cannot be sustained.[6] Economic activity may, therefore, be thought of as a constantly dynamic and politically determined series of rounds of production, exchange and consumption of value through which further circuits of value may take place.

But what are the spaces and places through which these economic geographies may be constructed and so realised? Colonialism was a means of extending the spaces across which circuits of value could be developed to sustain the value requirements of the colonising powers. Though based firmly on territorial conceptions and practices of (national) political space, economic geographies of colonialism are relational spaces. They are the geographies produced through the construction of the circuits of value deemed necessary or desirable for the consumption, production and circulation of value of the colonisers.

The converse is also true. The economic geographies of postcolonialism are relational in the same sense, not only in that they are geographies made through, and necessary for, the construction of circuits of value but also because diverse geographies are necessary even to realise let alone to sustain the diverse economies that become possible in a postcolonial world. But, here again,

---

6 And the level of this inherently necessary exploitation is determined not merely by subsistence – or greater – quantities of value but by the value necessary to enable desired or acceptable or enforced levels and forms of social justice in producing, circulating and consuming value. Circuits of redistribution are always necessary in any economy unless the economically weak or incapable are, for whatever reason, simply to be allowed to fade away. Furthermore, the amount of value to be absorbed in the attempt to improve the quality of life, health, illness and death is central to notions of a just society but is, of course, acutely political as it implies uneven levels of exploitation.

the materiality of these geographies presents constraints around what might be thought of as unavoidable 'sunk costs'. Spaces of economy are not immediately or costlessly transformable and so postcolonial spaces involve significant redundancy thereby further constraining change and diversity. Such materialities are unavoidable and must, therefore, be fully incorporated into a postcolonial politics of power. However, the sheer imperative of economy for social life combined with the social and environmental threats to the sustenance of circuits of value necessarily involves the imagining, design and implementation of alternative economic geographies. The imperative of economy means that there simply is no alternative to alternatives.

This necessary materiality of economy (necessary both in the sense that circuits of value are always economic geographies – there can be no such thing as economies, only economic geographies – and in the sense of the imperative of economy) is the iron hand in the velvet glove of what Gibson-Graham (2006: 165) calls '"intentional community economies" in which social interdependency (economic being-in-common is acknowledged and fostered'. But materiality is, of course, not all. For Gibson-Graham (2008) such a project involves ethical thought as well as action. The 'performativity of our [i.e. academic subjects] teaching and research' transforms ontology into 'the effect rather than the ground of knowledge' (620) and involves 'three techniques of *doing thinking* . . . [O]ntological reframing: producing the ground of possibility . . . (620) [R]eading for difference: excavating the possible . . . (623) [and] Creativity: generating possibilities' (625). These are all inherently postcolonial projects and all are necessary here as well as there. They also imply new academic practices and performances – beyond as well as within the academy and involving 'the enactment and support of community economies' (627).

In short they all involve the postcolonial impulse.

Concluding comments: economic geographies and the possibility of a postcolonial politics of power?

The notion of diversity is integral to a potentially transformative politics of economic life and, through the economic imperative allied with the impossibility of any kind of economic life separate from social relations, cultural interpretations and political contestation, of great significance for a transformative politics, *tout court*. This politics lies as much in the performative incorporation of a diversity of values into all forms of economic activity as it does in a reflexive theoretical construction or promotion of alternative forms of economic practice (see Leyshon *et al.* 2003; Fuller *et al.* 2010). Diversity refers not just to differences among economic geographies – extant or yet to be created – but differences within economic geographies. It is the job of the politics of power to cover over, or at least to marginalise, both kinds of difference. And this is because postcolonial economic geographies are immanent in both and because of the inseparability of economic and social life. Hardly surprising, then, that the mainstream recognises its own vulnerability, especially at times of systemic crisis when the threat to mainstream universals is at a height and the emergence of others comes a distinct step closer. Postcolonial economic geographies are, in other words, always emergent notwithstanding both the repressive tendencies of the politics of power, here as well as there. Indeed, they demolish this particularly pernicious geography of difference and so make continuously possible a postcolonial politics of power.

References

Barnes, T. J. (2006) 'Saying yes without saying yes to progress', *Progress in Human Geography*, 30: 580–4.

Brenner, R. (1986) 'The social basis of economic development', in J. Roemer (ed.), *Analytical Marxism*, Cambridge University Press/Editions de la Maison des Sciences de l'Homme, Cambridge, pp. 23–53.

Chakrabarty, D. (2000) *Provincialising Europe Postcolonial Thought and Historical Difference*, Princeton University Press, Princeton, NJ.

Coe, N. M., Kelly, P. F. and Yeung, H. W. C. (2007) *Economic Geography: A contemporary introduction*, Blackwell, Malden MA.

Fuller, D., Jonas, A. and Lee, R. (eds) *Interrogating Alterity: Alternative economic and political spaces*, Ashgate, Farnborough.

Gibson-Graham, J. K. (1996) *The End of Capitalism (As We Knew It): A feminist critique of political economy*, Blackwell, Oxford.

— (2006) *A Postcapitalist Politics*, Minnesota University Press, Minneapolis, MN.

— (2008) 'Diverse economies: performative practices for "other worlds"', *Progress in Human Geography*, 32(5): 613–32.

Gregory, D. (2004) *The Colonial Present*, Blackwell, Oxford.

Harvey, D. (2006) 'Editorial: The geographies of critical geography', *Transactions of the Institute of British Geographers*, 31: 409–12.

Hobsbawm, E. J. (1979) 'The development of the world economy', *Cambridge Journal of Economics*, 3: 305–18, 310.

Lee, R. (2006) 'The ordinary economy', *Transactions of the Institute of British Geographers*, 31: 413–32.

— (2010) 'Economic society/social geography', in S. J. Smith, R. Pain, S. A. Marston and J. P. Jones (eds), *The Sage Handbook of Social Geographies*, Sage, London, pp. 205–21.

— (2011) 'Within and outwith/Material and political? Local economic development and the spatialities of economic geographies', in A. Pike, A. Rodríguez-Pose and J. Tomaney (eds), *A Handbook of Local and Regional Development*, Routledge, London, pp 193–211.

Leyshon, A., Lee, R. and Williams, C. C. (eds) (2003) *Alternative Economic Spaces*, Sage, London.

Livingstone, D. (2007) 'Putting progress in its place', *Progress in Human Geography*, 30: 559–79.

Mackinnon, D. and Cumbers, A. (2007) *An Introduction to Economic Geography*, Pearson, Harlow.

Mandel, E. (1975) *Late Capitalism*, New Left Books, London.

Martin, R. L. (2010) 'The "new economic geography": Credible models of the economic landscape?', in A. Leyshon, R. Lee, P. Sunley and L. McDowell (eds), *Handbook of Economic Geography*, Sage, London.

Martin, R. L. and Sunley P. (2001) 'Rethinking the "economic" in economic geography: Broadening our vision or losing our focus', *Antipode*, 33: 148–61.

— (2006) 'Path dependence and regional economic evolution', *Journal of Economic Geography*, 6: 395–438.

Mitchell, T. (2002) *Rule of Experts Egypt, Techno Politics, Modernity*, University Press Berkeley, California.

Ogborn, M. J. (2007) *Indian Ink Script and Print in the Making of the English East India Company*, Chicago University Press, Chicago.

Peck, J. (2005) 'Economic sociologies in space', *Economic Geography*, 81: 129–76.

— (2008) 'Remaking laissez-faire', *Progress in Human Geography*, 32(1): 3–43.

Rankin, K. N. (2004) *The Cultural Politics of Markets*, Pluto Press, London.

Sedgwick, E. (2003) *Touching Feeling: Affect, pedagogy, performativity*, Duke University Press, Durham, NC.

Sheppard, E. S. (2009) 'Economy', in D. Gregory, R. Johnston, G. Pratt,

M. J. Watts and S. Whatmore (eds), *The Dictionary of Human Geography*, Wiley Balckwell, Chichester, 184–5.

Sheppard, E., Porter, P. W., Faust, D. R. and Nagar R. (2009) *A World of Difference Encountering and Contesting Development*, Guilford Press, New York.

Suzuki, T. (2007) 'Accountics: Impacts of internationally standardized accounting on the Japanese socio-economy', *Accounting Organizations and Society*, 32: 263–301.

Tieu, C. (2010) 'Les images fausses des Occidentaux Interview', *Sud Ouest*, 13 February, available at: www.sudouest.com

Turner, A. (2009) 'The financial crisis and the future of financial regulation', The Economist's Inaugural City Lecture, 21 January.

4

Economic geographies as situated knowledges

Wendy Larner

Introduction

I am a 46-year-old New Zealander, who completed a Canadian PhD, returned to Aotearoa New Zealand to establish her academic career, and who now works in a geography department in the UK while continuing to actively research New Zealand-based topics. How is this simple statement of academic biography reflected in what I do and how I do it? What does this tell you about my intellectual theory and practice? More specifically, what does this mean for my understanding of the possibilities offered by postcolonial approaches to the economy? This chapter begins by showing that situated political and academic experiences have framed my intellectual approach. It then develops a broader argument about the benefits and challenges of theorising economic geographies as situated knowledges. In the final section I illustrate my theoretical and political claims through a discussion of some of the recent scholarship on neoliberalism. Rather than focusing on the understandings of post-colonial[1] theory offered by cultural

---

1 I am aware of the distinction often made between post-colonial as a literary field, and postcolonial as periodisation. As will become evident, I am not advocating an engagement between literary theory and economic geography, and it is doubtful that a former settler colony such Aotearoa New Zealand could ever be fully postcolonial. That said, I retain the term postcolonial as a useful shorthand for diverse attempts to challenge hegemonic forms of knowledge production.

theorists (Said 2003, or drawing on the work of social theorists from the Global South to try to dislodge the conceptual hegemony of the Global North (Connell 2007), the aim of this chapter is to first and foremost position postcolonialism as a politics, then show how and why this politics has implications for the geographies of knowledge production. In doing so, I am engaging with Spivak's (2008) observation that the 'postcolonial question' gets produced in different ways in different places.

Beginning the chapter with my own story is not simply a self-indulgent exercise, nor is it to equate place, identity and knowledge in any straightforward way. Rather it is an analytical entry point that allows me to emphasise that theories are developed and distributed through networks that do not always take the forms we might expect or flow in the directions we would predict. As geographers Eric Sheppard (n.d.) and Jim Glassman (2009) have recently argued, there are varied spatialities of international knowledge production. I use my own experiences to illustrate these increasingly diverse geographies of academic knowledge production and circulation, and then explore their implications for geographical theorisations of the economy. More specifically, I want to move away from the claim that theory is produced by metropolitan scholars, and that the periphery remains the site of case studies and data production (Sheppard n.d.). Rather I begin from the assumption that the knowledges of both metropole and periphery are more diverse than is often assumed, and then show how this starting point might encourage economic geographers to think in new ways about their discipline in general, and research on the economy in particular.

Debates about positionality have underpinned a recent focus on diverse patterns of academic location and movement. It is increasingly recognised that social experts (including economic geographers and other social scientists) are embodied individuals who carry their histories, geographies and social relationships with them (Kothari 2009). Moreover, as Richard Le Heron and Nick Lewis (2007: 5), argue, 'Our awareness of the works and work of economic geography is, to echo both Nigel Thrift and Doreen Massey, very much influenced by our a-where-ness'. To date, however, the majority of commentaries on these issues have tended to reinscribe stories of hegemonic places, languages and experiences and underline the ongoing marginalisation of geographic, linguistic and cultural 'others'. While sympathetic to such claims, the difficulty with this reading of the geographies of knowledge is that it makes invisible the increasing numbers of us who are multiply placed in such accounts. Because of the changing geography curriculum, more diverse hiring practices, and the internationalisation of the academy itself, increasing numbers of economic geographers working in the US and the UK are not from the academic traditions and high-profile departments that constitute the 'disciplinary heartlands'. One consequence is that we are placed in to disciplinary histories and intellectual formations that are only partly ours. How might we expose the fact that in both metropole and periphery there are multiple disciplinary and intellectual formations, shot through with relations of power? How can we reveal the discipline of economic geography as 'different in itself' understanding that it was always already so? And what work is required in the effort to proliferate these critical disciplinary genealogies and geographies? This is the task I have set myself in this chapter.

Situating myself

This chapter begins in Aotearoa New Zealand. Those who know something of the recent history of the country will recognise that the one-line biography that opens the chapter tells you a great deal about my political formation. For many New Zealanders of my generation, the Springbok Tour of 1981 was a defining experience. The decision by a conservative New Zealand government to let the South African rugby team tour the country at a time when there were international sanctions in place against the apartheid regime saw widespread mobilisation against the tour, crystallising a wider discontent with the status quo across a broad range of progressive social movements. Students, feminists, Maori, civil rights activists and unionists were among those who joined the anti-tour protests that took place in all the main centres. This politics initially took the form of an international solidarity movement against the apartheid regime in South Africa, but as the movement developed so too did attention increasingly focus on domestic issues. In particular, Maori activists challenged Pakeha[2] anti-tour protesters to recognise their own racism and the issues of internal colonisation that had been largely ignored over the previous century.

This was an extraordinarily challenging time for me; I was an 18-year-old Pakeha university student living away from home for the first time. I had grown up in a small conservative farming community in which rugby was one of the few social activities that brought Maori and Pakeha together. While I joined anti-tour marches with my student peers, I knew all too well that my father and many of my former school friends would be among those spectators jeering the protesters. Over the course of that year many Pakeha New Zealanders – both pro-tour and anti-tour – were forced to recognise that not only were sport and politics indelibly intertwined (despite the claims of the then Prime Minister Rob Muldoon) but also that New Zealand was far from being the ethnically integrated paradise that many of us imagined.

This formative experience means that postcolonialism is for me, and has been since 1981, a political aspiration rather than a theoretical approach or particular intellectual formation (Larner and Spoonley 1995; Larner 2006). It is a politics that demands all New Zealanders recognise the disjunctive and deeply contested historical geographical processes – including colonial conquest, settler capitalism, racialisation, globalisation – through which our place in the world and our multiple relationships with others have been constituted. Today living in no longer colonial, but certainly not postcolonial, Aotearoa New Zealand means working in a context where there are multiple, and sometimes incommensurate, understandings of personhood, community and property, which often need to be judged on their cultural context and political efficacy rather than their theoretical correctness (Larner 1995, Frankenberg and Mani 1993). The distinctive political processes, institutional formations and cultural understandings that have emerged through and against contestations over indigeneity, biculturalism and multiculturalism are sometimes difficult to

---

2 New Zealanders of European descent.

negotiate and can be particularly challenging for newcomers.[3] However these claims and the conflicts that surround them also represent an ongoing and explicitly situated politics of knowledge, place and identity.

This biography also tells you something about my academic orientation in general, and my approach to economic geography in particular. I came to economic geography not through knowledges associated with the expansion of the British Empire, the quantitative revolution, and the challenges of Marxism (to briefly rehearse conventional UK-centric chronological accounts of the sub-discipline), but rather through the heterodox theorisations of feminism and post-structuralism. The crucial course was a second-year paper, taught by feminist geographer Ann Magee in 1982. Ostensibly an urban-economic geography course, Ann's primary intellectual aim was to expose her provincial New Zealand undergraduate students to theories of feminism, Marxism and anarchism. Her efforts were complemented by those of the late Evelyn Stokes who had a long-standing commitment to Maori geography (as opposed to the geography of Maori). Her efforts, both in the classroom and for the New Zealand land claims process, put the questions of 'who researches whom' firmly on the intellectual agendas of many New Zealand geographers well before the discipline as a whole began to ask these questions (d'Hauteserre 2005). Many of my cohorts revelled in this radical curriculum, and eventually the discipline of geography itself mutated as the politics of feminism and biculturalism began to reshape local academic debates (Stokes *et al.* 1987). In retrospect it is also notable that many of us went on to be involved in grass-roots political movements of various sorts, both locally and nationally. Ann herself left the academy not long afterwards and has since become one of the leading figures in New Zealand's pursuit for sustainable development.

As young New Zealanders tend to do, I left the country after finishing my undergraduate degree and spent most of the next

---

3 My most recent experience of this was at a conference on the future of New Zealand science. A high-profile international key-note speaker privately expressed complete bewilderment at the very idea of 'Maori science', whereas for the vast majority of New Zealanders it would now be impossible to contemplate holding such a conference without this content.

five years working and travelling in Australia, Europe, Africa and
Asia. My eventual return to New Zealand at the end of 1987 was
marked by profound culture shock. During the time I had been
away the country once known internationally for its 'cradle-to-
grave' welfare state had been transformed by a dramatic state
sector restructuring programme, and was subsequently described
in an editorial by *The Economist* as the 'mother of all reformers'
(*The Economist* 1993). The economy had been deregulated, agricultural subsidies had been removed, the highly regulated post-war
manufacturing sector had been placed on a 'level playing field'
with its international competitors through tariff reductions, and
major state assets such as post, telecommunications, electricity,
railways, mines and forests had been sold to offshore investors.
Closer inspection also revealed the huge social cost associated
with this restructuring – at the time unemployment was at record
levels, government services were being cut, and social inequality
of all forms was more visible. But perhaps the most puzzling to
me was the way in which political–economic identities had also
shifted; choice, flexibility, empowerment and self determination had become an integral aspect of the way in which many
New Zealanders talked of themselves and their relationships with
others.

In many respects my academic work over the last twenty years
reflects my efforts to understand the content of this profound
economic, political and social transformation and its ongoing
consequences. Initially, however, I struggled to find appropriate
analytical tools for this intellectual project. Was New Zealand's
experience simply a South Pacific version of that associated with
Thatcherism and Reaganism? Should the blame for these changes
be placed squarely at the feet of the fourth Labour government?
Or were there broader economic processes at work? How could
I conceptually grasp the significance of shifting identities? It was
the discipline of geography, both nationally and internationally,
that offered me useful ways to think about the broader processes
of economic restructuring (Britton 1991; Britton; Le Heron and
Pawson 1993; Lancaster Regionalism Group 1985; Massey 1984)
but it was in feminist literatures that I found scholars engaged
in the difficult debates over questions of identity, difference and

subjectivity (James and Saville-Smith 1989). I was drawn into these discussions and began self-directed reading in an effort to straddle political economic and feminist concerns. This took me from economic geography to development geography, from Esther Boserup (1970) to Chandra Mohanty (1988), and from gender as social category to gender as discursive formation.

It was the governmentality literature (first encountered in Rose and Miller 1992) that eventually allowed me to draw together my longstanding interests in feminist and post-structuralist theorising, and to reconceptualise the economic and political processes associated with neoliberalism. Following my engagement with this literature during my doctoral studies in Canada, I became part of a loose network of Canadian, British, Australian and Scandinavian scholars whose engagements with the then relatively obscure lectures of a dead French theorist began to reshape social science research (Larner 1998). On my return to New Zealand, together with my colleagues Richard Le Heron and Nicholas Lewis, I began to use the label 'post-structuralist political economy' as a means of signalling broader ambitions to reconceptualise the economy (Larner and Le Heron 2002a, 2002b). Our research trajectory was based on a shared commitment to situated theorising (beginning from the understanding that where we were mattered to how we understood the world), and a growing conviction that New Zealand was experiencing messy and contradictory neoliberalising processes not readily explained by the analytical resources to hand in more conventional economic geography and political economy literatures. It was this engagement that led us in due course, both individually and collectively, to contest universalising assumptions of globalisation, to highlight the specificity of neoliberal political projects, and to conceptualise the rise of new economic and political forms as heterogeneous assemblages in our efforts to understand the emergent economic and political formations of the 'new New Zealand'.

Situated knowledges and postcolonial economies

What does this embodied story of politics, academia and theoretical improvisation mean for the question posed by this book? It should

already be clear that postcolonial theorisations of the economy
are not more familiar forms of development geography under a
new name, even if such scholarship takes the form of revisionist
analyses centred on the politics of contestation and resistance
rather than hegemonic expressions of power (Pollard *et al.* 2009).
Nor is it to privilege analyses of colonialism, developmentalism
and globalising neoliberalism in academic accounts about the relationships between 'here' and 'there' although this is an important
start. Indeed, if this is the project of postcolonial economies, then
this intellectual project has failed in its own terms as it remains
an account that reinscribes the hegemony of the metropolitan
places and knowledges. Rather, postcolonialism is an approach
that has long asked us to be conscious of the situatedness of our
own knowledges, and to interrogate what that might mean for
our scholarship (Spivak 1988). As Jennifer Robinson (2003: 650)
succinctly argues, 'Postcolonialism is a project to disabuse social
theory, and perhaps spatial theory, of its claims to universalism'.
What might this mean for efforts to develop more challenging
retheorisations of the economy?

I began this chapter by narrating my political, academic and
intellectual formation because it underlines my first point; namely,
that the issues we address as social scientists are often underpinned
by (usually unstated) personal experiences, concerns and passions.
In this context it is useful to begin by connecting the search for
postcolonial approaches to the economy to the gradually increasing demographic diversity of the metropolitan academy. As more
social scientists from 'other' places, including ever-so-slowly
increasing numbers from the Global South and postsocialist settings, find intellectual niches in these theory-driven departments
will this force broader recognition of the specificity of purportedly
universal knowledges? Will these scholars be interested in claims
about multiple knowledges? Or will many of these (often highly
numerate and technically sophisticated) diasporic scholars be
forced to practice 'intellectual assimilation' (Sheppard n.d.) in
order to gain acceptance, or forced in to the now often hard-to-
fill slots of applied research and quantitative methods? Relatedly,
as more metropolitan scholars are exposed to 'other' people and
places, because 'gap years' have become a rite of passage for

increasing numbers of young people from the Global North, international travel has become easier and cheaper, and academic labour markets are rapidly internationalising (across both national and linguistic boundaries), will this change the content of economic geography? What connections are there between places of origin, formative personal experiences, and subsequent academic endeavours? Sheppard (n.d.) argues that at present these trends are giving rise to demographic, not intellectual, hybridity but will this change as the discipline diversifies, and more economic geographers understand themselves to be both here and there (Glassman 2009)?

Secondly, I traced my academic formation in order to underline the point that we need to think carefully about the disciplinary stories we tell ourselves and others. Those of us working both outside and inside the disciplinary heartlands often find ourselves cast in the roles of translator and mediator. When we are outside we expose ourselves, our colleagues, and our students to the 'international' debates and literatures, and then explore what intellectual purchase these debates might have in our own places. But when we are inside (either temporarily or permanently) what academic interventions do we then make? Too often, I suspect, we give in to the temptation to frame ourselves and our concerns as paradigmatic case studies. This allows us to demonstrate to colleagues from bigger and/or more important places that not only can we relate the most recent theoretical developments to our concerns, but we can also argue for the empirical relevance of our place. Yet the risk is that we too reinscribe the problematic distinction between the theory-driven metropole and the peripheral, data generating, case study. We need to be clear with ourselves, as well as others, that it is not good enough to simply study 'here' using the analytical tools of 'there'. It is also important to be wary of the search for authenticity – including the rediscovery of local knowledges or indigenous scholarship – although in some settings such exercises of recovery will be a crucial first step (Connell 2007). In short, postcolonialism demands we recognise that problems, knowledges, concepts and categories have multiple historical geographies. This encourages us to ask ourselves: How do I know what I know? What is the geography of my Geography? Who are my audiences? And how does it compare to the Geography of others?

Thirdly, and more substantively, this starting point underlines the need to think harder about the analytical resources we use to conduct geographical research on the economy. While for some economic geographers turning to post-colonial theory might be an important step in efforts to decentre conventional understandings of the economy, there are already a raft of theoretically informed economic geographies that draw on post-structuralist literatures to develop anti-essentialist accounts of economic entities, processes and actors. The diverse approaches associated with cultural economy, diverse and community economies, post-development studies, and ethnographies of the economy, among others, all offer ways of moving beyond universalising economic knowledges. Thus it may be that in the ambition to develop postcolonial readings of economies, geographers actually need less theory or at least not more theory of particular kinds. It may be more useful to use theory to new ends, heeding Connell's (2007) call for 'dirty theory'. As she explains, 'The role of dirty theory is not to subsume but to clarify; not to classify from the outside, but to illuminate a situation in its concreteness' (p. 207). Once we get 'dirty' in this way it is highly unlikely that what we see will foster universal claims, grand narratives, or even be theoretically and politically consistent.

In short, rather than privileging reified accounts based on abstract concepts and macrolevel processes in the search for post-colonial approaches to the economic, I am arguing for approaches to the economy that use careful theorising and innovative methodologies to document how analytical and empirical links between 'there' and 'here' have come to constitute economies in particular forms. In many ways this is to echo Doreen Massey's (1993) long-standing call for power geometries; the careful tracing of connections wherever they take us and to be explicit about why making these different economic geographies visible matters politically. The geographical processes through which problems, knowledges, concepts, categories, actors, discourses, techniques and so forth travel and are translated are not smooth processes of diffusion from the metropole to the periphery, but rather involve multiple and heterogeneous geographies. Moreover, almost inevitably the focus on concreteness will mean acknowledging and working with disjuncture and ambiguities.

These claims lie at the heart of my assertion that rethinking economic geographies demands situated knowledges. This is neither an argument about the local as the key site of knowledge production, nor a suspicion about generalisation *per se*. Rather it is an approach that begins from the assumption that the objects and subjects of economic knowledge have specific constitutions, emerge from multiple origins and travel in disjunctive circuits. I am proposing a closer examination of processes of constitution, articulation, translation and mutation that comprise these geographies. In the section that follows I give some concrete examples of what such situated economic geographies might involve.

Towards situated economic geographies

Alternative approaches to theorising the economy could focus on the disjunctive formation of 'actually existing' economic knowledges. Why is it that particular professional, technical and lay economic knowledges takes particular forms in particular places, and what does that mean for the economic formations that ensue? Indeed, it could be argued that postcolonial readings of the economy emerged first in practice rather than in theory, as economic, juridical and legal structures in various places have struggled to reconcile diverse understandings of land, kinship and use. What happens if we broaden the learning derived from these explicitly postcolonial settings (one obvious example is the contested debates over indigenous land claims), and begin from the assumption that economic knowledges are always situated, multiple and hybrid no matter where they are found? While we now recognise that modernity was not a pattern produced in Europe and exported to the rest of the world (Connell 2007), we have yet to fully bring this understanding to our conceptualisations of the economy.

These alternative economic geographies could be disciplinary projects. In this context, the focus would be on travelling theories and circulating concepts, showing how certain academics, texts and ideas have become what science and technology scholars call 'mutable mobiles' (Law and Mol 2001) and examine the work that they do in assembling particular actor-networks. These economic geographies are quite different from conventional 'history of ideas' projects premised on notions of the diffusion or generalisation of certain knowledges. Rather the aim is to reveal that concepts and categories themselves have diverse histories, geographies and sociologies. There are already accounts that show us that concepts and categories are not taken up by the same scholars in different contexts, and they are not asked to do the same intellectual work (Cusset 2008; Lendvai and Stubbs 2009). Indeed, Spivak (2008) argues that postcolonialism itself is a situated concept; stressing that exiled Palestinian scholar Edward Said's work emerges from the politics of his time and place and his training in nineteenth century British literature, and that her own intellectual forma-tion involves understanding complex alliances between British colonialism, Indian nationalisms and feminisms, the importance of Indian colonial discourse studies, and the role of Indian intel-lectuals in the study of hybridity and transnationality. Importantly, she also argues that current models of postcolonial theory may not necessarily travel well. Ideas arrive (or not!) in specific contexts in embodied forms, and then are made and remade through multiple connections and contestations.

In economic geography Trevor Barnes (2001, 2002, 2006) has begun this work, but it needs to be extended well beyond the mainstream economic and quantitative knowledges with which he is concerned. What happens if we proliferate such accounts? This would encourage us to think harder about why certain concepts are privileged in particular settings, and to focus on why this varies across space, time and disciplinary context. It would require not only robust, geographically sensitive, genealogies of concepts and categories, but also a nuanced understanding of local politics. To return to my own intellectual trajectory to illustrate the kinds of questions such an approach might generate: How did Latin American dependency theory shape accounts of New Zealand's experience of settler capitalism? Why were New Zealand geog-raphers such early participants in globalisation debates? Why were my Quebecois colleagues so sceptical of Foucault? Why did British, Australian and Canadian sociologists begin to engage the governmentality literature in the early 1990s, whereas most Anglo-American economic geographers did not come to this literature until a decade later? What intellectual and political work did continental philosophy do for Australian feminists during the 1980s, and why is that so different to the work it now does for British non-representational geographers in the 2000s?

These alternative economic geographical projects could also be more empirically oriented projects. The approach I am advocating demands that we think much harder about how economic entities – markets, firms, industries, sectors – are produced in particular forms in particular settings. There are existing studies that indicate what might be learned with such an approach. Tomo Suzuki's (2007) work on post-war accounting in Japan, Timothy Mitchell's (2002) on the modern Egyptian state, and Tania Li's (2007) work on community forestry in Indonesia are diversely positioned in disciplinary and theoretical terms, but these scholars all focus on showing how specific conceptions of the economy were assembled in particular places. What happens if we turn a similar lens on New Zealand's export development strategies, eco-town schemes in the UK, and new forms of financial regulation in the US? How have economic discourses, strategies and techniques travelled, and what has happened as they have mutated on these travels? Such work also encourages us to pay heed to particular problemisations, serendipitous encounters, local appropriations and the selective reworking of particular economic approaches. In my view, such a focus would tell us a great deal new about economies, and how it is that we come to know them in the diverse ways that we do. In doing so it would also help 'provincialise' economic knowledge (Chakrabarty 2000), by showing how concepts and categories travel and do particular work in specific places.

For example, in the seminar series on which this book is based I outlined an argument about the co-constitution of the New Zealand fashion industry. Drawing on research conducted with my New Zealand colleagues I showed how this industry has been assembled in a distinctive form as it had been mobilised by the diverse political projects of the fifth Labour Government including globalisation, the knowledge economy, creative cities, social development (Larner, Lewis and Le Heron 2009;

Lewis, Larner and Le Heron 2008). 'Ah yes', the response from the audience was, 'we have the creative industries here in the UK as well and they are doing the same work.' But is this actually the case? Do creative industry processes and practices really mean the same thing in different places? Subsequently Russell Prince has shown that the creative industries projects in New Zealand and UK are distinctive assemblages; emerging in particular times and places and in response to particular problems (Prince 2008). His work also highlights how these projects are associated with the travelling knowledges, the formation of new epistemic communities, and the emergence of distinctive forms of expertise. In short, we might see the increasing ubiquity of the creative industries as the global diffusion of a neoliberal 'fast policy' (Peck 2004) or we might focus on the specificity of these processes in order to show how this particular economic entity has come to be known in particular ways in particular places. In sum, understood in this way, the empirical is not simply yet another case study but the location from which we theorise.

More generally I have long argued that there are multiple versions of neoliberalism and called for a greater focus on the messiness of particular neoliberal projects (Larner 2000, 2003). Drawing on diverse theoretical influences and with multiple political motivations, economic geographers and others have begun to do the hard work that situates neoliberalism, examining its multiple origin points, and interrogating the distinctive political formations that have emerged. In short, we have begun to more carefully follow our object of study rather than assuming we already know the contours of its geographies and sociologies. For example, Jamie Peck (2008) has recently shown that the rise of neoliberalism involves a complex transnational historical geography through his study of the embodied networks that constituted the Chicago School. More broadly, focusing variously on political–economic theories, spatial imaginaries, political technologies and subjectification, diverse contributors to this research field have been concerned to trace how particular understandings emerge and are articulated into the political configurations in which they are now found (see, among others, Bockman and Eyal 2002; Czarniawska and Sevon 2005; Hoffman *et al.* 2006; McCann 2008;

Swain 2006). Despite important conceptual differences between these accounts, the shared emphasis is on examining the specificity of the political–economic processes involved, and the contingent nature of the 'global assemblages' (Ong and Collier 2005) that result.

Of particular interest to me is how diverse economic actors (including academics, consultants, policy-makers, technocrats and activists) have travelled across sectors and borders, and the ideas and practices they embody. Such embodied studies are a major challenge to the broader literature on neoliberalism which tends to focus only on emblematic figures such as Hayek and Friedmann, Thatcher and Reagan. These subjects include the telecommunications engineers, who were made redundant from the newly privatised Telecom NZ during the 1980s because they did not fit the private sector mould, but then set themselves up as privatisation consultants and began to travel the Pacific (Larner and Laurie 2009). They also include the new 'strategic brokers' who have backgrounds in social movements, but are now working in both local and central government inventing and sustaining the local partnerships that are proliferating in the social policy arena (Larner and Craig 2005). They encompass the businesswomen such as Karen Walker who lie behind New Zealand's success-ful designer fashion industry (Larner and Molloy 2009), Mike Moore (a New Zealander who started off as a member of the Young Socialists and came to head the WTO during the Doha round) (Larner 2009), and indeed even diasporic citizens such as myself who are being enrolled into new economic development strategies (Larner 2007). Seen together, these projects have shown how a diverse range of New Zealanders are being encouraged to look outwards, build relationships, create new knowledges and constitute new domains. I would argue strongly that in order to understand the specificity of new forms of governance we need to interrogate the negotiated tensions that are constitutive of these new formations, and embody political–economic processes rather than seeing them as externally imposed.

But how else has neoliberalism gone global? What about the role of its critics? To date we know much less about the roles that academic and activist networks have played in centring 'strong theory' (Gibson-Graham 2008) accounts of neoliberalism. What would we see if we positioned critical economic geographer Jamie Peck and the University of Madison-Wisconsin, rather than neoclassical economist Milton Friedman and the University of Chicago in an analysis of neoliberalism as a travelling concept? What role has the global social justice movement played in proliferating analyses of neoliberalism? Did social movements and community organisations 'prefigure' practices we now associate with new forms of governance (Sharma 2008)? I am certainly not suggesting that economic geographers, political activists and social movements are somehow proponents of neoliberalism, but I am suggesting that if we take the concept of multiple origins seriously we need to be more attentive to the conceptual implications of our critiques. Relatedly, our fixation with neoliberalism has blinkered us to other, equally significant, expressions of power, including authoritarian, neo-colonial and disciplinary forms. Why haven't we traced the practises that have moved from the Global South to the Global North in our efforts to untangle contemporary political formations? For example, what are the flows, networks and mobilities through which microfinance has travelled from India to Germany? What other forms of economic experimentation are taking place and where? How have these economic discourses and practices mutated *en route*? Again, answering these questions will demand specific stories, requiring careful attention to the empirics, rather than programmatic statements.

Of course we will need to be very careful in developing such analyses. How we analyse the current conjuncture matters, not least because it carries political significance. We must not be content with smooth stories that recreate global hegemonies, but nor should we ignore the important role of political contestation in framing those hegemonies in particular forms. We need to reveal contradictions and contestations, and the aim is to show that it always could have been otherwise. In this context we need to be selective about our origin points, and make informed decisions about what discourses, policies, techniques and subjects we follow and to where. But we also need to understand that these travels may not begin where we think they do, and they make take us to places we do not expect to find ourselves. Indeed, we may find that it becomes much more difficult to think of 'here' and 'there' in a context where comparison, networking and global processes have become more integral to contemporary knowledge formations.

Conclusion

Throughout my academic career an ongoing engagement with New Zealand empirics has been central. Despite my best efforts I find it very difficult to make programmatic statements about the nature of the contemporary world; rather my intellectual ambition is to show how concepts and categories come to take particular shapes in particular places. This trajectory is what I have tried to illustrate in this chapter using the term 'situated knowledges'. My claim is that intellectual trajectories, academic projects and conceptual questions take specific forms and that this has implications for the economic geographies that ensue.

So what does all this mean now that I am located in the UK in a department some would see as being at the very heart of the hegemonic disciplinary project? Is my ambition for postcolonial economic geographies now an impossible dream? While I have built a transnational life, intellectual approach and academic career from a small South Pacific economy,[4] I am conscious that I now relate a chronological disciplinary narrative to my Year One economic geography students, which starts with Chisholm's Handbook of Commercial Geography (1889) and ends with Allen Scott's (2000) argument that economic geography should be seen as an intellectual palimpsest rather than a united front. In doing so I am re-narrating a disciplinary history in ways that erase the discontinuities between my own intellectual formations and hegemonic accounts of the discipline. But when I tell my students that this is a disciplinary history, not the disciplinary history, they don't get it. It is difficult to unsettle their taken for granted understandings of the nature of the academy when their textbooks reinscribe the idea that all the important and interesting economic geographers are found in the UK or North America, and have only

---

4 Herein is a question for my New Zealand colleagues: when did we start thinking of ourselves like this?

just begun to explore the idea that 'the economy' is a historically and socially constructed idea (Coe *et al*. 2007).

Yet my move to the UK has further underlined the need to think about situated knowledges. Issues that I previously understood to be conceptual differences (for example, my relatively optimistic reading of the political possibilities of contemporary forms of partnership working (Larner and Butler 2007)) have turned out to be empirical differences. I now understand why many of my British colleagues see government–community partnerships as top–down and tokenistic initiatives. Indeed, a comparative project focused on the implications of partnerships for forms of activism in Manchester and Auckland has forced me to recognise that the new governmental forms in the two cities are simply not the same (Milligan *et al*. 2008). The government-sponsored forums that go under the name of partnership in the UK offer very different political possibilities when compared to the more inventive spaces that have emerged in the New Zealand setting, in part because of the way in which big P Partnership of biculturalism in Aotearoa New Zealand has informed the debates about these proliferating little p partnerships. This underlines my broader point that the 'geography of geography' matters when we make claims about the utility or otherwise of concepts such as neoliberalism, partnership and community-based activism.

What has also become clear to me is that big ideas travel much more easily than detail. For example, despite the increasing influence of Timothy Mitchell's groundbreaking work in the contemporary economic geography literature (Mitchell 2008) how often do we remember that his original research was set in Egypt? And there are very real challenges associated with making big conceptual claims from an empirically small place. To this day my New Zealand colleagues and I struggle to persuade international publishers, referees and commentators that our country case is interesting and relevant to the broader political–economic debates in which we participate. At the same time, many of our local colleagues would prefer to see more straightforward accounts of the New Zealand experience; strong stories that might serve as the basis for clear political actions. And of course we shouldn't overlook the very real political economies that underpin this; the unequal distributions of resources, the 'brain grab', the commercial imperatives of the publishing industry, the linguistic hegemony of English, the complex relationships that those from outside Anglo-American networks have with dominant forms of knowledge.

But I am not alone or even unusual in grappling with these dilemmas. Increasing numbers of us have diversely constituted intellectual formations. My point is that economic geographical knowledge is always already multiple. In trying to make visible these multiple knowledges we need to be careful not to simply rehearse disciplinary histories that recentre Western knowledges and underline the intellectual hegemony of particular places, thereby making invisible those of us who are already here. That said, there are not enough of us in the British Academy, and certainly not enough in economic geography. Indeed, what is striking to me is how many geographers working on the economy in this part of the world have found homes for themselves in development studies. So I conclude with a fairly mundane observation; if we broaden our definition of who economic geographers are then we will find that many of us are already doing the research that is captured under broader ambition for postcolonial economic geographies. The challenge is to both recognise and foster this diversity, both demographic and intellectual. Indeed, if postcolonialism is a condition in which we live with the economic, political and cultural legacies of colonialism, then perhaps in our differentially globalised world it would be useful for us all to explore what that might mean for the geographies of our scholarship.

Acknowledgements

Thanks to Mark Jackson, Richard Le Heron and the editors for their very useful comments.

References

Barnes, T. (2001) 'In the beginning was economic geography: A science studies approach to disciplinary history', *Progress in Human Geography*, 25(4): 521–44.

— (2002) 'Performing economic geography: Two men, two books, and a cast of thousands', *Environment and Planning A*, 34: 487–512.

— (2006) 'Geographical intelligence: American geographers and research and analysis in the Office of Strategic Services 1941–1945', *Journal of Historical Geography*, 32(1): 149–68.

Bockman, J. and Eyal, G. (2002) 'Eastern Europe as a laboratory for economic knowledge: The transnational roots of neoliberalism', *American Journal of Sociology*, 108(2): 310–52.

Boserup, E. (1970) *Women's Role in Economic Development*, George Allen and Unwin, London.

Britton, S. (1991) 'Recent trends in the internationalisation of the New Zealand economy', *Australian Geographical Studies*, 29(1): 3–2.

Britton, S., Le Heron, R. and Pawson, E. (1993) *Changing Places in New Zealand: A geography of restructuring*, New Zealand Geographical Society, Wellington.

Britton, S. and Le Heron, R. (1987) 'Regions and restructuring in New Zealand: Issues and questions in the 1980s', *New Zealand Geographer*, 43(3): 129–39.

Chakrabarty, D. (2000) *Provincializing Europe: Postcolonial thought and historical difference*, Princeton University Press, Princeton, NJ.

Chisholm, G. (1889) *A Handbook of Commercial Geography*, Longman, Green and Co., London.

Coe, N., Kelly, P. and Yeung, H. (2007) *Economic Geography: A contemporary introduction*, Blackwell Publishing, London.

Connell, R. (2007) *Southern Theory*, Polity Press, Cambridge.

Cusset, F. (2008) *French Theory: How Foucault, Derrida, Deleuze and Co. transformed the intellectual life of the United States*, University of Minnesota Press, Minneapolis, MN.

Czarniawska, B. and Sevon, G. (eds) (2005) *Global Ideas: How ideas, objects and practices travel in the global economy*, Liber and Copenhagen Business School Press, Copenhagen.

D'Hauteserre, A.-M. (2005) 'Embracing postcolonial geographies: Contributions of Dame Evelyn Stokes to the development of postcolonial geography in New Zealand', *New Zealand Geographer*, 61: 102–9.

The Economist (1993) 'The mother of all reformers, New Zealand economic reform', Editorial, 16 October.

Frankenberg, R. and Mani, L. (1993) 'Crosscurrents, crosstalk: Race, "positionality" and the politics of location', *Cultural Studies*, 7(2): 292–310.

Gibson-Graham, J.-K. (2008) 'Diverse economies: Performative practices for "other worlds"', *Progress in Human Geography*, 32(5): 613–32.

Glassman, J. (2009) 'Critical geography I: The question of internationalism', *Progress in Human Geography*, Online First 1–8.

Hoffman, L., De Hart, M. and Collier, S. (2006) 'Notes on the anthropology of neoliberalism', *Anthropology News*, 47(6): 9–10.

James, B. and Saville-Smith, K. (1989) *Gender, Culture, Power*, Oxford University Press, Auckland.

Kothari, U. (2009) 'Re-building the empire: From colonialism to development', in M. Duffield and H. Vernon (eds), *Development and Colonialism: The past in the present*, James Currey, London.

Lancaster Regionalism Group (1985) *Localities, Class and Gender*, Pion, London.

Larner, W. (1995) 'Theorizing "Difference": Geography and feminism in Aotearoa/New Zealand', *Gender, Place and Culture: A Journal of Feminist Geography*, 2(2): 177–90.

— (1998) 'Sociologies of neo-liberalism: Theorising the "New Zealand Experiment"', *Sites*, 36: 5–21.

— (2000) 'Neo-liberalism: Policy, ideology, governmentality', *Studies in Political Economy*, 63: 5–26.

— (2003) 'Guest editorial: "Neoliberalism"?', *Environment and Planning D: Society and Space*, 21(5): 309–12.

— (2006) 'Brokering citizenship claims: Neoliberalism, Tino Rangatiratanga and multiculturalism in Aotearoa New Zealand', in E. Tastsoglou and A. Dobrowolsky (eds), *Women, Migration and Citizenship: Making local, national and transnational connections*, Aldershot, Ashgate.

— (2007) 'Expatriate experts and globalising governmentalities: The New Zealand diaspora strategy', *Transactions of the Institute of British Geographers*, 32(3): 331–45.

— (2009) 'Neoliberalism, Mike Moore and the WTO,' *Environment and Planning A*, 41(7): 1576–93.

Larner, W. and Butler, M. (2007) 'Strategic brokers and the politics of partnership: After neoliberalism in Aotearoa New Zealand', in H. Leitner, E. Sheppard and J. Peck (eds), *Contested Urban Futures: Neoliberalisms and their discontents*, Guilford, New York.

Larner, W. and Craig, D. (2005) 'After neoliberalism? Community activism and local partnerships in Aotearoa New Zealand', *Antipode*, 37(3): 402–24.

Larner, W. and Laurie, N. (2010) 'Travelling technocrats, embodied knowledges: Globalising privatisation in telecoms and water', *Geoforum*, 41(2): 218–26.

Larner, W. and Le Heron, R. (2002a) 'From economic globalisation to globalising economic processes: Towards post-structuralist political economies', *Geoforum*, 33(4): 415–19.

— (2002b) 'The spaces and subjects of a globalising economy: Towards a situated method', *Environment and Planning D: Society and Space*, 20(6): 753–74.

Larner, W. and Molloy, M. (2009) 'Globalization, the new economy and working women: Theorizing from the New Zealand designer fashion industry', *Feminist Theory*, 10(1): 35–59.

Larner, W. and Spoonley, P. (1995) 'Post-colonial politics in Aotearoa/New Zealand', in D. Stasulius and N. Yuval-Davis (eds), *Unsettling Settler Societies: Articulations of gender, race, ethnicity and class*, Sage, London.

Larner, W., Le Heron, R. and Lewis, N. (2007) 'Co-constituting "After Neoliberalism?": Political projects and globalising governmentalities in Aotearoa New Zealand,' in K. England and K. Ward (eds), *Neo-liberalization: States, networks, people*, Blackwell Publishing, Oxford.

— (2009) 'The state spaces of "After Neoliberalism": Co-constituting the New Zealand designer fashion industry', in R. Keil and R. Mahon (eds), *Leviathan Undone?: Towards a political economy of scale*, University of British Columbia Press, Vancouver.

Law, J. and Mol, A.-M. (2001) 'Situating technoscience: An inquiry into spatialities', *Environment and Planning A*, 19: 609–21.

Le Heron, R. and Lewis, N. (2007) 'Globalising economic geography in globalising higher education', *Journal of Geography in Higher Education*, 31(1): 5–12.

Lendvai, N. and Stubbs, P. (2009) 'Assemblages, translation and intermediaries in South East Europe: Rethinking transnationalism and social policy', *European Societies*, 11(2): 1–23.

Lewis, N., Larner, W. and Le Heron, R. (2008) 'The New Zealand designer fashion industry: Making industries and co-constituting political projects', *Transactions of the Institute of British Geographers*, 33(1): 42–59.

Li, T. (2007) 'Practices of assemblage and community forest management', *Economy and Society*, 36(2): 263–93.

Massey, D. (1984) *Spatial Divisions of Labour: Social structures and the structure of production*, Macmillan, London.

— (1993) 'Power-geometry and a progressive sense of place,' in J. Bird (ed.), *Mapping the Futures: Local cultures, global change*, Routledge, London, pp. 59–70.

McCann, E. (2008) 'Expertise, truth, and urban policy mobilities: Global circuits of knowledge in the development of Vancouver, Canada's "four pillar" drug strategy', *Environment and Planning A*, 40(4): 885–904.

Milligan, C., Kyle, R., Bondi, L., Fyfe, N., Kearns, R. and Larner, W. (2008) *From Placards to Partnerships: The changing nature of community activism in Manchester UK and Auckland NZ*, ESRC Research Report.

Mitchell, T. (2002) *Rule of Experts: Egypt, techno-politics and modernity*, University of California Press, Berkeley.

— (2008) 'Rethinking economy', *Geoforum*, 39: 1116–21.

Mohanty, C. (1988) 'Under western eyes: Feminist scholarship and colonial discourses', *Feminist Review*, 30: 61–88.

Ong, A. and Collier, S. (2005) *Global Assemblages: Technology, politics and ethics as anthropological problems*, Blackwell Publishing, Oxford.

Peck, J. (2004) 'Geography and public policy: Constructions of neoliberalism', *Progress in Human Geography*, 28(3): 392–405.

— (2008) 'Remaking laissez-faire', *Progress in Human Geography*, 32(1): 3–43.

Pollard, J. McEwan, C., Laurie, N. and Stenning, A. (2009) 'Economic geography under postcolonial scrutiny', *Transactions of the Institute of British Geographers*, 34(2): 137–42.

Prince, R. (2008) 'Assembling the "creative economy": Epistemic communities, policy transfer and the geography of expertise', PhD thesis, School of Geographical Sciences, University of Bristol.

Robinson, J. (2003) 'Postcolonialising geography: Tactics and pitfalls', *Singapore Journal of Tropical Geography*, 24(3): 273–89.

Rose, N. and Miller, P. (1992) 'Political power beyond the state: Problematics of government', *British Journal of Sociology*, 43(2): 173–205.

Said, E. (2003) *Culture and Imperialism*, Random House, London.

Scott, A. (2000) 'Economic geography: The great half century', *Cambridge Journal of Economics*, 24: 483–504.

Sharma, A. (2008) *Logics of Empowerment: Development, gender and governance in neoliberal India*, University of Minnesota Press, Minneapolis, MN.

Sheppard, E. (n.d.) *Critical Geography's Contemporary Quandries*, Mimeo.

Spivak, G. (1988) 'Can the subaltern speak?', in C. Nelson and L. Grossberg (eds), *Marxism and the Interpretation of Culture*, University of Illinois Press, Urbana, IL.

— (2008) *Other Asias*, Blackwell Publishing, London.

Stokes, E., Dooley, L., Johnson, L., Dixon, J. and Parsons, S. (1987) 'Feminist perspectives in geography: A collective statement', *New Zealand Geographer*, 43(3): 139–49.

Suzuki, T. (2007) 'Accountics: Impacts of internationally standardized accounting on the Japanese socio-economy', *Accounting, Organizations and Society*, 32(3): 263–301.

Swain, A. (2006) 'Soft capitalism and a hard industry: Virtualism, the "transition industry" and the restructuring of the Ukrainian coal industry', *Transactions of the Institute of British Geographers*, 31: 208–23.

Section 2

Postcolonial understandings of the economic

5

Cultural econo-mixes of the bazaar

Nitasha Kaul

> So, now I beg you, fairies all,
> To patronize each separate stall,
> And while the bazaar lasts out to try
> And see how many things you can buy . . .
> Good fairies all to try, try, try,
> And see how many things you can buy . . .
> Bring out your fairy coins we pray
> And buy, buy, buy all we've got to-day!
>
> (Currey 1934)

Introduction

This paper situates 'bazaar' as a site of multifaceted exploration. It is as much an enquiry into a bazaar ('Janpath' in New Delhi) as it is into the modes of knowledge about the bazaar. Challenging the representation of the postcolonial bazaar as a bizarre relic of the past or the pure theoretical market, I make the case for viewing it as a socioeconomic site of modernity. A site that is populated with the evocations, expectations, and histories of the various implicated and often contested human constituencies.

Bazaars are integral to cultural imaginaries, and I start by presenting some of the ways in which they have functioned to excite fantasy and fear. In spite of this, bazaars are often conceptualised primarily as an economic space to 'truck, barter and exchange'. I suggest that in this characterisation there is a problematic slippage between the market and the bazaar. The bazaar is not simply another market. Neither is the market itself any much more than a convenient fiction for the purposes of an abstract deductive political economy which obtains its purchase on the 'economic' realm by a perpetual erasure of subjectivity and particularity under the signs of objectivity, generality and science. While, even to many anthropologists, the appeal of judging the bazaar against a pervasive ideal of the market continues to be irresistible, I argue that the bazaar offers a valuable site to challenge the culture/economy separation that characterises much thinking about the economic realm. It is to this effect that the paper travels to re-member the coming into being of a specific bazaar – the Janpath. What makes this travel interesting is the forays it makes into issues of governmentality, patriarchy, livelihoods under capitalist globalisation, nationstatism, in other words, the spatial and symbolic contexts of postcolonial modernity in India.

A visit to the bazaar

It is a family scene. Mr and Mrs Dunford with their children are preparing to visit 'our English Bazaar' in Soho Square. Theodore, 'a fine boy of about ten years of age', asks 'Pray Papa, what is the meaning of the word Bazaar?'. The reply is quite detailed:

> The term Bazaar is given by the Turks and Persians to a kind of Market or Exchange, some of which are extremely magnificent; that of Ispahan, in Persia, surpasses all the European exchanges, and yet that of Tauris exceeds it in size. There is the old and the new Bazaar at Constantinople, the former is chiefly for arms, and the latter for different articles belonging to goldsmiths, jewellers, furriers, and various other manufacturers.
>
> (Anon. 1818: 3)

The father Mr Dunford proclaims the virtues of the bazaar especially for the way in which it provides a means of living to women in society who have no other sustenance.

As might be expected in an instruction book for English children written in 1818, the family's visit to the bazaar is an opportunity to acquire good manners along with lots of commodities. The bazaar also functions as a domain to illustrate the 'coarseness' of bargaining – the Dunfords never haggle. The 'short fat coarse looking woman' who unsuccessfully tries to bargain from five shillings to three or the 'odd-faced' woman who bargains at the umbrella shop serve to highlight the contrast with the well-bred affluent Dunfords who only ask for goods and pay the price, never interacting with the sellers. For them, the bazaar is a site of knowledge and a place of sampling from among myriad commodities. It is a showcase of the world to them, and yet a display which only confirms their own sense of superiority when it comes to artistic accomplishments.

Around a century later, when consolidation of the Empire meant that contacts with the 'showcase' of the world had become more concrete, the bazaar also turned into a vile and threatening place. For instance, Anglo-Indian women (British women in India) 'avoided the bazaar out of a fear that they would be charged exorbitant prices and thus lose status' (Procida 2003: 129). Thus, the bazaar could either be a magnificent visual display showcasing the world's goods on offer at 'home', or it could be a shocking and vile 'native' space unsuited to the presence of a British lady.

Bazaar as a site of extraordinariness also offers a certain flâneur-like freedom to the person who is at once in society but not of it (the reflective wanderer, the outsider). The bazaar can prompt what cannot be 'normal' in society, and it can lead to discoveries about oneself and the world that one would not make in the normal business of life. In a novel *Janpath Kiss* (Jha 1991), the central character Sadanand Misra is an engineer trapped by a duplicitous society and its expectations, and he often walks through the Janpath bazaar, as that space to him symbolises a certain kind of freedom from the city, an alternative world where rules can be just a little remade and fantasies lived. One day he suddenly kisses a girl in the bazaar for no apparent reason other than the actioning of a strange impulse. The appeal of the unclassifiable 'Janpath dream', the 'Janpath magical world', the 'desire to touch a Janpath girl' (73) is a symbolic peg for a kind of space, a space right in the middle of the city where promises of freedom and encounters with otherness lurk, hanging brightly along with all the clothes and shiny stones that sell not just material objects but symbolic dreams – of an urban global fashion and freedom that the bazaar walking person can really be a part of.

Like the fictional Indian Sadanand prey to 'some power' beyond his control '[t]here on Janpath' (70), even the real Westerner Goldstein (2002) finds something of the unexpected in Janpath. Describing a 'strange happening' during his travels in 1967, Goldstein writes: 'I was in New Delhi, walking down Janpath Lane to the airline office, when some force or energy stopped me in my tracks. I was simply unable to take another step forward' (87), a 'peculiar event' which prompted him to go to the Hindu holy place of Benares. Less magical is Galland (1990), with whom we see an October 1986 visit to Janpath – 'a busy main street in Delhi. I stood next to a cow at the street corner. Taxi horns blared. Scooters, auto-rickshaws, buses, cars, bicycles, pony-drawn tongas clipped by' (127). The narrator impatiently refuses an insistent shoeshine boy whose memory haunts her later (why did I not give to this one?).

All these visits to the bazaar highlight its affective dimension, as a space for the arousing of emotions through the interplay of visuality, social custom, desire and sensuality. Yet, most social scientific accounts of the bazaar view it simply as an economic realm in which questions of identity and culture do not arise, except when they are reflected in monetary terms. It is well-worn commonsense that money has no colour or creed. As Redfield and Singer (1954: 69) put it, 'it is not to the interest of the (Jewish) baker, the (Turkish) carpet-dealer, the (French) hand laundry, that the American Christian customer looks when he patronizes them, but to his own'. In this vein, the bazaar is seen merely as a form of the 'market'. Before proceeding further with a discussion on bazaar, let me briefly outline the way in which the term 'market' has been employed in political economy, and critique this for its generalising and universalising gesture which neglects the socially constructed instrumentality of market institutions.

It would seem that the word 'market' is at once worthy of the double distinction of evoking numerous variants of socio-economic interaction, and at the same time problematic enough to have defied an unchallengeable definition. Indeed, even economists, who might be considered to be well within the province, have puzzled with questions such as 'What [exactly, after all] is a market?'. While '[m]any economists tend to find markets almost everywhere on earth and in history', there are numerous overlapping ways of characterising markets in empirical, functional and structural terms (Rosenbaum 2000). In the general literature on the subject, market is taken to be a kind of concept that has accumulated enough history to be, at once, a physical place for humans to truck, barter and exchange; a metaphorical term for an institution that has persisted through human history; a realm where things or even attributes can be valued in some way; a medium of purely financial transactions; a humanist designation of those things economic; and an abstract category in economic theory. It is, in short, a conceptual fiction that has served many purposes. One such important purpose in our times has been to carve out an 'economic' space over which economics as a social science has an overweening purchase.

This general idea of the economic space as being purely 'economic', as devoid of considerations of identity or culture can be understood and critiqued broadly in two ways. First, we can challenge how the contours of the so-called economic space are fashioned from the general societal existence (see Mirowski 1989, 1994). Secondly, by drawing attention to the recent body of postcolonial scholarship in economics (see Zein-Elabdin and Charusheela 2004), we highlight the ways in which economic experiences have an intimate relationship with culture, history and power relations. At this point we can ask the question – Can we situate an anthropology of the bazaar, which, in its multifaceted relation to identity and culture, can challenge the hegemony of the abstract economic market?

How bizarre is the bazaar?

The 'bazaar' is very rarely an object of scrutiny in its own right. Bazaar is not only a market, but a 'something else', an alternative socioeconomic structure whose fundamentals, operation and reproduction cannot be explained by the anodyne characterlessness of the 'economic market'. In our times, the economic 'market' is a fiction born of the barren recesses of abstract economic theory (see Callon 1998). Illustrative of pedagogic truisms, it serves the ends of an equally abstract 'economy', and is capable of carrying political policy messages in the garb of technical facts.

When scholars have gone in search of the 'bazaar', they have tended to see it primarily as a special kind of place for trading, and have often tried to explain what they observe in the bazaar in terms of how different it is from (our) standard market. This observed departure of the bazaar from the 'norm' of the market 'as it should be', is then explained either in terms of the universal structural characteristics that take on a peculiar form in that context, and therefore the bazaar is a rational economic organisation evolved to deal with these peculiarities (see Geertz 1978), or in terms of the teleology of the market evolution, so that business sense and economic structures are in a different stage in the (primitive/pure) bazaar type economic trading (Fanselow 1990).

For Geertz (1978), the bazaar is a trading institution where information is poor, scarce, maldistributed, inefficiently communicated and intensely valued – so that for the bazaaris the main task is to search for information. It is due to this characteristic of information search that various elements of bazaar institutional structure have evolved in certain ways. However, such attempts to first identify and then explain away the 'bizarreness' of the bazaar can be problematised not just for its lack of interrogation of how the economic context comes to be defined, but also for the way in which they do not consider the bazaar as a dynamic space with many different kinds of selling that interact with visual and vocalist display. For example, in the Janpath bazaar, while there are shops and stalls that display their goods and bargain with customers, there are also sections of the bazaar where goods are displayed and the seller's designates shout out the price repeatedly, and where there is no bargaining. It is not just a question of access to information being costly to acquire, it is also a question of what is being sold (the type and quality of the good), and how the contest for meaning and persuasion plays out in the relationship between the seller and the buyer.

Fanselow (1990) rightly rejects attempts to portray the bazaar as an exotic business practice. While providing a sophisticated analysis, he remains anchored within the project of explaining away the 'apparent irrationality' of the bazaar, and rescuing from moral judgment the infamous 'unscrupulousness' of its traders (his point being that these misperceptions owe to the lack of understanding of markets in unstandardised non-substitutable goods). The structural limitations and properties of goods transacted in the bazaar lead to bazaar stereotypes of 'limited scale of operation, proliferation of traders, the unity of household and business, and the spatial aggregation of businesses dealing with the same kind of commodities' (Fanselow 1990: 263).

I propose to move the argument beyond the problematic polarities of the bizarre bazaar, and offer an explanatory account, that not only absolves the average (especially 'otherplace') bazaar fellow from centuries of suspicion of irrationality and lack of common/business sense, but also provides us with a way of bringing out into the open the questions of culture, identity and meaning as they relate to the economic realm. The bazaar does not need to be explained in line with the modernist logic of rational structures and transparent actors, but understood for the specific systems of meanings that inhere in a bazaar and how they fashion an 'economic' context out of the imbroglio of desire, power and interests. How does the bazaar function as a structure of meanings, and as a site for the construction of contested economic identities in the shadow of culture and history?

In this chapter, it is asserted that society is not a neatly sliced object of knowledge and intervention where we can discern the administrative, social, political and economic dimensions. Rather, a construct such as the bazaar is in itself a living formation, and not simply a sieve for the right-sized concepts to fill in its holes of explanation. In terms of what I have elsewhere argued for as 'contextual social political economy' (Kaul 2008), the concept of 'bazaar' is not a map waiting to be comprehended and filed away into the annals of economic knowledge till evidence of irrationality or new theory wakes us up, rather it is a particular socioeconocultural way of life (cf. Jain 1998; Ostor 1984) that needs understanding from the ground-up, or in its own right.

Why should the bazaar be understood as a lived system of meanings, and why not simply as an apriori economic structure which can be explained in terms of conventional economic categories? The answer is that what is at stake is the very link between theory and the world since conventional explanatory accounts would have us keep faith in the *a priori* separability of the economic and the cultural, a separation which is presumed universally available. The separation of spheres of the 'cultural' and the 'economic' (see McDowell 2000) needs to be examined because it plays an important part in structuring what counts as what kind of knowledge and how do we get access to it. What is valid 'knowledge' of the bazaar as an object of study? And how is that distinguished from mere 'experience' of the bazaar? In actively resisting cultural/economic characterisation and separation, one is questioning the modernist rendition of knowledge that does not allow the spheres of culture and economy to be seen as artificially separated, and consequently does not allow them to be identified as only contingent and in context. One is rethinking the very sphere of the economic genealogically (Butler 2000: 277–8) and rethinking circulation as a cultural phenomenon (Lee and LiPuma 2002).

In this endeavour, the importance of deconstructing economic theory and drawing attention to the many slippages between the terms economy, economic and economics (see Kaul 2002, 2003, 2008) is crucial. For instance, we can point out how not only is circulation seen as mere transmission without any cultural constitution, but that economic theory (discipline of economics) which claims to provide an account of that circulation also studiously avoids areas 'where meaning is itself a socially constructed object of scrutiny' (Fine 1999: 419), which includes consumption, globalisation, and so on (see also Dowd 2000). In this way, the connections between the logic of economic theories and the economic logic can be traced to destabilise the separation of identity and the economic, culture and economy. The economy is not a single, simple, universal entity that is omnipresent and lends itself to total comprehension. The economy itself is recognised as a creative metaphor which needs to be filled with particular meanings at particular situations.

How is the 'fact' of the entity 'bazaar' put together? In what ways does it draw upon a symbolic archive, a repository of images, on ideologies of nationalism, orientalism, colonialism and capitalism, on received ways of explaining economic structure, on the primacy of the economic category through which other motives are filtered, on histories and lived realities? How are these disparate concerns reconciled in the fact of the bazaar at any point in time?

There are precedents in this endeavour, often coming from different disciplines. Ray (1988) examines the bazaar as a network of credit and exchange but one which is imbricated in the socio-cultural fabric of Indian society; this telling of the rise of Indian capitalist class in the depression years is interpellated with a sense of the economic as being only available in terms of a cultural totality. Similarly, for Yang (1998) the bazaar is situated as the distinctive scene of interrogation for posing questions about Indian society under colonialism and narrative history. Though it was not the subject of systematic study, 'both as an analytical unit and at a metaphoric level, bazaars speak the language of exchange and negotiation, of movement and flow, of circulation and redistribution . . . of extracommunity or supracommunity connections and institutions' (16–17). In this context, as Ostor (1984: 124) rightly notes, space is only one aspect of the bazaar as a culturally constructed, multivocal symbol, the other is specific relationships between people.

Travelling to Janpath

Against the backstory of these bazaar tellings, here I want to 'travel', briefly, to Janpath bazaar. Unlike most of the bazaars studied by scholars so far, this is an urban (metropolitan) bazaar, one that is rigourously subjected to the governing technology of the state in terms of permit, planning and architecture, and one that strongly reveals highly gendered practices.

My stories of Janpath will concern the following. What does the Janpath bazaar say about how a postcolonial urban space is historically and culturally coded economic, and gendered masculine, in a narrative that includes the relative power and status of different lives in the bazaar? This is a project tangential to any 'proper' disciplinary investigation of the functioning of an economic space such as the bazaar. For, the multiple pathways taken here explore how economic space is crafted out of material and symbolic resources of the various implicated constituencies. What are the ways in which the Janpath bazaar as a symbolic space articulates economy and society in a postcolonial context? What does it say about the hybridity of the supposedly economic processes, and their implication in identity and history, about the interpretation and 'making one's own' of such spaces by the actors involved, about the chaining of these endeavours with the larger civic theatre of modernity – the state and the power of governmentality and the policy logic of administration.

The (post)colonially inherited cityspace

Janpath bazaar is located at the heart of India's capital. Several key government, corporate, commercial, religious and civic society organisations are located in the vicinity. The initial settlement of Janpath is one of many changes that were part of the large-scale remaking of the urban space of New Delhi in the ending years of the colonial rule. The word 'Janpath' literally means 'People's way' (Jan/people and Path/way) in Hindi, and this name was given to the area of the city which was called 'Queen's way' prior to Indian Independence. The Janpath bazaar (which is only one end of Janpath) is a name given to a nested set of lanes and roads where shops of various kinds sell their goods in the central area of New Delhi. The bazaar is a central feature of the city and as such can be said to play a significant role in the urban landscape.

Janpath bazaar: the site of the gaze

Within the area of the Janpath bazaar, there are different kinds of shops and settlements. This diversity is a prominent feature of the bazaar. I have identified four clearly distinguishable levels of the bazaar and their characteristic features are summarised in Table 5.1 below.

Thus, the main differences between the different levels of the bazaar can be seen along the lines of: gender, type of buyers and variation in merchandise, structure of the shops, their prominence and visibility in the area, ethnicity of the sellers, legality of the settlement and the mode of selling (level of bargaining or oral communication).

Table 5.1

Levels of the Bazaar	History, Gender and Ethnicity	Goods and Buyers	Legality and Profitability
I. The pucca Janpath shops (also known as Tibetan bazaar)	Part of Refugee settlement, run solely by men, largely Punjabi	Variation in type of merchandise and prices. Foreigners and relatively well off native buyers	Legal and profitable site for business. Level of bargaining is little. Very prominent and visible business
II. The *Tehbazaari* (municipal license) holders (Janpath bazaar or *Tehbazaari* lane depending on who one speaks to)	Organic growth in subsequent decades, run solely by men, largely Punjabi	Very little variation in the type of goods or prices. Largely young middle-class urban buyers	After being illegal for many years, they were partly legalised after the Thareja Commission report. Some extensions are semi-legal. Profitable site for business. Famous for a very high level of bargaining. Prominent and visible as businesses
III. The mobile migrant sellers (on the *Tehbazaari* lane)	Organic growth due to livelihood pressures on the migrants, mostly men who are from smaller towns in Uttar Pradesh and Bihar	Some variation in type of goods, but largely lower priced than the rest of the bazaar. Varied buyers, but average (lower) middle-class buyers	Illegal. Not a lot of profit margin, some bargaining. Visibility and prominence very low
IV. The Gujarati women sellers (the Gujarati bazaar)	Settled over the years (some second generation women sellers), some men have moved into the area recently	Some variation in the type of goods, little variation in prices. Tourist buyers or urban middle-class family buyers	Some legal and some semi-legal. Access to services (like electricity) is varied even when paying the same rent. Profitable site for business, not a lot of bargaining. Visibility and prominence low but variable

Source: Author's research

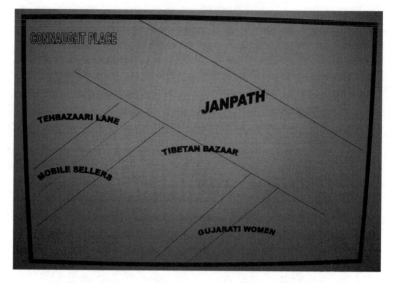

Figure 5.1 Janpath bazaar: the site of the gaze

During my numerous visits to this bazaar, I have been struck by its organicity and the sense-experiences it affords (for a discussion on multivocality of Indian bazaars in general, see Padmanabhan 2001), be it the loud and rhythmic calls of the garment sellers, the colourful displays, or its many un/pleasant smells. The bazaar has been changing in many ways over time, for instance recently there has been the increasing display of Hindu (and some Buddhist) religious symbols (paintings, little statues, and so on). Despite long years, for its poorer long time sellers, there is no feeling of permanence in the bazaar. As Raj Bahadur Sharma, an ice slab-seller in the area for forty years, said about the tehbazaari shops 'kayi baar lagi aur ukhdi' ('many times they set up and were uprooted'). There was a general feeling that the change of political parties in power does not really affect the overall mechanism of the state. People expressed this in different ways, but their concerns almost always were the little infrastructural immediacies and long-term legal grievances. Many poorer sellers saw themselves as victims of a state that favoured the rich shops, yet at the same time, they were keen and conscious agents who realised the value of knowledge interventions in policy terms.

Many trajectories and imaginaries constantly collide in Janpath bazaar. If this bazaar is a liberatory space, this experience is not even, and varies with gender and class. It holds open a special kind of possibility for the male spectator who can just 'hang out' in the bazaar. For example, Favero's informers strike him with their fascination with Janpath and other similar bazaars – 'Here . . . there's everything, you have women, foreigners, everything' (2003: 554). Intoxicated by the 'everything' that Janpath has to offer, individuals, especially men, can just 'hang out' and sit by the sides of the pathways and along corners sampling the scene so multiply loaded with meaning. The inescapable fact in these pictures, especially of Janpath, is the securely gendered and sexualised nature of the street occupation. The transnational public sphere symbolised by the Janpath bazaar imaginary is a space where the viewing of most commodities is coded feminine, but the viewing of people, the 'bazaar gaze' (if one might call it that) is certainly coded masculine. The women looking at the objects on display being simultaneously the visual objects of the men's bazaar gaze (the 'desirable Janpath girls' in Jha's novel 1991), imbues a reflective sense to the scene where commercial and symbolic imaginaries are in traffic. However, if some modes of street life are gender and class differentiated, all modes of such street life dwelling are in their own way a challenge to the utilitarian ethic of a capitalist order.

Gendered nature of the struggle for space

The urban bazaar is an intensely political space for the post-colonial society. It is an arena where earning a livelihood is most fragile in juridical terms, and where complexly layered itineraries of planned modernity have demonstrated particular blind spots in relation to class and state power. What is especially remarkable is that aside from activist organisational work, there has been very little by the way of theory/story research on the issue of gender in the bazaar. Perhaps some of this neglect owes to the perceived 'economic' nature of the bazaar space, so studies have seen disembodied agents devoid of an identity. The argument here is that this gender dimension is an extremely important component of the story, even if it is absent by consent from mainstream disciplinary knowledge accounts.

The bazaar landscape seen in terms of a place with a reflection of human meanings is both the symbolic site for a gendered gaze, and also the physical site for an intensely masculine imaginary of the economic trade and commercial transactions. Nonetheless, many women resist this symbolic and physical figuring, and still manage to trade in the bazaars even if this means being confined to the least profitable and most vulnerable forms of trading (as in the case of mobile fruit sellers), or being segregated both socially and geographically (as in the case of the Gujarati women on Janpath Lane; see also Rai 1999).

I spoke to some of the Gujarati women sellers in Janpath at length and they were keen to share their experiences. While they were faced with multiple difficulties, such as taking care of children and coping with the harsh environment of sun and rain in the absence of any shade, in conversing with them one could not help noticing their hopes and awareness of agency. The places under the odd tree on the lane were seen as being very valuable, as most women had to sit in the open for the whole day. They wanted their children (they stressed, 'I have only two') to study and 'get a job', for themselves they wanted 'chappar' (shade) and 'roshni' (light), two things that affect their trade most. The streetlights in the lane do not work, something I saw in 2004, and subsequently read in Rai as being the case also in 1999. The women were very aware of the importance of education, organisation and unionisation, yet spoke of the efforts to organise in the lane failing. One woman put their desire for the trade evocatively when she expressed the wanting of a 'dukaan jaisi personality' ('shoplike personality'). This was simultaneously a desire for a something and to be someone – craving for the identity that is correlative of a shop, and to have a shop with identity.

Bazaar: plans, policies and policing in a lived space

As a lived urban space, Janpath is subject/ed to the regime of planning and policing in the city. The encultured socio-economic site of Janpath is an 'urban' space in a postcolonial third world megapolis. It is marked by a contest over competing notions of space and livelihoods. Let us examine this briefly.

Both the physical and the symbolic space of Janpath are seen as arena for control by the state (municipality and the police). For the planners in the municipality, it is a space with a national history and heritage, which needs to reflect the ideal planned city. Against the usual planned vista of unpeopled beauty in nature and architecture, for example presented in New Delhi Municipal Corporation's film *New Delhi: A Garden City*, Delhi continues to throb as a living city (with a heterogenetic culture where layers of history have developed alongside and on top of each other) and one that accordingly frustrates the planner architects especially in the resisting will of thousands of people who make a livelihood off its streets. The existence of these street vendors is a significant feature of most cities in the world, and is everywhere marked by an unending struggle against the governmental mechanisms within which they are reflected as placeless encroachers. A majority of people who earn their livelihood in the Janpath bazaar would fall into this category. Indeed, as I discussed before, with the exception of the pucca shops in the Tibetan bazaar, the other sellers in Janpath are either 'tehbazari' municipal licence holders, unlicenced mobile sellers, or the women sellers on Janpath Lane (some of whom are licenced). The street vendors struggle against not just poverty, but equally against a civic urbanism, that accelerated especially in preparation for the Commonwealth Games 2010, that tends to favour 'beautification' and 'cleanliness' drives which uproot and dispossess them. The Master Plans of the cities in India (as in other countries) did not have a provision for what is known as the urban informal sector. The existence of street trading was seen as an activity that was unorganised and needed to be banished from the planned urban city, which was primarily modelled along the lines of Western cities. And this continues to be a majority view. However, this so-called informal sector is actually a highly organised segment of business and social life of the city (see articles in *Seminar* 2000), and contrary to the expectations of development economics, it has not been absorbed into the formal sector of the economy with increased growth. Quite the opposite, with the onset of what is termed 'liberalisation' in India as a part of

Figure 5.2 Janpath Lane (author's photograph)

Figure 5.3 Tehbazaaril Lane (author's photograph)

the wider 'globalisation' process, and the accompanying closure of various factories and workshops, the formal sector jobs in the cities have led the way to a greater number of the unemployed taking to the streets for livelihood.

This story of urban dispossession of people in search of life chances is an important story of the bazaar. It is a story that figures the multiple presences of the state (as New Delhi Municipal Corporation, as the legal system, as the police), the functioning of power at a time when the 'economy is opening up', and the desperation in the search of a livelihood. In the post-colonial era, the larger national state as an entity has functioned with the colonially inherited institutions of subjection and control, which were designed to see the 'population' as an entity in need of planned intervention. This exercise of state power derived its legitimacy from the degree to which it was able to administer its peoples in line with planned nationalist grand schemes of modernity. The nationalist state was to usher a rational modernity that would be able to compete with the universal norm as embodied in the 'developed' states. Thus, the cities were to be the paradigmatic modern urban spaces drawn with planned residential complexes, governmental seats of power, the commercial districts, and the historical monuments celebrating the achievements of independent nationalism. This laudable narrative of urban modernity, however, was born of the imperial imagination and as such did not recognise that the 'public places' in India are invariably places where people trade personally, and where people have always been drawn in search of making a living. The postcolonial city was not so easily split between the commercial, the residential, the scenic – but that it was miscellaneous everywhere. The people in the middle-class housing areas needed commodities, the masses of lower grade administrative government workers needed to eat in the afternoons and buy things after work, people in the slums and the settlements needed to buy things that they could not afford at formal shops, and that there was domestic entrepreneurship at every level of society, especially at the level of the bazaars which sprang up in the interstitial spaces of the city. These bazaars are sometimes stable; sometimes they spread; sometimes without a boundary as they spill; and sometimes eternally mobile as in the weekly

Figure 5.4   Janpath at night (author's photograph)

markets that appear at a different locality in the city on different days. The governmental objective has been largely to control if not eradicate these vendors who are seen as spoiling the scenic beauty of the city. This ties in to the larger ambition of the state in recent times, to be a worthy destination for globalisation.

For instance, a very skewed imagination was at work in a proposal put forward by Housing and Urban Development Corporation (HUDCO) which aimed to make Janpath the 'Oxford Street' or the 'Champs Elysees' of Delhi (Raghuvanshi 2004). According to this Grand Plan, Janpath would be remodelled as a tourist spot for foreigners and a leisure area for (a well-off section of) the locals. It included plans for a shopping colonnade, art gallery, shopping malls, multiplexes, restaurants, fast-food joints and offices, but the transportation focus was on car parking facilities and neglected the bus services. As the head of HUDCO, Rana explained, '[t]he idea is to restore Connaught Place to its former glory as a market with historical importance and creating an area that would represent India to the foreigners. Janpath, with its location and position as a popular tourist spot, is best suited for such a transformation'

(Raghuvanshi 2004). The former (read colonial) glory of the area is to be recreated and it is to be patterned after a Western city to represent India to the world. This process of conscious promotion of a display culture marks the shift from public sphere to public stage [Urry] – wherein structures of governance vie in a 'global culture of self promotion', and '[l]ocal economic regeneration [is] . . . left to the local planning level' (Dicks 2003: 17, 35).

People who function at the intersection of such institutions face a diffuse exercise of power through the multiple faces of the state. In recent times, the Indian judicial system has tended to take an activist stance in the interests of promoting social justice. A prominent example of this lies in the landmark Janpath verdict of the Supreme Court case (*Sodhan Singh vs New Delhi Municipal Committee* [NDMC] 1989; also *Genda Ram vs Municipal Corporation of Delhi* [MCD] 1992), whereby it was ruled that, within reasonable restrictions, a person had a fundamental right to vend on street pavements. This led to the Thareja Committee which was tasked to allocate 'tehbazaari licences' to genuine vendors (a similar Chopra Committee was set up for the MCD areas).

However, there is no straight line from the law to the action, and what resulted was a long and complicated process whereby the vendors had to fill in forms and show written paperwork including challans/notices of illegality issued to them over the years. In an ironic twist, the pieces of paper stating their illegality were to procure legal rights for the bazaar sellers! Not everyone had these pieces of paper for every year, and missing even a single document could make or break the case. Licences were to be allocated on a cascading yearwise basis with priority given to the pre-1977 vendors. Sometimes the vendors did not get the licences, sometimes they got the licences but NDMC did not give them a space, and sometimes they got neither space nor the paper. Even with the licences (which are themselves obfuscatory and sometimes omit names or else abbreviate the names of the bazaars in a problematic manner – for example 'SB' could indicate two very different bazaars, Sadar bazaar or the Sunday bazaar), the people in the bazaar are harassed by the police and municipal enforcement agencies who are widely known to take routine bribes from the sellers.

Closure of these avenues of livelihood will be a blow to the life chances of those most vulnerable in society. The bazaar, far from being an empty conceptual category, a historical curiosity, an exotic marginalia as it is figured in much theory, is full of stories that connect culture and the economy. While Geertz may have unpeopled his bazaar to make it suitable for an 'economic' writing (his piece discussed here was published in the *American Economic Review*); Fanselow may have thought that all bazaar shops are equally dingy, and all bazaar traders are secretive (1990: 256); and the literary imagination have a fear-and-fantasy relationship to it (the inscrutable Orient, the dirty native place, the fascinating objects, the showcase, the place of discovery), knowledge of the 'fact' of the bazaar must combine both the theories and the stories.

By way of conclusion

The bazaar has been an exotic site and its rationality has been the subject of rescue endeavours in much research. In contrast, I have argued that we need to see the bazaar as a fertile ground – a hybrid space for stories, for theories and for explorations of the nation-state, capitalism, colonialism, globalisation and governmentality. In particular, the Janpath bazaar provides us with a site for exploring diverse postcolonial subjectivities under the influence of a weighty history and the diffuse operation of coercive power. If we see it as a space unrarefied by the disciplinary boundaries of culture, economy, history, theory, literature and activism – it can be the site for exploring several interconnected issues as they are lived, experienced and observed. This chapter has travelled to transgress the story/theory modes of enquiry in the hope of presenting the poetics and politics of bazaars in general, and the Janpath bazaar in particular, as contested spaces with many layers of meaning that undo the pervasive and problematic separations of culture and economy in modernity.

References

Anon. (1818) 'A visit to the bazaar', by the author of *The Little Warbler of the Cottage*, etc., John Harris, London.

Butler, J. (2000) 'Dynamic conclusions', in J. Butler, E. Laclau and S. Zizek (eds), *Contingency, Hegemony, Universality*, Verso, London.

Callon, M. (1998) 'Introduction: The embeddedness of economic markets in economics', in M. Callon (ed.), *The Laws of the Markets*, Blackwell, Oxford.

Currey, S. M. (1934) *Bazaar in Fairyland: A fairy playlet – specially written for bazaar openings*, The Epworth Press, London.

Dicks, B. (2003) *Culture on Display: The production of contemporary visitability*, Open University Press, Maidenhead.

Dowd, D. (2000) *Capitalism and its Economics: A critical history*, Pluto Press, London.

Fanselow, F. S. (1990) 'The bazaar economy or how bizarre is the bazaar really?', *Man*, 25(2): 250–65.

Favero, P. (2003) 'Phantasms in a "Starry" place: Space and identification in a central New Delhi market', *Cultural Anthropology*, 18(4): 551–84.

Fine, B. (1999) 'A question of economics: Is it colonizing the social sciences?', *Economy and Society*, 28(3): 403–25.

Galland, C. (1990) *Longing for Darkness: Tara and the Black Madonna*, Century, London.

Geertz, C. (1978) 'The bazaar economy: Information and search in peasant marketing', *American Economic Review*, 68(2): 28–32.

Goldstein, J. (2002) *One Dharma: The emerging Western Buddhism*, Rider, London.

Jain, K. (1998) 'When the gods go to market: The ritual management of desire in Indian "Bazaar Art"', *Communal/Plural*, 6(2): 187–204.

Jha, A. (1991) *The Janpath Kiss*, Chanakya Publications, Delhi.

Kaul, N. (2002) 'A critical "post" to critical realism', *Cambridge Journal of Economics*, 26(6): 709–26.

— (2003) 'The anxious identities we inhabit . . . post'isms and economic understandings', in D. K. Barker and E. Kuiper (eds), *Toward a Feminist Philosophy of Economics*, Routledge, London.

— (2008) *Imagining Economics Otherwise: Encounters with identity/difference*, Routledge, London.

Lee, B. and LiPuma, E. (2002) 'Cultures of circulation: The imaginations of modernity', *Public Culture*, 14(1): 191–213.

McDowell, L. (2000) 'Acts of memory and millennial hopes and anxieties: The awkward relationship between the economic and the cultural', *Social and Cultural Geography*, 1(1): 15–24.

Mirowski, P. (1989) *More Heat than Light: Economics as social physics, physics as nature's economics*, Cambridge University Press, Cambridge.

— (1994) *Natural Images in Economic Thought: Markets read in tooth and claw*, Cambridge University Press, Cambridge.

Ostor, A. (1984) *Culture and Power: Legend, ritual, bazaar and rebellion in a Bengali Society*, Sage Publications, Delhi.

Padmanabhan, M. (2001) 'Introduction', in D. Khanna (ed.), *Bazaar*, Viking, New Delhi.

Procida, M. (2003) 'Feeding the imperial appetite: Imperial knowledge and Anglo-Indian discourse', *Journal of Women's History*, 15(2): 123–49.

Raghuvanshi, G. (2004) 'Janpath: Oxford Street in the making', *The Hindu Business Line*, 10 April, available at: http://www.thehindubusinessline.com/2004/04/10/stories/2004041001710100.htm (accessed 8 September 2009).

Rai, S. M. (1999) 'Fractioned states and negotiated boundaries: Gender and law in India', in H. Afshar and S. Barrientos (eds), *Women, Globalization and Fragmentation in the Developing World*, Macmillan Press, London.

Ray, R. K. (1988) 'The bazaar: changing structural characteristics of the indigenous section of the Indian economy before and after the Great Depression', *The Indian Economic and Social History Review*, 25(3): 263–318.

Redfield, R. and Singer, M. (1954) 'The cultural role of cities', *Economic Development and Cultural Change*, 3: 53–73.

Rosenbaum, E. (2000) 'What is a market? On the methodology of a contested concept', *Review of Social Economy*, 58(4): 455–82.

Seminar (2000) Special Issue on *Street Vendors: A symposium on reconciling people's livelihood and urban governance*, July (491).

Yang, A. A. (1998) *Bazaar India: Markets, society, and the colonial state in Gangetic Bihar*, University of California Press, Berkeley.

Zein-Elabdin, E. O. and Charusheela, S. (eds) (2004) *Postcolonialism Meets Economics*, Routledge, London.

6

Bridging the legal abyss: *hawala* and the *waqf?*

Hilary Lim

Introduction

This interdisciplinary chapter explores some of the complex postcolonial geographies bound up in the encounter of two Islamic financial institutions – *hawala* and the *waqf* – in the legal landscape of Britain. Conducted against a background of the 'War on Terrorist Finance', this encounter between official and unofficial law is not merely a story of surveillance of the frontier and exclusion of these institutions, or further testimony to the plural and contested theory and practice of 'economy'. Instead, this chapter maps the particularities of the encounter between English state legal discourse and these two Islamic institutions in order to make visible the potential for other multi-dimensional maps and new terrains. These encounters are suggestive of shards of contemporary possibilities for economic empowerment, resource mobilisation and redistribution. Such possibilities may be inclusive and alternative and their reception by British law needs to be interrogated in order to understand their potential.

Viewing law through the lens of space, identifying the ways in which law both produces and legitimises certain social and physical spaces, as well as the process through which law is itself shaped by spatial politics, gave rise over the last two decades to geographies of law. Unfortunately, as noted recently by Benda-Beckmann et al.

(2009), this spatial lens has relatively rarely been fixed upon plural legal conditions. In less developed states, clear instances of legal pluralism are recognised and identified, where customary and religious legal systems are co-presences with state law, but examples of legal pluralism also exist elsewhere. For example, British Muslim individuals and communities are on the one hand faced with the modern Western official legal system and on the other hand Islamic law (*shari'a*) which binds the conscience of Muslims wherever they are living, moulding their experiences, whether or not the state 'officially' implements it.[1] This 'living law' finds institutional expression in quite widespread ad hoc unofficial *shari'a* courts, alongside more recently officially sanctioned, but relatively autonomous, Muslim tribunals[2] and the official court system, with individual choices being made about the forum for a dispute or the deployment of extra-legal bargaining opportunities. The conventional concern of legal geography is though more with the relations of state law and space, as opposed to the diverse, untidy, overlapping, sometimes seemingly incompatible, legal orders which are frequently traversed and negotiated to form social behaviour in postcolonial settings.

One continuous thread of analysis, within the broader discussions of law and space, has been organised around mapping law and this has provided opportunities for exploring legal pluralism. In particular, the visualisation of the discourse of law through the map, when used by writers seeking to examine directly the power of law, has the consequence of revealing the exclusionary nature of the discourse, serving also to disclose and recognise those legalities

---

1 Islam is not monolithic and *shari'a* is not static or immutable; the sources of Islamic law are divine but it is human interpretation (*bashari*) using highly developed methods of reasoning (*usul al-Fiqh*) which 'actualises' it. With the exception perhaps of Saudi Arabia and Iran, where Western legal influences have been largely resisted and exclusivity of Islamic laws are professed, other Muslim communities and countries represent a greater hybridity of legal cultures, dependent on specific historical, colonial and postcolonial contexts, as well as state ideologies, customary and secular laws.

2 Muslim Arbitration Tribunals (MAT) were set up in 2007 in a number of UK cities under the Arbitration Act 1996. They deal with a range of disputes including family and inheritance matters, as well as those raising commercial issues and debt. It is interesting to note that according to Hirsch (2010) a small but significant number of non-Muslims are using the MAT to arbitrate their commercial disputes.

which lie on the borderlands or beyond the edges of the map. Some twenty years ago, de Sousa Santos (1987) used the metaphor of the map in a sustained way, pointing out the extent to which the process of (orthodox) cartography distorts 'reality'. Maps are projections which filter out those details which are determined to be unimportant for technical reasons, such as the requirement to be flat and the need for scale. They are also inscribed with the ideology of the cartographer. The map maker has to make decisions about which specifics of the real world to distort, of which the gross deflation of the whole size of the African continent in maps produced under British imperialism is an obvious example. For de Sousa Santos, there are striking resemblances between legal distortions of reality and those within cartography and the process of ideological projection can be detected in legal systems, notably in determining what would be/is recognised as law and therefore as being 'on the map'.

For de Souza Santos every map has a centre and a periphery, with the centre of bourgeois state legality clearly occupied by contractual principles, dominating legislation, legal training and legal ideology. While other fields of law, such as family, welfare or housing law may be outposts on the margins,[3] other normative systems outside state legality may be missing from the map altogether. For instance the 'law of the oppressed', as uncovered in earlier research by de Sousa Santos (1995: 123–249), lies arguably beyond the boundaries of most legal maps.[4] He detailed an internal functioning legality of dispute prevention and resolution found in an 'illegal' Brazilian favela, separate from, excluded by and sometimes in conflict with the official state legality; a further instance of what has since been termed deep legal pluralism (Woodman 1998).

More recently, de Sousa Santos has deployed a different spatial analysis and legal cartography of radical abyssal lines of exclusion

---

3 For a fuller discussion of this see Lim (1996: 130–5) and Bottomley and Lim (2007: 3–5)

4 The field research on 'Pasargada' – the name given to the relevant squatter settlement – was carried out in 1970. The research was published in a variety of forms, but in 1995, it was published with a mirror chapter providing an autobiographical account of the research.

dividing one realm of social reality and territory – 'this side of the line' – from another – 'the other side of the line'. This analysis too encompasses normative fluorescence. Modern law, he argues, represents one of the two most important representations of 'abyssal thinking'; which is rooted in the effective eradication and rejection of whatever lies on the 'other side of the line'.[5] For him, modern law establishes 'this side of the line' through its organising principle, which is the distinction between what is legal and what is illegal according to official state law. An invisible abyssal line, thereby, separates the territory of law from the territory of the 'lawless, the a-legal, the non-legal, and even the legal or illegal according to non-officially recognised law' (2007: 3).

The 'other side of the line' was at one historical stage a fixed territorial location – the colonial zone – and there was a literal cartography of precise global legal lines separating the New World from the Old World.[6] '[T]reaties, peace and friendship applied only to Europe, to the Old World, to the area on this side of the line' (Schmitt 2003: 93). This was succeeded more recently by a metaphorical cartography of lines separating the realm of law from a non-area, an unthinkable terrain of rejected, relegated and incomprehensible experiences and beliefs. However, the lines drawn are no longer the carefully policed and 'neat' divide of literal cartography. They are rather meandering, ragged and 'closer to home'. De Sousa Santos uncovers what he terms the 'return of the colonial', in postcolonial territories, but more specifically metropolitan societies, in 'three main forms: the terrorist, the undocumented migrant worker and the refugee' (2007: 7). The colonial violates those 'metropolitan spaces that were demarcated from the beginning of Western modernity as this side of the line' (2007: 7) and the

---

5 A further radical line is drawn between modern science with its monopoly on distinguishing what is true and false and 'popular, lay, plebeian, peasant or indigenous knowledges' (de Sousa Santos 2007: 2).

6 de Sousa Santos (2007) highlights the 'amity lines – the first one of which may have emerged as a result of the 1559 Cateau-Cambresis Treaty between Spain and France. Circling the globe along the Equator or the Tropic of Cancer in the South and longitudinally through the Azores and the Canary Islands, or both, these lines were important principles of international law for the Protestant and Catholic kings of Europe.

response from the 'abyssal metropolitan' is to draw and redraw lines 'at as close a range as is necessary to guarantee security' (2007: 7). This manifests itself physically, for instance, in the fences of gated communities and the Israeli wall erected along the 'borders' of Palestinian territory. However, other manifestations include the 'state of exception' (2007: 7) in the widespread anti-terrorist legislation which frequently suspends traditional constitutional rights and guarantees of 'this side of the line'. This chapter thus explores the interface between the official legal system and the deeply observed unofficial Islamic norms, concepts and institutions, which only in relatively rare cases break the surface of the official civil legal system and its regulatory frameworks. It does this through an examination of the drawing and redrawing of the abyssal line in the micro-context of modern British state law's 'reception' of two 'unofficial' financial institutions of importance to Muslims and which have connotations and consequences for sustainable development: *hawala* (value transfer) and the *waqf* (Islamic endowment).

Muslims in Britain have become skilled legal and cultural navigators across the seemingly unbridgeable chasm (Pearl and Menski: 1998: 52) between official state law and unofficial Muslim law, finding ways to avoid official law or, where unavoidable or necessary, to accommodate it within unofficial internal hybrid regulatory systems, *angrezi shariat*.[7] However, analysis of the creation and development of *angrezi shariat* has been largely confined to discussions about family law, demonstrating how English law mechanisms are used where practical, and new techniques developed to satisfy official legal requirements and those of religious law (Yilmaz 2005: 80). In terms of considering abyssal thinking, engagement with the *hawala* and the *waqf* by British state law provides a particularly interesting focus. Both mechanisms were swept up in the demonisation of Muslim communities and organisations in the so-called 'war on terror' and more particularly the war on terrorist finance. They are marked as key institutional

---

7 *Angrezi shariat* is of considerable diversity reflecting particular trans-local connections, community customs and pre-existing distinctiveness in Islamic law (see Pollard et al. 2009).

elements in the sophisticated 'subterranean universe of secrecy, subterfuge and criminal endeavours' (Raphaeli 2003: 59) of the Muslim terrorist-financing network. However, the respective encounters of these unofficial institutions with British state law are specific, distinct and complex with legal pluralities played out on shifting spaces and terrain.

Islamic charities are presented as inherently dubious, in the discourse of the war on terrorist finance, irrespective of the particular Muslim community or society concerned with their establishment, operating as covers for the mobilisation and funnelling of money to terrorists through simultaneously mingling humanitarian work with illegal conduct (Napoleoni 2003: 168; Raphaeli 2003). While Islamic charities and Islamic banking systems may be vilified at times, the alternative value transfer system of the *hawala* institution has attracted possibly even greater opprobrium. It is deemed innately suspect because of its successful operation, previously largely 'hidden' from public (metropolitan) view and seemingly functioning outside the corporate Western banking framework. Raphaeli (2003: 59), for instance, doubts the possibility of stemming the flow of money to terror organisations 'so long as there is someone who operates a *hawala* system from the back of a store'. The key response from the state has been to ensure that these institutions are fully subject to regulations designed as anti-money laundering or to counter the financing of terrorism, preventing illegitimately acquired funds from being used or legitimately acquired funds being used for illegitimate purposes.

In the maelstrom of hysteria surrounding Islamic finance, it is striking that both *hawala* and *waqf* have important implications for debates around sustainable development and alleviation of poverty. As part of wider migrant networks, based largely on kinship and trans-local identities (Waldinger and Fitzgerald 2004), *hawala* is a key informal mechanism for transferring funds from first- and second-generation migrants (whether documented or undocumented) to low income and low-middle income countries and communities. Migrant remittances to less developed countries are estimated by the World Bank to have been US$316 billion in 2009. Their sheer scale, which in many contexts may outweigh all other forms of external finance for recipients' countries, including funds from conventional overseas aid programmes, has raised inevitable questions as to whether remittances are a potent resource for development (McKinley 2003; Sorensen and Van Hear 2003; Heilman 2006). The *waqf* also has an important and growing contribution to make in mobilising and channelling charitable funds for medical, educational, cultural and entrepreneurial activities, within the Muslim world and Muslim communities.

It is widely acknowledged that person-to-person remittances are an important survival tool for those in receipt of these funds, sometimes their only income, with much of the money transferred being used for family consumption (Myhre and Nurse 2004), as well as a primary means to secure education, healthcare and housing. However, the 'remittances euphoria' (De Haas 2005) may be misplaced. The extent to which remittances can be an engine for economic growth, respecting environmental as well as socio-economic goals, is hard to calculate (Brown 2006; De Haas 2005), not least because of the methodological problems in assessing the specific development impact of remittances. As Maimbo (2005) indicates, remittances are by their nature fungible and difficult to associate with particular outcomes or effects, which may be multiple. Empirical analysis is also hampered by the fact that data on remittances has serious pitfalls (Ratha 2005). For instance, as the World Bank freely admits, their own estimates of remittances may have serious defects, and there are suggestions that informal unofficial transfers of funds, through *hawala* and similar instruments, could be equal in value to transfers taking place in the official sphere (Gammeltoft 2002). This is not surprising since the financial benefits alone of using an informal transfer scheme, such as a *hawala*, when compared banks or official remittance products – such as Western Union – are considerable.[8] Furthermore, it is

---

8 Ballard (2006: 8) suggests that the average transfer for most migrants is 'no more than a few hundred dollars'. Such transfers are of little interest to the formal banking centre and *hawala* shops offer preferential transfer and foreign exchange rates. In a study conducted for the IMF (Passas, 2005) a comparison was made between a range of formal systems, bank and exchange house drafts, telegraphic transfers and Western Union with a *hawala* scheme for transferring US$100 to South Asia from Dubai. The *hawala* was the only scheme that involved no transfer fees, compared to charges of between US$1.32 to US$27 for the other systems and it offered by far the most favourable exchange rate for the transfer fee.

somewhat 'unlikely and disrespectful' (Ivancic 2008) to expect individual migrants to invest in developing countries as they struggle to meet the basic needs of their own families.[9] Indeed, some argue that although its effects may be difficult to isolate and quantify, it is the directness of a remittance in sending funds to the periphery, rather than the centre, which is one of its most positive features (Ballard 2003), often fostering local entrepreneurial activities, particularly when accompanied by micro-finance initiatives (Azad 2005).

As will be discussed in more detail below, the *waqf*, which has a history of more than 1,000 years as a pivotal Islamic financial and philanthropic institution, suffered a period of widespread decline, decay and disarray during the colonial and early post-colonial period. There are continuing debates as to the effectiveness of the *waqf* for meeting development goals, but the institution is enjoying a contemporary revival, with efforts across the world to create 'new' pious endowments which are efficient and avoid the administrative abuses of the past. For instance, as Benthall and Bellion-Jourdan (2009: 35–6) have recently documented, in Turkey 'since 1967, legislation inspired by both Islamic and American law has facilitated the founding of "new waqfs" with precautions against the administrative abuse of the past'.[10] As they conclude (2009: 44), '[the] rich heritage of the waqf remains available today as an ideological "tool-kit" for building new Islamic institutions'. While much is anticipated for such initiatives and for leveraging remittances for sustainable development, questions remain as to their potential. Research has tended to centre on the effectiveness of these Islamic institutions in delivering 'at the

---

9   This has not prevented individual states from trying to control and maximise the flow and impact of remittances through macro-economic mechanisms that seek to secure future transfers, for instance through the issuing of diaspora bonds to raise finance from overseas migrants or more simply through arrangements with specific banks for remittance products that reduce transfer costs.

10 Banks and non-governmental organisations (NGOs) are offering products whereby the wealthy may deposit funds as a *waqf* (endowment), which is managed by the bank or NGO for benevolent purposes (Sait and Lim 2006: 188). In the UK the charity Islamic Relief offers a *waqf* bond which donors can choose to direct towards a range of philanthropic projects for relief and emergency, health, education and so on.

grassroots', with less emphasis on their reception and functioning in 'sender' countries. This chapter maps the particularities of the encounter between English state legal discourse and Islamic institutions – the *waqf* and the *hawala* – in order to make visible the potential for other multi-dimensional maps and new terrains. The former, though buried by some academics in a 'colonial unconscious', has traversed the abyssal line, adopting the simulated face of the English trust. However, it will be argued that the latter has been resisted, denied and relegated to the 'other side of the line', as is evident from the specific story of Mr Azam's attempt to obtain protection from state law for his *hawala* transaction.

'Flying Money'

In September 2004, Mr Azam, living in England, took a decision to transfer funds to Pakistan in order to pay for his mother's medical treatment. He did not choose a conventional bank transfer, *Western Union* or *Travelex*, but an informally grounded debt transfer facility or *hawala* run by Madina Express, one of a number of businesses under the trading name 'Madina Travel'. On the eighteenth of the month Mr Azam paid £12,000 to Madina Express in the form of a bank draft, together with a £5 fee, on the understanding that an equivalent sum in rupees, at an agreed exchange rate of 105.75 rupees to the pound, would be credited to the account of his sister in Pakistan. He received a receipt from the *hawaladar*, the 'broker' who ran the business, confirming these basic details.

Under the *hawala* system money can be transferred to any specified location, however geographically distant from the transferor. Its attractions for a customer such as Mr Azam include its relative speed and cheapness when compared to other methods. From a technical perspective, a *hawala* requires nothing more than a mobile phone and a fax machine or internet connection to operate and many facilities are managed from small offices or kiosks, internet cafes or, as in Mr Azam's case, within a travel agency. With deep roots in early medieval business dealings in the Muslim world, which were hampered by shortages in currency, *hawala* depended and depends upon close relationships of trust built around kin, culture and shared religious belief (Schramm and

Taube 2003). Similar systems of informal debt and value transfer exist in non-Muslim communities,[11] however, the *hawala* is an important institution for many Muslims and was recognised by several Muslim legal scholars.[12]

Hawala remains an important element in the unofficial 'trans-local' and 'trans-national' networks that diasporic Muslims maintain with Muslim communities across the globe. In particular, it enables 'connected individuals' to transfer funds easily and efficiently to geographical locations often identified as 'home',[13] while relying also on the 'inclusive domain' of shared faith and experience, the *umma*, which displaces space and territory and unites Muslims. Moreover, the *hawala* has been described as having 'a hardy adaptability to difficult circumstances' (Viles 2008: 28) and it is an arrangement which can deliver money to a remote rural area with no effective banking system or even to one experiencing the challenges of conflict or a natural disaster. For instance, research in 2003 for the World Bank estimated that approximately $200 million of emergency aid and relief had been channelled through *hawala* transactions into and around Afghanistan by 127 international and 467 local NGOs since the removal of the Taliban regime (Maimbo 2003).

The basic financial building block of the *hawala* is debt transfer as explained by Schramm and Taube (2003) in the following manner:

> Person X owes a debt to Person Y, who in turn owes a similar sum to Person Z. In a *hawala* transaction, Person Y signs over his claim on Person X to Person Z. For X and Z there is a change in identity of their respective business partners, but not the amount of their obligation or claim. Y, on the other hand, has balanced his demands and

---

11 For instance, after the tsunami in 2004, expatriate Tamil communities utilised a similar informal value transfer process to *hawala*, known as *undiyal* (piggy bank), to channel funds into Eastern Sri Lanka (Cheran and Aiken 2005). Chinese migrant workers use similar systems, called fei-chien or fei-ch'ien ('flying money') (Ballard 2006: 8). In India such value transfer systems are known as *hundi*, in the Phillipines as *padala*, in Hong Kong, *hui kuan* and in Thailand, *phei kwan* (see El-Qorchi et al. 2003; Viles 2008).

12 This is despite strict Islamic legal rules regarding written contracts, witnesses and record keeping.

13 For a fuller discussion see Pollard et al. (2009) and Yilmaz (2005).

obligations through this transaction and is therefore eliminated from the economic chain of interaction

However, what has emerged through this simple transfer of a debtor's charge to another is not only a complex financial system, but also an 'elegant social' system (Viles 2008: 29) of 'coalitions of reciprocity', 'dynamic alliances' and 'translocal networks of absolute interpersonal trusts' (Ballard 2006: 9) capable of enabling inter-regional and intra-regional trade and business. The facilitators of the system, the *hawaladars*, use similar processes of consolidation, deconsolidation and settlement to a conventional bank, but with few operational costs. In a simplified form and contrary to conventional views that *hawala* operate wholly outside the corporate banking sphere, the individual *hawaladar* consolidates funds from individual customers, often as with Madina Express using a conventional bank, in that case *Barclays Bank*. When exchange rates are favourable the *hawaladar* (A) will convert the consolidated fund into dollars and enter into a back to back swap of value with another *hawaladar* (B). The dollar fund will be transferred to wherever specified by the *hawaladar* (B), often in a further 'almost subliminal' (Schramm and Taube 2003) use of conventional banking a dollar bank account in a key financial centre such as Wall Street, in return for a similar tranche of value in the currency of choice paid to the agent of *hawaladar* (A) by *hawaladar* (B), for instance in Rupees in Pakistan.

In practice there are chains of deals and sub-deals or back-to-back 'swaps' involving networks of actors in different geographical locations. Ballard (2006: 8) describes the *hawala* network as 'pulsing' on a daily basis. Mega deals are conducted with tranches of money (at least $100,000) between specialist consolidators, particularly in Dubai, to facilitate the value flows through the network of capillaries in these highly complex transfers. However, value channels through the system only because the participants exchange and distribute information using phones, fax or the internet in an atmosphere of mutual trust, which ultimately ensures that, via the chain, payments are made to the appropriate recipients. As a consequence, the mass of data, which needs to be stored and recorded for transfers of value in the formal banking sector, is unnecessary. In theory at least, *hawala* requires no use of documentation and can take place outside public/government regulation and control.[14]

Unfortunately, in Mr Azam's case the exchange of value in the form of funds into his sister's account did not take place. On the 23rd of September, under a restraint and receivership order, the assets and property of the *hawaladar* were placed under a receiver.[15] The *hawaladar* was prosecuted for money laundering, although two years later all charges against him were dismissed. Mr Azam sought the return of the £12,000 from the receiver, but in December 2004 was told that no payment could be made to him. The crucial factor in this decision being that, as is common practice for the operation of a *hawala*, the £12,000 paid by Mr Azam was consolidated with the monies of other customers such that a total payment of £64,355 was made into a sterling bank account in the name of Madina Express (with Barclays Bank). The entire sum in the sterling account was then transferred into a US Dollar account, also in the name of Madina Express. The effect was that on the date of the receiver's appointment the sterling account into which the £12,000 had been paid was overdrawn to the extent of £9,388.33, leading the receiver, citing an earlier legal authority, to deny the return of the £12,000 to Mr Azam. Most transfers through a *hawala* are for considerably less than the £12,000 in this case, often consisting of the small regular remittances made by migrant workers to their families[16] who can ill afford the high charges of the formal sector. However, given the

---

14 Zagaris (2007) estimates that there are about 800 specifically registered standalone informal money transmission systems in the UK, most of which have fewer than five employees. These have to be registered with Customs and must meet certain standards designed to prevent money-laundering and the financing of illegitimate activities, including keeping records for at least five years, confirming the identity of their customers, having anti-money laundering systems in place and training staff.

15 The order was made under the Criminal Justice Act 1988 and the Drug Trafficking Act 1994.

16 Ballard (2004: 144) estimates, for instance, that between £500 million and £1 billion are transferred as worker remittances to families in Pakistan each year, 'the greater part of these funds' being delivered by means of a *hawala* network, with similar systems in place for remittances from the United Kingdom to Bangladesh, Pakistan, Afghanistan, Iran and Somalia.

size of the payment Mr Azam made to Madina Express it is perhaps unsurprising that he persisted in seeking the return of his funds.[17] Mr Azam's argument was that the *hawala* should be conceived as an English trust of which he was the beneficiary.

Despite their long history, geographical spread and complexity, *hawala* systems, although subject to some regulation, were firmly 'on the other side of the line' without any 'need' for any particular exclusion, unrecognised and largely invisible outside specific communities linked by kinship. The *hawala* institution made few if any incursions into official legal orders. There were no direct attempts either to banish *hawala* from, or appropriate it into, discourses on 'this side of the line'. More recently, with the 'discovery' of new forms of financing terrorism, *hawala* has generally surfaced in the criminal and not the civil courts,[18] in cases concerned with terrorism-related activity, including money laundering and drug trafficking. Such cases tend to support the reification in political discourses of Islam with terror (Viles 2008; Atia 2007), but the drawing of the exclusion and partition, of what is legitimate and illegitimate, is by no means simple. A perfect division is not made between one side of the line, the law-abiding, clean, Western financial world, and the other side of the line, the shadowy, illegal or a-legal networks of surreptitious flows of money through the Muslim sphere. As Atia (2007: 461) suggests 'the outside and the inside are constructed, defined, "enframed" [and] produced through a variety of tactics'. These cases are largely concerned with questions as to whether *hawala* networks have been used to facilitate the movement of criminal funds, but it is notable that they generally contain a judicial pronouncement or confirmation to the effect that *hawala* systems are not by their nature illegal. For instance, Lord Justice Toulson states that: 'There is nothing unlawful or irregular *in itself* about a hawala banking system'.[19] *Hawala* mechanisms are then all potentially tainted and open to abuse, but a (small) legitimate space of

17 *Azam v Iqbal and another* [2007] EWHC 2025 (Admin).
18 See for instance *R v Liaquat Ali, Akhtar Hussain and Mohsan Khan Shahid Bhatti* [2005] EWCA Crim 87 and *Liaquat Ali, Akhtar Hussain v Revenue and Customs Prosecutions Office* [2008] EWCA Crim 1466.
19 *R v Abbas Hussain Khanani* [2009] EWCA Crim 276, emphasis added.

operation and manoeuvre is admitted, left available should such an instance arise.

There are cases in the civil courts referring to *hawala* and the reiterative association of *hawala* with shadowy or furtive money may be quite explicit. For example, a *hawala* transaction arose tangentially in *Hill Street Services Co Ltd v National Westminister Bank plc*,[20] where the claimant was bringing a claim against the bank that £135,750 had been removed from its bank account without authorisation. In the course of explaining the source of some money, Peter Smith J states the following:

> . . . Mr Shroff was indulging in evading the Indian exchange regulations. The monies did not actually come from Mr Shroff, they came from a third party (Mr Mehta). This was a transaction called a 'Hawala'. It is a well-used method of evading exchange control regulations. A person wishing to evade the regulations pays money to someone else within the relevant jurisdiction who has access to foreign monies. That person then uses the foreign monies for the benefit of the national and then achieves an export of monies for the benefit of the national contrary to the regulations.[21]

Here, there is no reference to a legitimate sphere for *hawala*, potential or otherwise, rather what occurs in this passage is a fetishising of difference, such that it appears to be a foreign oddity, a 'wondrous strange' outpost and just an unlawful activity of a marginal, criminal, even barbaric, culture. Thus the rhetoric of this case is caught into the broader inflationary spiral of panic created by media and politicians about terrorists, economic migrants and funds whirling through shadowed spaces into the hands of criminals or Al-Qaida.

The appearance of a *hawala* transaction in Mr Azam's case stands out because he was taking his claim, based on principles of equity, firmly inside the official legal system, with a request that it be not merely legitimated but read, understood and assimilated within the state framework. His request that his transaction receive the security and the protection of the state was relatively unfamiliar and distinct from the generally 'criminal' cases in

---

20 [2007] EWHC 2379 Ch
21 Ibid. at para 42.

which the state sought to prevent money laundering and other
illegitimate activities. The question of whether a *hawala* was
in fact a trust had been considered on a previous occasion in a
civil court, in the case of *Re H*.[22] The judgment of Moses J in
that case was relied upon in *Azam*, yet *Re H* took place in the
context that the *hawaladar* had been convicted of conspiracy to
launder the proceeds of drug trafficking and there was no claim
by any customer or customers, equivalent to Mr Azam, to be a
beneficiary or beneficiaries under the trust. Mr Azam specifically
claimed on the basis of a *Quistclose*[23] trust. Such a trust often
occurs against a background of impending personal or corporate
insolvency and strikingly, with respect to *hawala*, brings together
in one transaction what Gummow LJ in *Re Australian Elizabethan
Theatre Trust*[24] described as the 'distinct and disparate norms' of
debt and trust.

The majority of trusts can arise informally, with equity looking
to intent rather than form, without the need for the word 'trust' to
be used.[25] What is required is evidence of intention on the part of
the settlor (the person creating the trust) to place another person
(the trustee) under a binding obligation with respect to property,
(as opposed to a mere moral obligation), which is to be held for
the exclusive benefit of another (the beneficiary). In the case of a
Quistclose trust, the required evidence of intention is that of mutual

---

22 [2003] EWHC 3551 (Admin).
23 The *Quistclose* trust takes its name from *Quistclose Investments Ltd v Rolls Razor (in
liquidation)* [1970] AC 567. Moffat (2009: 807) has recently described the *Quistclose*
trust as 'a modern enigma wrapped in a mystery' that 'has held a fascination for
trust lawyers for almost forty years'. An effective summary of these debates can be
found in Moffat (2009).
24 (1991) 102 ALR 691.
25 A trust can be created even in circumstances where the parties concerned have no
knowledge of the concept. In *Paul v Constance* [1977] 1 All ER 195, a man was found
to have declared an express trust of funds in a bank account, held in his name, for
himself and his cohabitee in equal shares. Scarman L. J. recognised that the man
in question had no knowledge or understanding of a trust, describing him and his
partner as 'simple people unaware of the subtleties of equity', but considered that
his repeated statements to the effect that the money in the bank account was 'as
much yours as mine' amounted to a trust declaration. And on somewhat similar
facts in *Rowe v Prance* [1999] 2 FLR 787 where on very limited evidence – verbal
references to 'our boat' – the court again found an express declaration of a trust,
although on this occasion with respect to a yacht.

intention between the settlor and the trustee that the property in question is to be used only for a specified purpose and most importantly will not become part of the general assets of the trustee. In the event that the purpose is not carried through then the property results back to the settlor.[26] It was argued, therefore, that against a background of mutual trust the *hawaladar* (as a trustee) was bound to use the £12,000 handed to him by Mr Azam, (as settlor), for a specific purpose, the money was not the *hawaladar's* to use as he pleased and when the purpose failed the *hawaladar* (trustee) was obliged to return it to Mr Azam in full as its true (beneficial/equitable) owner.

Mr Azam failed to establish a *Quistclose* trust parallel to the *hawala* relationship, with the court appearing to take the stance that not only was there no trust in the legal sense but also that the *hawala*, although not illegal, was inconceivable in the conceptual framework and discourse of English law. Sullivan J concluded that 'the *hawala* system, as practised . . . by the claimant in the present case, [was] totally inconsistent with the existence of a trust'. Despite Mr Azam's claim that he had never considered that the money handed to Madina Express would become part of its general funds, there was, it was reasoned by the court, no evidence of an intention shared with the *hawaladar* in this regard, as required for a *Quistclose* trust. It was admitted that existing case law on the creation of informal express trusts did not require that the relevant money had to be kept in a separate bank account in order to be bound by a trust obligation, but 'the fundamental obstacle' for Mr Azam and indeed for any similar customer was that 'it is inherent in the *hawala* system . . . that the sums paid by customers wishing to transfer money are *not* kept in a separate account distinct from the "general funds of the company"'.[27] At the same time the system could not be equated with 'conventional banking', although the relationship of banker and customer 'was far more analogous to the

---

26 One of the key areas of debate surrounding the *Quistclose* trust is whether in fact the money 'results back' to the settlor upon failure of the purpose, on a secondary or resulting trust, or whether in fact unless and until such time as the purpose is carried out beneficial ownership remains with the settlor.

27 See n 16, para 29.

relationship between the *hawaladar* and his customer than that of trustee and beneficiary'.[28] This is not merely the grudging statement that *hawala* transactions are not innately illegal, but the law 'on this side of the line' hermetically sealing itself against penetration by 'other' norms and recognition or adaptation to diverse ways of life and finance, casting *hawala* if not into the abyss at least into legal limbo.

The *waqf* in trust

Encounters between trusts and Islamic legal mechanisms are, however, not new and there is good evidence to suggest that the roots of the Anglo-American trust in fact lie in the *shari'a* and another institution by implication demonised in the 'War on Terror Finance' – the *waqf* (Islamic endowment). The *waqf* (pl. *awqaf*) is a key Islamic institution and a legal mechanism, recognised and developed in Islam for more than 1,000 years. It permits an owner to permanently settle property to the use of beneficiaries for specific purposes. At its heart the Islamic endowment is connected firmly with the religious precept of charity. Charity towards economically dependent members of family, community and society is one of the five fundamental principles of Islam. Islam obliges Muslims to pay *zakat* (charitable levy) (*Qur'an* 9: 60). Benthall and Bellion-Jourdan (2009: 9) emphasise that this is a form of 'financial worship' without which 'the efficacy of prayer is negated'. Land settled within a *waqf* may be colloquially referred to as 'religious land', thereby demonstrating the vital relationship between the religious obligation and the institution as one of the key vehicles a Muslim may use to comply with this charitable expectation. The investment of Muslim communities over time into the *waqf* institution is enormous. *Awqaf* amounted, for instance, to about one third

---

28 At around the same time as the decision in this case, the rights of the customers in a 'Christmas Club' were considered in the *Farepak Foods and Gifts Limited* [2006] EWHC 3272, but again no *Quistclose* trust was found since such an interpretation was at odds with *Farepak's* business model and the directors attempts to set up a trust were deemed to be an attempt at preferring a particular group of creditors.

of the Islamic Ottoman Empire and wherever there was a substantial Muslim community one was likely to find a *waqf*. Their
development was largely due to a conservative view of the role
of government, which was seen as supporting and subsidising
but not carrying out welfare activities. Services like health and
education in the Ottoman Empire were privately financed and
organised through the *waqf* system, as a part of public policy
(Arjomand 1998).

On the surface, at least, the *waqf* shares most of its essential
characteristics with the trust and its predecessor the *use*; in
particular the division between 'administration' and 'beneficial
enjoyment' of property. Cattan (1955: 212) regards the trust as
directly comparable to the *waqf*, describing their similarities as
'striking'. Similarly, Avini (1996: 1161) has argued that 'both institutions shared the same structure – the *waqif* is analogous to the
person making the *enfeoffment* (settlor); the *mutawalli* is the same
as the *feoffee to uses* (trustee); and the beneficiaries [*mustahiqq* pl.
mustahiqqun] (both present and future) exist in both institutions'.
Superficially, at any rate, there is a likeness in the distinction
between private and public trusts and that between a *waqf ahli*,
which is an endowment for the benefit of the family of the *waqif*
until the extinction of her descendants, whereupon it is diverted
to a charitable purpose, and the *waqf khairi*, which is a purely
charitable endowment (Avini 1996).

Cattan (1955: 212) takes the view that even an assessment
of the differences between the trust and the *waqf* only serves to
confirm their 'close similarity'. While it is the case, for instance,
that the trustee becomes the legal owner of the property, while
the *mutawalli* does not, in practice both roles are to administer
property on behalf of beneficiaries or beneficial purposes. The
very nature of a *waqf*, with the word literally meaning detention,
is that property is being permanently tied up in perpetuity, while
private trusts are subject to the rule against perpetuities. This
principle, incidentally, means that a cash *waqf*, as opposed to
those consisting of land, has proved a matter of challenge to, and
debate within, Islamic law, although *awqaf* which involve tying up
money and using the income from it for social or pious purposes
have been an important factor in modern Islamic philanthropic

developments. However, as Cattan (1955) points out, the trust in its earlier form – the *use* – could be made in perpetuity.[29]

Orthodox trust textbooks rarely make reference to the *waqf*, but where they do it is in the context of a search for the origins of the trust. There is a dominant line of argument, rooted in a structure of (Western) global historical time which converts 'history into a "waiting room" from which non-Western economies' (Pollard and Samers 2007: 325) and legal systems will eventually emerge into modernity, reflected in Maitland's frequently quoted view that the development of the trust idea is 'the greatest and most distinctive achievement performed by Englishmen in the field of jurisprudence' (Hayton 1998). Goodhart (1996), for instance, adopts an imperialist view that: 'It is at least possible that the trust will in the 21st century join those other English inventions, such as football and the steam engine, which have swept the world'. However, there are academics, such as Moffat (2009) that provide glimpses of another hidden history of the 'invention' of the trust (see also Hudson 2010). He refers to the article discussed above by Avini (1996), in support of his 'allegation' that the 'source' of the trust may lie in Islamic law, although Avini makes a more complex and subtle argument about the 'origins' of the *use*/trust than is perhaps evident from Moffat's brief passing comments. The former suggests that it may be helpful to think of the two institutions having a 'convergent evolution', rather than to search for the 'source' of the trust, avoiding 'conjectural findings of causation'. Nevertheless, Avini (1996) does conclude that if there was an external model for the English trust, he concurs with the Islamic theory that the *waqf* was the greatest influence upon the trust, imported into England by Franciscan friars who were active in the Middle East during the thirteenth century and where there is good evidence both that the *waqf* was already firmly established

---

29 There are other ways in which the technical rules concerning *waqf* endowment and the trust seem to coincide. For instance, Islamic law makes provision for the situation where a charitable purpose has become extinct or disappeared, in which case the benefit of the *waqf* is applied to another charitable purpose, in a manner which bears some resemblance to the doctrine of *cy pres* in the English law of trusts. Nevertheless, it should be acknowledged that there are differences in this area for the *waqf* is, by its very nature, dedicated to charity and may be reapplied without having to place close attention, as with the trust, to the particular settlor's intention.

as a widely used legal device and widespread possibilities for cultural exchange.[30] There is every possibility that the well-acknowledged Islamic contribution to the so-called 'European awakening' in medicine and mathematics was accompanied by a similar contribution to the discipline of law (Avini 1996: 1159).

However, given the encounters between legal cultures of the colonial engagement, it is perhaps not a matter of surprise that the *waqf* is rarely considered in Western texts, particularly as a possible inspiration for the trust. Those colonial encounters were almost the literal opposite of the Islamic theory of the origins of the trust. The colonisation of the *waqf* by the legal concept of the trust, coupled with more general attacks upon it from the colonial powers contributed to a pre-existing decay and decline. It is argued that much of the decline of the *waqf*, can be laid at the door of Islamic legal doctrine (Schoenblum 1999). As Benthall and Bellion-Jourdan (2009: 33) summarise: '[the] aim of permanence to the Day of Judgement was not achieved: the majority of *waqfs* suffered in practice from fragmentation, neglect, diversion to other beneficiaries, of confiscation; and they were often a cause for bitter dispute'. In particular, the principal of perpetuity with respect to the *waqf ahli*, where as generation succeeded generation the number of beneficiaries increased to a point where individual benefits were insignificant, meant that property often fell into disuse or ruin (Carroll 2001). There is also evidence to suggest that *waqf* property came increasingly under the administration of poor and unsuitable *mutawallis* (Layish 1994). The colonial powers, particularly the British, found the *waqf*, neither public nor private land, to be inscrutable and began to reconstruct *waqf* law through an elaboration of common-law family, trust or public laws.[31] Seizing on the argument that the *waqf* was inefficient, inequitable and uneconomic, and thereby a cause of backwardness, *awqaf* had their status altered or extinguished, although the experience varied between Muslim countries. *Waqf* land itself was viewed as a vast resource of 'non-private' land that could easily be harnessed by the

---

30 A comprehensive legal treatise on the *waqf* was compiled by Al-Khassaf much earlier in the ninth century (trans. Verbit 2008).
31 For a fuller discussion, see Sait and Lim (2006: 159–61).

colonial powers for other purposes. Where there was any lack of certainty about the status of *waqf* property, as was the case where old Ottoman records were incomplete, lands were siphoned off by the colonial and later the postcolonial state (Raissouni 2005). The *waqf* continued its decline in the postcolonial period, as Muslim states, in a move welcomed in the West as underpinning land market economics and private property, sought to abolish or nationalise this institution rather than modernise it. In Tunisia, for instance, after independence all *waqf* property was seized by the state and similar processes took place across the Arab world, including Syria and Egypt[32] (Sait and Lim 2006: 162–4).

The relegation of *waqf* law to a sub-terrain of rejected, incomprehensible experiences and beliefs, beyond the abyssal line, forever in the waiting room, endures. Waters (2006: 218) in a recent and lengthy discussion of the global stretch of trust and trust-like 'fiduciary property administration' tours jurisdictions of Europe, central and south America, South Africa, Quebec, Louisiana, Japan, Korea and China, before touching briefly on 'Trusts in Islamic Law' which he considers may be 'traditionally . . . comparable to the role of a common law charitable or public trust'. However, in the spirit of Maitland, Waters goes on to state that while the 'analogies with the trust are obvious . . . it seems hardly possible to contend that the *waqf* is itself a functional model of the trust concept', perhaps because he takes the view also that the 'application of the *waqf* to commercial or business purposes has not to date taken place'.

Contrary to Water's view, where *aqwaf* have flourished often they involve or are linked to trade and business, as in Bangladesh where they include a shopping centre in Dhaka and a large herbal medicine institution *Hamdard Foundation* (Sadeq 2002). As Benthall and Bellion-Jordan (2009) have recently argued, 'Islamic finance and charity are interdependent in forming a circle of seamless discourse'. Moreover, there is a resurgence of interest and promotion on the *waqf* (Organisation of the Islamic

---

32 The enduring 'effectiveness' of this centralisation is perhaps evident from El Daly's presentation of new research to the Philanthropy and Development Conference in Egypt, where she said that many people in the country thought that the meaning of *waqf* was government property (quoted in Douara 2007).

Conference 2000), as a third sector, independent of government and purely profit-motivated individuals, particularly with respect to plans for sustainable development (Emman 2008) and microfinance (Ahmed 2007). Developments involving the cash *waqf* are an important element in such innovatory rethinking. Products which combine investment through a *waqf* with charitable endeavour are becoming more common. The International Union for Conservation of Nature West Asia has, for instance, created an innovative financing mechanism whereby donated funds are collected and placed into a *waqf*, invested and then the proceeds used for sustainable development projects.[33]

Like the *hawala*, the *waqf* has no specific recognition in English law and remains unrecognisable in the existing framing of the dominant legal discourse. Unlike the *hawala*, and despite its designation as 'other' by some Western academics such as Waters, the *waqf*, or at least the idea of the *waqf*, seems to have quietly, almost surreptitiously, passed through the abyssal line under the legal cloak of the English charity. According to the Charity Commission's Faith and Social Cohesion Unit (FSCU) there are 486 registered Muslim charities in Greater London alone, recognised and regulated by the state. To acquire charitable status, which carries with it considerable tax benefits, Muslim institutions, like other charities, must be shaped into an accepted legal form, usually a charitable trust or registered corporation, managed by persons designated as trustees or directors. This process has been largely administrative and without legal conflict, yet the terms *waqf* and trust are evident in the registered names of a small number of contemporary registered Muslim charities. With respect to some charities, particularly those established by Bangladeshi communities, this collage of terms can be perhaps explained through trans-local associations and familiarities, tapping into the richness of consciousness and understandings of the *waqf*. The sign 'waqf' may also be an effect of increasing Muslim pride in the survival and revival of the *waqf* as an institution. For instance, large Saudi foundations 'describe themselves as waqf in Arabic

---

33 See http://www.iucn.org/about/union/secretariat/offices/rowa/iucnwame_our-work/iucnwame_waqfinitiative/ (accessed 21 January 2011).

language publications [although] they would more recognizably be characterised as "parastatals" or . . . Government Organised Non-Governmental Organisations' (Benthall and Bellion-Jordan 2009: 36).

The appearance of the word '*waqf*' in charities' names may hint at something deeper, a repressed complexity, a continued, if partially hidden, deeper observance of unofficial Islamic norms, concepts and institutions, as well as 'traffic' between cultures. As discussed above, there are few noteworthy areas of obvious legal conflict between the 'shell' of the English trust and the *waqf* (Thompson 1999). The aims and activities of Muslim organisations may have been transformed by the required formulations of official state law, in order to acquire charitable status. However, it does not mean that the *waqf* is not alive, albeit usually hidden from outside view, within the informal legal culture, influencing how the donation of funds, their management and distribution are 'thought through'. Trustees' reports and accounts for some of East London's Muslim charities deposited with the Charity Commissioners indicate that while meeting the requirements of English Law they are operating underneath with a distinctively Islamic framework and legal culture. The language of the 'seamless discourse' of Islamic finance and philanthropy discourse is scattered through these reports, with one of the largest trusts in East London, the London Mosque fund, making reference to *zakat* and *fitra* collection and distribution, as well as *Qard-e-Hasanah*, a specifically Islamic benevolent interest-free loan (Pollard et al. 2009: 153–6). The *waqf* bonds issued by Islamic Relief, which invests funds in a manner which is *shari'a* compliant, and used for philanthropic purposes, is a much more explicit and particular appearance of this Islamic institution in the English context. Moreover, the exoskeleton of the trust and the transparency of the administrative processes, to which charitable trusts must adhere, may provide a valuable degree of protection for Islamic philanthropy. Benthall and Bellion-Jourdan (2009: 84) highlight a Charity Commission official defending Islamic Relief Worldwide for its humanitarian work and condemning unwarranted 'allegations . . . made against such charities because they are 'Muslim' and most of the time without evidence'. At the same time they emphasise the 'Islamic character of the organisation', particularly the religious identity and practice of its personnel.

Conclusion

This chapter has explored the encounter between key economic institutions developed within Islamic law, which offer splinters of opportunity for innovation in economic empowerment, resource mobilisation and redistribution, with English state legal discourse. The 'War on Terrorist Finance' is the backdrop for this encounter between official and unofficial law, but it is not just a story of frontier policing and exclusion of these institutions to 'the other side' of the abyssal line. State legal discourse does carry persistent reminders of existing stereotypes of 'migrants' and 'terrorists', as well as associated disturbance with respect to that which is or appears to be undocumented, such that *hawala* is positioned and framed as not belonging and unrecognisable before its 'arrival' in state law's field of vision. The *waqf* enjoys no specific state recognition and there may be distortion and uneasiness in the integration of the 'idea' of the *waqf*, through administrative regulation and within the sleeve of the charitable trust or company, into a Western legal and philanthropic discourse 'on the other side of the line'. However, plural legal relations in this context, particularly with respect to the ideology of the *waqf*, while constrained, even hidden, are also somewhat untidy and more unruly, suggesting alternative mappings.

Many Islamic institutions have chosen to cross the abyss and use the state framework, with a range of reasons and motives, thereby raising potential for an alliance of the charitable obligation and redistributive elements of the Islamic framework, at a time of widespread renewal of the *waqf*, with flourishing Western models of fund raising and deployment. Moreover, the legal requirements of a legal charity may confine, but they have also supplied valuable, if largely accidental, security and protection in an environment of widespread accusations that Islamic philanthropy is merely a cover for subversive political or religious aims. If the development potential of the *waqf* and indeed the remittances transferred through *hawala* are to be fully realised, their reception on the legal plane in sender countries requires further analysis. The complex and long history of relations between the trust and *waqf* inhibited the development of the latter. However, more recently it has offered possibilities for innovative development strategies, including microfinance, which holds out promise also for institutions like *hawala* if approaches to the seamless discourse of Islamic finance and charity can go beyond fearful reaction and exclusion.

References

Ahmed, H. (2007) 'Waqf-based microfinance: Realising the social role of Islamic finance', paper written for the International Seminar on Integrating Awqaf in the Islamic Financial Sector, 6–7 March, Singapore, available at: http://info.worldbank.org/etools/docs/library/240137/Paper_Microfinance%20&%20Waqf%28Dr.%20Habib%29.pdf (accessed 28 April 2010).

Arjomand, S. A. (1998) 'Philanthropy, the law and public policy in the Islamic World before the modern era', in W. F. Ilchman, S. Katz and E. L. Queen II (eds), *Philanthropy in the World's Traditions*, Indiana University Press, Bloomingon, pp. 109–132.

Atia, M. (2007) 'In whose interest? Financial surveillance and the circuits of exception in the war on terror', *Environment and Planning D: Society and Space*, 25: 447–75.

Avini, A. (1996) 'The origins of the modern English trust revisited', *Tulane Law Review*, 70: 1139.

Azad, A. K. (2005) 'Migrant workers' remittances: A source of finance for micro-enterprise in Bangladesh', in S. M. Maimbo and D. Ratha (eds), *Remittances: Development impact and future prospects*, World Bank, Washington, pp. 120–132.

Ballard, R. (2003) 'Remittances and economic development', papers for the Centre of Applied South Asian Studies, University of Manchester, UK, available at: http://www.casas.org.uk/papers/pdfpapers/selectctte.pdf (accessed 26 April 2010).

— (2004) 'Delivering migrant workers' remittances: The logistical challenge', *Journal of Financial Transformation*, 12: 141–53.

— (2006) 'Hawala: criminal haven or vital financial network', Newsletter, International Institute of Asian Studies, University of Leiden, October Issue: 8–9.

Benda-Beckmann, F., Benda-Beckmann, K. and Griffiths, A. (2009) 'Space and legal pluralism: An introduction', in F. von Benda-Beckmann, K. von Benda-Beckmann and A. Griffiths (eds), *Spatializing Law: An anthropological geography of law in society*, Ashgate, Aldershot.

Benthall, J. and Bellion-Jourdan, J. (2009) *The Charitable Crescent*, I. B. Tauris, London.

Bottomley, A. and Lim, H. (2007) 'Feminist perambulations', in H. Lim and A. Bottomley (eds), *Feminist Perspectives on Land Law*, Routledge-Cavendish, Abingdon, pp. 1–30.

Brown, S. S. (2006) 'Can remittances spur development? A critical survey', *International Studies Review*, 8: 55–75.

Carroll, L. (2001) 'Life interests and inter-generational transfer of property: Avoiding the law of succession', *Islamic Law and Society*, 8(2): 245–86.

Cattan, H. (1955) 'The law of *waqf*', in M. Khadduir and H. J. Liebsney (eds), *Law in the Middle East*, William Byrd, Richmond, pp. 203–222.

Cheran, R. and Aiken, S. (2005) 'The impact of international informal banking on Canada: A case study of Tamil transnational money transfer networks (*Undiyal*), Canada/Sri Lanka', Working Paper, available at: http://publications.gc.ca/site/eng/313590/publication.html.

De Haas, H. (2005) 'International migration, remittances and development: Myths and facts', *Third World Quarterly*, 26(8): 1269–84.

de Sousa Santos, B. (1987) 'Law: A map of misreading: Towards a postmodern conception of law', *Journal of Law and Society*, 14: 279–302.

— (1995) *Toward a New Common Sense*, Routledge, New York.

— (2007) 'Beyond abyssal thinking', *Eurozine*, available at: http://www.eurozine.com/articles/2007-06-29-santos-en.html.

Douara, D. (2007) 'Philanthropy and development conference presents new research, calls for waqf revival', *The Daily Star*, 2 March, available at: http://www.dailystaregypt.com/article.aspx?ArticleID=5922.

El-Qorchi, M., Maimbo, S. and Wilson, J. (2003) *Informal Value Transfer Systems: An analysis of the informal hawala system*, IMF-World Bank Occasional Paper No. 222, Washington DC, IMF.

Emman, A. (2008) 'Islamic waqf and management of cultural heritage in Palestine', *International Journal of Heritage Studies*, 14(4): 380–5.

Gammeltoft, P. (2002) 'Remittances and other financial flows to developing countries', *International Migration*, 40(5): 181–211.

Goodhart, W. (1996) 'Trust law for the twenty-first century', in A. J. Oakley (ed.), *Trends in Contemporary Trust Law*, Oxford University Press, Oxford, pp. 257–72.

Hayton, D. J. (1998) *The Law of Trusts*, Sweet and Maxwell, London.

Heilman, C. (2006) 'Remittances and the migration-development nexus – Challenges for sustainable governance of migration', *Ecological Economics*, 59(2): 231–6.

Hirsch, A. (2010) 'Fears over non-Muslim use of Islamic law to resolve disputes', *The Guardian*, 14 March.

Hudson, A. (2010) *Equity and Trusts*, Routledge-Cavendish, London.

Ivancic, T. (2008) *Remittances for Development: Hawala or Western Union?* Naider, available at: http://www.naider.com/ateneo/articulo_blog.asp?id=318 (accessed 25 April 2010).

Layish, A. (1994) 'The Muslim *Waqf* in Jerusalem after 1967: Beneficiaries and management', in F. Bilici (ed.), *Le Waqf dans le monde musulmna contemporain (XIXe-Xxe siecles)*, Institut Francais d'Etudes Anatoliennes, Istanbul.

Lim, H. (1996) 'Mapping equity's place: Here be dragons', in A. Bottomley (ed.), *Feminist Perspectives on Equity and Trusts*, Cavendish, London, pp. 125–48.

Maimbo, S. M. (2003) *The Money Exchange Dealers of Kabul: A study of the hawala system in Afghanistan*, World Bank, Washington DC.

— (2005) 'Migrant labour remittances in South Asia', World Bank, Washington DC.

McKinley, B. (2003) 'International migration and development – the potential for a win-win situation', presentation at G77 Panel for Migration and Development, International Organization for Migration, New York.

Moffat, G. (2009) *Trusts Law*, 5th edition, Cambridge University Press, Cambridge.

Myhre, D. and Nurse, K. (2004) 'Crossfire', *Small Enterprise Development*, 15(1): 4–8.

Napoleoni, L. (2003) *Modern Jihad: Tracing the dollars behind the terror networks*, Pluto Press, London.

Organisation of the Islamic Conference (2000) 'Promoting *waqfs* and their role in the development of Islamic societies', Report of the Secretary General to the Twenty-seventh Session of the Organisation of the Islamic Conference, Kuala Lumpur, Malaysia, June, 27–30.

Passas, N. (2005) 'Formalizing the informal? Problems in the national and international regulation of hawala', in *Regulatory Frameworks for Hawala and Other Remittance Systems*, IMF, Washington DC. pp. 7–16.

Pearl, D. and Menski, W. (1998) *Muslim Family Law*, Sweet and Maxwell, London.

Pollard, J. S. and Samers, M. (2007) 'Islamic banking and finance and postcolonial political economy: decentering economic geography', *Transactions of the Institute of British Geographers*, 32: 313-330.

Pollard, J., Lim, H. and Brown, R. (2009) 'Muslim economic initiatives: Global finance and local projects', in R. Phillips (ed.), *Muslim Spaces of Hope*, Zed Books, London, pp. 139–262.

Raissouni, A. (2005) 'Islamic waqf Endowment – Scope and Implications', trans. by Abderrafi Benhallam, revised by Ahmed Alaoui, Islamic Educational, Scientific and Cutlrual Organisation, (ISESCO), available at: http://www.isesco.org.ma/pub/Eng/WAQF/waqf.htm.

Raphaeli, N. (2003) 'Financing of terrorism: Sources, methods and channels', *Terrorism and Political Violence*, 15(4): 59–82.

Ratha, P. (2005) 'Workers' remittances: An important and stable source of external development finace', in S. M. Maimbo and D. Ratha (eds), *Remittances Development: Impact and Future Prospects*, World Bank, Washington, p. 19.

Sadeq, A. M. (2002) '*Waqf*, perpetual charity and poverty alleviation', *International Journal of Social Economics*, 29(1/2): 135–51.

Sait, S. and Lim, H. (2006) *Land, Law and Islam*, Zed Books, London.

Schmitt, C. (2003) *The Nomos of the Earth in the International Law of the Jus Publicum Europaeum*, Telos Press, New York.

Schoenblum, J. A. (1999) 'The role of legal doctrine in the decline of the Islamic *waqf*: A comparison with the trust', *Vanderbilt Journal of Transnational Law*, 32: 1191–230.

Schramm, M. and Taube, M. (2003) 'Evolution and institutional foundation of the *hawala* financial system', *International Review of Financial Analysis*, 12(4): 405–20.

Sorensen, N. N. and Van Hear, N. (eds) (2003) *The Migration-Development Nexus – Evidence and Policy Options*, International Organization for Migration, Geneva.

Thompson, H. A. (1999) 'The best legal structure for Muslim charities', available at: http://www.wynnechambers.co.uk/pdf/IslamicCharitableTrust. pdf (accessed 21 January 2011).

Verbit, G. P. (2008) (trans. and ed.) *A Ninth Century Treatise on the Law of Trusts*, Xlibris.

Viles, T. (2008) 'Hawala, hysteria and hegemony', *Journal of Money Laundering Control*, 11(1): 25–33.

Waldinger, R. and Fitzgerald, P. (2004) 'Transnationalism in question', *American Journal of Sociology*, 109(5): 1177–95.

Waters, D. W. M. (2006) 'The future of the trust: Part I', *Journal of International Trust and Corporate Planning*, 13(4): 179–223.

Woodman, G. (1998) 'Ideological combat and social observations: Recent debate about legal pluralism', *Journal of Legal Pluralism and Unofficial Law*, 42: 21–59.

Yilmaz, I. (2005) *Muslim Laws, Politics and Society in Modern Nation States: Dynamic legal pluralisms, England, Turkey and Pakistan*, Ashgate, Aldershot.

Zagaris, B. (2007) 'Problems applying traditional anti-money laundering procedures to non-financial transactions, "parallel banking systems" and Islamic financial systems', *Journal of Money Laundering Control*, 10(2): 157–69.

7

Postcolonial geographies of Latin American migration to London from a materialist perspective

Cathy McIlwaine

Introduction

London is a city of opportunities to work, but at the same time it is very sad. You arrive here like a 'chicken' that doesn't speak English, you look at the houses, the buses driving on the wrong side of the road. For a long time, you feel completely lost, people try and talk to you in the street and you don't understand what they're saying, you're completely out of your orbit.

Mario, irregular Bolivian migrant

Over a decade ago it was noted that although immigrants and ethnic minorities were quintessential 'postcolonial subjects', research on the geographies of migration had yet to engage fully with postcolonial debates (Samers, 1998). While theorising transnationalism has adopted and adapted many dimensions of poststructuralist epistemology in terms of the importance of challenging binary interpretations of movement of capital, labour and people, as well as highlighting the importance of plurality and hybridity, explicit postcolonial interpretations of mobility drawing on empirically grounded work remain quite scarce beyond work on diasporas (Keown *et al.* 2009; Mitchell 2003). Yet, a postcolonial perspective can be fruitful in relation to the mobility of people because by its very nature it actively encourages 'anti-essentialist conceptualisations of space, place and identity' (Silvey 2004: 501; Yeoh 2003). However, while patterns of international migration are hugely diverse in terms of the nature of flows across the globe, there remains a distinct pattern of people moving from countries in the Global South with fewer socio-economic opportunities to those where there are perceived to be more (International Organization for Migration 2008; Li and Teixeira 2007).

Therefore, while many postcolonial interpretations of mobility focus on identity formation and processes of hybridisation at an abstract level, they also need to stress the deep-seated inequalities that underpin international migration from the Global South (Bailey 2001). Drawing on qualitative research with Latin American migrants (from Colombia, Ecuador and Bolivia) in London, this chapter suggests that a postcolonial perspective can provide useful insights into international migration experiences as long as an explicitly materialist interpretation is adopted (McEwan 2003). Such an interpretation recognises that mobility reflects not only the constant reconfiguration of identities, but also that this movement is underpinned by global processes of uneven development. The materialist perspective highlights that although an examination of the lives of migrants needs to take the negotiation of diasporic identities into account, it is the material realities of their lives that drives their ability to live in cities of the Global North.

Interpreting international migration from a postcolonial perspective

At the outset, and without rehearsing the complex debates around definitions of postcolonialism or unravelling the 'tangled skein of intellectual threads' (Yeoh 2001: 456), it is important to highlight some of the foundational aspects of postcolonialism that are especially relevant in relation to international migration. Acknowledging that there are many types of postcolonialisms (internal, transnational, imperial) (Sidaway 2000), the complex negotiation of power underlies them all (King 1999, 2003). Also of relevance here is that a specifically spatial rather than temporal take on postcolonialism can provide a more accurate picture of global relations (Blunt and McEwan 2002). Perhaps of most importance, is that a revised interpretation of postcolonialism that situates issues of identity, meaning and consciousness within a material and political reality is of most use in understanding international mobility (Blunt and McEwan 2002; King 1999; McEwan, 2003; Yeoh, 2003). This also helps in appeasing the over-emphasis on the historical, cultural and theoretical abstraction in some conceptualisations of postcolonialism that have been widely critiqued by those concerned with concrete inequalities and poverty (Simon 2006, 2007). However, although a much more politicised and engaged interpretation of postcolonialism has taken root in recent years (Ashcroft 2001; McEwan 2003), studies of international migration from such a revised perspective are less common.

Indeed, it is somewhat surprising that an explicit postcolonial approach has not received more attention in studies of international migration (Bailey 2001; Samers 1998; Yeoh 2003). This said, a broad poststructuralist, if not always postcolonial perspective has been central to conceptualisations of transnationalism (Bailey *et al.* 2002; Basch *et al.* 1994; Guarnizo 1997; Samers 1997). In particular, the notion of movement across borders as fluid and interconnected has complemented the need to account for the role of the changing nature of global capitalism in the movement of people. In addition, transnationalism has recognised that migrant identities are constructed in relation to more than one nation-state as well as different discourses and difference (Glick Schiller *et al.* 1995; Mitchell 2003). From a cultural perspective, explorations of transnationalism have focused on issues of hybridity, plurality and in-betweeness (Bhabha 1994). Yet while this work has been important in challenging binary interpretations of circulation, there remains considerable scope to consider much more systematically how economic inequalities underpin movement (Bailey 2001; Blunt 2007). This is especially notable from an empirical perspective as noted by Mitchell (2003: 82): 'without "literal" empirical data related to the actual movements of things and people across space, theories of anti-essentialism, mobility, plurality and hybridity can quickly devolve into terms emptied of any potential political efficacy'.

In particular, there are opportunities to combine this research with the long-standing work on transnationalism associated with the work of Alejandro Portes and others in relation to Latin American migrant settlement in the US from a largely political economy standpoint. As well as contributing to debates on conceptualising transnationalism (Portes *et al.* 1999), this research has explored various dimensions of interconnecting ties among migrants focusing on social, economic and political linkages (Itzigsohn *et al.* 1999; Vertovec, 2004a; see Levitt and Jaworsky 2007 for an overview). However, while this work has been critically important in elucidating the nature and processes of transnational linkages across the world, it is less helpful in exploring why people migrate in the first place.

Although postcolonialism cannot provide all the answers as to why people move, the fact that it aims to reduce the spatial and temporal distance between these parts of the world and to recognise them as integrally linked in unequal ways (McEwan 2003), can help to shed some light on the processes of such movement. Drawing on Stuart Hall's (1996) ideas about the world comprising a series of linkages between cultures and economies revolving around the 'metropole' of Europe as a colonial power and the powerless 'peripheries' of the world, a postcolonial perspective can help us to see how colonialism has generated multiple mobilities and diasporas, be they imperial, labour, trade and/or cultural (Yeoh 2003). While many of these colonial diasporas continue to multiply with today's forces of globalisation and the concomitant inequalities this process inheres (Samers 1997), others have much more complex colonial legacies and postcolonial histories (Yeoh 2003), as will be discussed in the current context in relation to Latin American migration to the UK.

As well as providing a historicised and contextualised interpretation as to why people migrate, a postcolonial interpretation also allows for a heightened recognition of migrant agency. In postcolonial terms, this viewpoint allows us to 'recover the lost historical and contemporary voices of the marginalized, the oppressed and the dominated' (McEwan 2002: 128) who have been subjugated by colonial and neo-colonial forces. Although international migrants from the Global South are rarely the poorest members of their societies (Datta *et al.* 2007a), they come from countries that are marginalised globally, and are often suffering from high levels of poverty and inequality. Ethnographic accounts that capture the voices of those who move provide an important counterpoint to grand narratives of mobility (Silvey and Lawson 1999; Lawson 2000). These stories can reveal the everyday practices that reflect complex constructions of migrant subjectivities that are variously influenced by gender, class and racial subject positions (Dyck 2005).[1] However, overemphasising migrant agency to the neglect of structure can also be erroneous leading to what Bailey (2001: 421) refers to as 'agency-heavy' and 'structure-light' conceptions (Lawson 2000; Silvey 2000, 2003).

Finally, it is important to reiterate that it is not necessarily a postcolonial perspective *per se* that has facilitated these challenges to hegemonic modes of thinking and doing. Instead, it reflects a wider trend towards seeking to work in engaged, participatory and ethical ways (McEwan 2001; Raghuram and Madge 2006). In part, and in the context of global relations this can be done by learning from those in the Global South (McIlwaine 2010). Of particular relevance here have been attempts to use conceptualisations developed to understand the lives of people in the Global South and how migrants cope with their new lives after they migrate to the North (Datta *et al.* 2007b; Kelly and Lusis 2006). This has especially important in relation to debates about coping practices and livelihoods (Wills *et al.* 2010).

Therefore, a materialised postcolonial perspective can be helpful in understanding international and transnational migration, not because it presents anything spectacularly new, but that it brings together a range of contemporary shifts in thinking in a range of fields (King 2003).[2] Thus, as a process international

---

1 Although it is important to remember that giving voice to migrants conceptually does not necessarily mean that migrants are agents themselves.

2 King (2003: 392) notes that '[T]he dangers are in attempting to use the concept in a totalizing fashion or, indeed, attempting to explain everything from a postcolonial framework or perspective'.

and transnational migration can challenge prevalent conceptions of distance between the North and South, it can confront and reinforce existing colonial orders, and it can show how historical patterns of development can be partially re-written in a quotidian sense by migrants. However, we must not lose sight of the material realities of many migrants who can often only exercise their agency within huge sets of constraints imposed personally, by national and global economies, and by nation-states. The remainder of this chapter focuses on research conducted with Latin American migrants who are not the classic postcolonial migrants normally associated with London or the UK more generally. However, as 'new migrants' from the Global South with no direct colonial ties with the UK, their experiences are still imbued with a 'colonial imprint' (Yeoh 2003: 375).

The discussion suggests that a materialist postcolonial perspective can provide a much more nuanced interpretation of the complexities of why people move that recognises the inequalities of uneven global development and the persistence of economic power in shaping people's decisions. Although this chapter highlights that people moved for a wide range of intersecting reasons, their choices were constrained by an exclusionary immigration regime that functions to maintain a low-paid labour force for the UK economy while providing a minimal provision of rights for migrants. The reasons for negotiating this regime were underpinned by peoples' economic needs (interpolated with political factors in the case of Colombians in particular) prompted by economic (and political) failures in their home countries. As migrants established themselves in their new surroundings which were often characterised by exclusion and discrimination, the focus on how they negotiated their lives in a new city tended to concentrate on dealing with and overcoming economic exigencies that required the mobilisation of a range of economic and closely interrelated social practices. Although cultural practices of ensuring belonging and carving out a cultural identity for Latin Americans in London was certainly a concern for many (Román-Velázquez 2009), it tended to be subsumed to the demands of survival in an often hostile city.

Contextualising Latin Americans in postcolonial London

Without entering into the debates about what actually constitutes a postcolonial city beyond one that is influenced materially, socially and culturally by its colonial and imperial past (Henry *et al.* 2002), London is clearly one of the premier postcolonial cities in the world (Eade 2000) as well as being a global city (Sassen 2001). Its roots lie in centuries of emigration and immigration that over time have seen London become home to a huge range and volume of foreign born people. Although Commonwealth migration has historically bolstered London's economy and society, in more recent times, its population has become ever more 'super-diverse' through the emergence of 'new migrant groups' from a wide range of different countries with no historical or colonial ties to the UK (Vertovec 2007). London is home to people from 179 different countries (from a total of approximately 195), with the majority from low-income nations. As labour markets have been deregulated, welfare systems been reformed and new immigration policies introduced, so many of these new migrants have filled jobs in the lower echelons of the urban labour market creating a distinct 'migrant division of labour' (May *et al.* 2007; Wills *et al.* 2010).

Latin Americans have been an important 'new migrant' group within this new migrant division of labour. Although many Latin American countries have a long relationship with the UK in terms of trading and providing refuge for political exiles including many founders of Latin American independence (Miller 1998), relatively large-scale Latin American migration to London is much more recent, dating back to the 1970s. At this time, Colombians arrived as a result of the work permit system to take-up elementary jobs in cleaning and catering. Once the work permit system was abolished, Colombians continued to arrive to join relatives and friends with a further increase after 1986 as people arrived seeking asylum as the conflict in their home country worsened (Bermúdez Torres 2003). Since the 1980s, increasing numbers of Ecuadorians, Peruvians, Brazilians, Argentineans and more recently, Bolivians have begun to arrive mainly as economic migrants (Carlisle 2006). Although there are currently no accurate figures as to how many

Latin Americans there are in the UK, the Labour Force Survey in 2006 estimated that there were 18,000 Colombians, 25,000 Brazilians, 4,000 Argentineans and 1,000 Chileans.[3] Unofficial estimates put the figure at between 700,000 and 1,000,000 (FCO 2007: 5), including 200,000 Brazilians, 140,000 Colombians, 70–90,000 Ecuadorians and 10–15,000 Peruvians. The majority resides in London (McIlwaine 2007).

The research on which this chapter is based draws on qualitative interviews conducted with 100 Latin American migrants in London using two samples between 2004 and 2007. Both used non-purposive sampling techniques identifying migrants through migrant organisations as well as snowballing techniques. The first sample entailed in-depth interviews with 30 Colombian migrants, most of who arrived in London between 1994 and 2004. The sample was evenly split between men and women with nearly half coming from Coffee Zone of Colombia. More than half were aged in their 30s, 40s or 50s and most were relatively well educated (13 had been to college or university). Of the 17 people who were employed, all worked in the cleaning sector in some capacity. In terms of immigration status, 20 out of the 30 migrants were regular, with the 10 undocumented migrants usually having overstayed their visas. In the second sample, 28 Colombians, 22 Ecuadorians and 20 Bolivians were interviewed and three focus group discussions were conducted with a further 17 migrants (also including Brazilians, Chileans and Peruvians), together with ten interviews with Latin American community leaders. Participant observation with a migrant organisation was also conducted for two years between July 2006 and October 2008. The profile of the second sample reflected the first in that the focus was on 'ordinary' migrants rather than elites. In addition, 26 men and 44 women were interviewed, with a concentration of those aged between 21 and 40. Again, the majority of migrants interviewed were quite well-educated (almost a quarter had completed tertiary education). Despite these high levels, migrants again worked in elementary jobs, with over half working in cleaning in banks, offices or houses, with a further eight working

---

3 Retrieved on 2 June 2008 from: http://www.statistics.gov.uk/StatBase/Source. asp?vlnk=358&More=Y.

in cafes or restaurants and three in childcare. The vast majority reported having legal papers (60), with only ten reportedly irregular. Twenty-two people had student visas, with a further 22 stating they had residence acquired either through asylum, marriage or Spanish passports (legally or illegally). The majority had arrived in the previous 10 years, with one-fifth arriving since 2006. In terms of place of residence among both samples, Latin Americans were dispersed throughout the city although there were concentrations in some areas of South London (Lambeth, Stockwell, Camberwell and Brixton), and North London (Holloway, Finsbury Park and Seven Sisters). Most lived in private rented accommodation, usually with other Latin Americans, often in over-crowded conditions.

The postcolonial geographies of migrating from Latin America to London

Foregrounding migrants' stories as a way of understanding migration processes is profoundly sympathetic to postcolonial interpretations. As noted above, such an approach reveals how movement from one country to another entails more than the creation of diasporic identities; there are also deep-seated economic, social and political inequalities at the heart of most mobilities from the Global South to North. Indeed, it is this type of movement that traces former colonial linkages in reverse that highlights the utility of a postcolonial perspective in particular. An analysis of how migrants experience postcoloniality over space also highlights just how pervasive the economics of migration can be, acknowledging how socio-cultural factors intersect in important ways with the material reasons that underpin mobility.

For Latin Americans moving to London, international migration involved a set of powerful negotiations that challenge the failures of their home countries in providing sustainable economic and political environments for people to make a living. As a result, Latin Americans exercised their agency to traverse a range of routes across international borders to ensure some form of betterment in their lives, few of which are linear or straightforward. These were simultaneously facilitated and constrained by the immigration regimes of nations.

While most migrants were motivated to migrate to London because of material factors, there were important differences according to country of origin. Reflecting the ongoing and pro-tracted armed conflict in their homeland, Colombian migrants were much more likely than Ecuadorians and Bolivians to have moved for politically-motivated reasons or threats of violence even though the lack of economic opportunities was important for all groups. The broader context for this was widespread socio-economic deterioration or stagnation in all three countries, with Bolivia the hardest hit with growth rates of GDP of only 1.3 per cent (ECLAC 2006a: 61). In terms of poverty, Bolivia had among the highest poverty rates in the continent with over 63.9 per cent of the population living below the poverty line in 2004 (an increase from 52.6 per cent in 1989). Rates were also high in Colombia (46.8 per cent in 2005) and in Ecuador (48.3 per cent in 2005) (ibid.: 64). Therefore, it is hardly surprising that people were leaving their homeland in search of better opportunities. Indeed, in Bolivia, in 2000, 4.1 per cent of the population had migrated, in Colombia, 3.4 per cent had emigrated, while in Ecuador, 4.8 per cent had left (ECLAC 2006b: 15).

The case of Esperanza echoes the situations and sentiments of many Latin American migrants to London. Esperanza was forty-three years old and had migrated from Colombia in 2000. She lived in the inner-city and worked as a cleaner in a block of flats for 5 hours a day. In Colombia, she was a single parent living with her mother and her daughter. She owned and ran a restaurant in her home town of Palmira in the department of Valle del Cauca. Although Esperanza admitted that she was better off economically than most people, she was exhausted by the work and still struggled to make ends meet. In addition, her husband had been killed in the armed conflict and she was left with sole charge of her daughter who was studying at college to become a doctor. Esperanza knew that she wouldn't be able to pay university fees so she resolved to migrate, leaving her daughter behind. In turn, her choice of London was because she already had a brother living there who had sought and secured asylum there as a result of escaping death threats from a paramilitary group because of his previous involvement as leader of a Leftist political group.

Esperanza, despite entering on a tourist visa, also claimed asylum because of the death of her husband and her brothers' situation. Her case was rejected although she did finally secure Indefinite Leave to Remain through the Family Amnesty programme.[4]

Esperanza's migration trajectory highlights how armed conflict, economic exigencies and social pressures intersected to prompt migration. However, her postcolonial imagination of London also played a part in that Esperanza and her brother were drawn to London by the potential promise of asylum. In many Latin American migrants eyes, London and the UK more widely was constructed in their imaginations as a place of refuge, of tolerance and of safety, in direct contrast to how many migrants portrayed their lives back home, especially the Colombians.

However, while most migrated directly to London, many also moved first to Spain highlighting an interesting take on subverting colonial ties. This movement has been part of a wider process of Latin American migration to Europe as entry to the US has become more restrictive, especially since 9/11 and as Spain has opened its borders due to increasing labour demand and a concomitant range of changes in immigration legislation (Bermúdez Torres 2006; Catarino and Oso 2000). This has been further facilitated for Latin Americans by the colonial legacy of the 'motherland' where language and cultural similarities can potentially assist migrants in establishing themselves more easily. This was certainly the case among the Latin Americans in London who had first moved to Spain, all of whom perceived Spain as a stepping stone where initial migration was easier but where economic opportunities were more limited. While the colonial heritage provided an initial pull and eased movement to a certain degree, especially linked with language, this swiftly disappeared once the material realities of life in Spain became clear.

Juana's migration experience illustrates this. Juana, who was thirty-eight years old and from Santo Domingo de los Colorados in Ecuador, initially left in an attempt to escape an abusive

---

4 The Family Amnesty programme gave those who had at least one dependent child in the UK and had claimed asylum before 2 October 2002 the right to apply for Indefinite Leave to Remain. This gave them full rights to remain in the UK and to work.

relationship with her partner. Not only had she lost her source of economic support but her former partner was also abusing their son: 'what really made me come here was that my son had problems with my partner, violence, my son was traumatised. I wasn't in a good economic situation so I decided to leave, to try and get something better, to improve my life, to not have to depend on a man'. At first leaving her son behind with her mother, Juana went to Spain on a tourist visa because she already had friends there and because of the language. However, when she couldn't find work in Madrid, she contacted another friend who lived in London who lent her $1000 to buy a false Spanish passport. Immediately after she arrived in 1999 she started work as an office cleaner. After a year, her son joined her in London after migrating first to Spain and then to the UK, also using a false Spanish passport.

For men in particular, there were limited job opportunities in Spain, exacerbated by widespread racism against Latin Americans. For example, Mario who was twenty-four years old and came from Santa Cruz in Bolivia migrated first to Valencia where he lived for three years before moving to the UK. Yet, Mario was disillusioned because he couldn't get decent work:

> But it's not the paradise that people say. There's no work there, most people work in agriculture, you have to harvest and you have to be really strong, also when it rains there's no work. You can't work in cleaning like here in London. Not everyone has the patience to look after the elderly. There's some work in construction, but you need papers and in my case, I didn't have them. The Spanish can be very racist against Latins; they treat them like slaves.

The migrant narratives of Esperanza, Juana and Mario therefore highlight how Latin Americans have negotiated their entry into Europe via the colonial motherland only to find that their situation in Spain was imbued with the racism of conquest as well as the continuing desire on the part of the state to use what was effectively postcolonial labour to fill the demand in the growing economy. While Spanish immigration legislation facilitated this flow of people, many Latin American migrants subverted this situation for their own ends by using EU passports as their entry point into the rest of Europe and in this case to the UK.

Therefore, immigration legislation can affect the transnational nature of movement across international borders, but also the ways in which migrant identities transform, mutate and are rebuilt (Varsanyi and Nevins 2007). In the UK, changes in immigration legislation have profoundly influenced the formation and histories of particular migrant groups and communities (Blunt 2007) especially among Latin Americans (Román-Velázquez 2009). The case of Colombian migration to the UK illustrates these changes very clearly. It is especially interesting that they were one of the first groups to benefit from changes in immigration legislation that had traditionally favoured former colonies. The 1971 Immigration Act abolished the voucher scheme that had been in force since 1962 whereby Commonwealth citizens could move to the UK, and replaced it with a work permit system. This was the first time that non-Commonwealth citizens had been given access to the UK on a more equal basis. Work permits were supposed to be limited to semi-skilled jobs, although exceptions were made for certain industries such as hotels, catering and domestic work. According to Cock (2009), the early waves of Colombian immigration focused on two employment agencies near Piccadilly Circus run by Italians. Acting as the main port of entry for Colombians, a man from Armenia, in the province of Quindío established a link between the Italians and Colombians from his home area through selling contracts and placing people in hotel and cleaning jobs in London. Although by 1980 work permits were withdrawn for low-skilled jobs, Colombian migration networks had already been established facilitating further migration (McIlwaine 2005). Again, a postcolonial perspective illuminates how historical patterns of development and the ties between the UK and the rest of the world, especially the developing world, have been retraced and redrawn by a particular migrant group for their own benefit albeit within the wider needs of a powerful nation in need of cheap labour.

Ximena's case shows how migration was facilitated by this changing immigration legislation within the wider context of uneven global development (Bailey *et al.* 2002; Duvell, 2003). Ximena's migration to London was based on one of these work permits. She had arrived in 1977 at the age of twenty-nine from

Palmira. She recounted how a local man who lived in London came to her community and sold work permits. Her husband bought one and after 6 months he received the permit giving him 15 days to present himself at a restaurant in Piccadilly. Six months later, Ximena joined him, working as a dishwasher in a restaurant, leaving behind her eight year old son in the care of her mother. Ximena describes her shock at arriving in London:

> Nothing was as he told me. It wasn't what I thought, imagined. I had never thought it could be dark at 3 in the afternoon, and even less at 8 or 9 in the morning when it was still dark. And it was so cold, horribly cold, for us it is so difficult to cope with the cold. In all my knowledge and experience, I didn't imagine that this was a reality – this is what I had seen on the films on television - when I talked steam came from my mouth.

Among the three nationalities discussed here, Colombians have been historically favoured through both work permits and the asylum system resulting in them being the most likely to have residence and citizenship status in the UK. In contrast, Bolivians were the most vulnerable with the majority being irregular. Somewhat ironically, they were also the only nationality who could enter the UK without obtaining a visa in their country of origin. However, what is also striking is that although only 20 people in both samples identified themselves as irregular, the majority of those interviewed had experienced irregularity at some point in their migration trajectory, or had waited for years to hear about asylum claims. Indeed, immigration status was much more than a structural constraint or facilitator, but it imbued the daily lives of Latin Americans in London in deleterious ways (see also Bailey *et al.* 2002; McIlwaine 2009).

Alba from Santa Cruz in Bolivia was thirty-four years old and lived in a hotel room in Finsbury Park in North London with her two small children and her husband. She arrived with her children in 2006, to join her husband who had moved 2 years previously. Although her husband had British nationality through a paternal grandfather, Alba entered on a tourist visa that had since expired. Although she had contacted various organisations to try and regularise her situation, it proved impossible. Such was her anxiety that it was affecting her health, exacerbated by the fact that she couldn't access health services: 'I am ill from nerves, I'm very stressed, everything gets to me, and unfortunately I can't go to the doctor because I'm illegal . . . I'm so scared that I'll be caught and arrested and deported'. She couldn't work because of her status beyond a few odd sewing jobs, and she felt completely dependent on her husband with whom she had a conflictive relationship.

Moving from Latin America to Europe was therefore part of a postcolonial project where migrants as agents of their own destinies retraced the steps of former colonial masters in reverse as well as challenging and renegotiating them. Yet moving to the North, and in this case to London, was imbued with inequalities as people tried to overcome severe problems that affected their lives in their home countries in order to provide for the needs of the economies of the Global North. This was done within the broader strictures of European immigration regimes that facilitated or denied entry to Latin Americans.

The everyday postcolonial practices of survival among Latin American migrants in London

While much work on transnational migration especially from a postcolonial perspective highlights the transformations in identity and consciousness as the result of moving from one culture to another and the hybridisation process that occurs, the realities of life for migrants invariably revolves around the need to make some form of living in order to ensure basic survival. The creation of a cultural and social life, while obviously closely bound-up and interrelated with many dimensions of 'getting-by' economically, was identified as a secondary consideration especially by migrants in the early years of settlement. Nonetheless, the development of a range of Latin American identities was in evidence in London with their economic options colouring some of these constructions. In particular, the fact that many Latin Americans worked in cleaning and catering had led to the creation of an identity around the 'Latin American cleaner' which was construed in largely negative terms. Although the vast majority of migrants began their working lives in London cleaning offices or working in a restaurant or café, most Latin Americans had never worked in such jobs before their move. For men in particular, cleaning was perceived as a necessary evil to be endured as well as one which undermined their masculine hegemonic identities (see also McIlwaine 2010).

Edgar arrived with his family from Pereira in Colombia in 1997 as a political refugee at the age of thirty-two fleeing death threats from guerrilla organisation, the FARC (Revolutionary Armed Forces of Colombia) because of his involvement with the Conservative Party. Once Edgar had secured asylum, his first job was cleaning offices like many of his compatriots before and since. Also like many others, Edgar was not used to this type of work, being educated to university level in Colombia and previously owning a string of different businesses, including a department store and a book distribution company. This made it very difficult for him to cope emotionally with cleaning: 'In my life, I tell you, I had never done any housework in my home, but to arrive and to have to dust, to wipe, to brush-up, it affects your self-esteem, you feel really, really bad, bad because you come with the idea of improving your life'. After 2–3 years working there, Edgar had saved enough money to establish a small Colombian shop.

Yet for women, the 'Latin cleaner' identity was less offensive linked with the fact that they were not transgressing hegemonic gender identities to perform these jobs as well as for practical reasons. Indeed, for women, cleaning jobs allowed them to balance child-care because of their part-time nature of (working 2–3 hours in each job, often outside normal working hours). Ximena had worked in cleaning for around 30 years. At the time of interview she had three cleaning jobs; she worked for 2 hours between 5 and 7am in the Department for Trade and Industry, then another 2 hours at City Hall, and then another in a shop in Mayfair. She was earning the minimum wage and had experienced many exploitative labour practices over the years, such as being dismissed without pay after a probationary period, or losing her job without notice. Such practices were often instigated by other Latin Americans in positions of supervisors, something which Ximena resented and which fuelled considerable levels of mistrust within the community.

As with migrant groups everywhere in the world, social networks both facilitated migration and assisted in settlement and survival once people arrived. Yet their historical construction as well as the exigencies inherent in the ways in which the immigration regime welcomed some migrants and rejected others meant that these social relations were fraught with difficulties. On one hand, social networks were critically important in helping people with initial housing and access to jobs (see also Landolt 2001; Nolin 2001). However, these were very limited in size in that people reported having very small friendship circles, almost exclusively with their own nationality or other Latin Americans. One of the most common comments people made their social life was '*yo no soy muy amiguera/o*' (I'm not a very friendly person). This notion of '*envidia*' or envy permeated the Latin American population rooted in competition over occupational and immigration status (see also Guarnizo and Díaz 1999; Guarnizo *et al*. 1999), with irregular migrants being especially frightened in case they were reported to the authorities – by British people as well as their own people in cases of disputes. Certain places were also associated with gossip and fear. Somewhat ironically, places such as the Elephant and Castle shopping centre in the south of the city and Seven Sisters market in north where the main Latin American shops, cafes and remittance agencies are located, were also identified as places to be avoided or visited only fleetingly for fear of gossip or the immigration services. Colombians in particular had to deal with stereotyping over drugs among themselves and between other groups as Julian, a janitor from Cali noted: 'When I first arrived at the building where I work, all they would say was "Colombia mafia, Colombia nice drugs". This is really difficult. Very few would every mention Colombia football, nice football, it was always mafia and drugs'.

Yet, migrants were not passive victims of economic and social hardship. They displayed some level of agency and collective action in the face of the difficulties they experienced reflecting Levitt's (2001) notion of 'mistrustful solidarity'. The church provided an important source of support for Latin Americans through both the Catholic and Protestant churches as they maintained and reconstructed their religious identities from back home.

In particular, the Evangelical churches such as the *Comunidad Cristiana de Londres* (Christian Community of London) were becoming incredibly popular with migrants, with several people who had been practising Catholics in their home countries converting to Evangelicalism in London. This was mainly because according to a pastor from the *Comunidad Cristiana de Londres*, they were one of the most important sources of support for migrants in providing one-to-one counselling in people's homes, as well as individual, group and family activities, all linked with Bible teaching. Also important were specific welfare organisations that provided assistance with immigration advice, welfare benefits, housing and language interpretation. In many cases, these organisations provided a lifeline for migrants. As Eduardo, an Ecuadorian noted about one such group: 'they . . . fight for you, like a lawyer fights for their client, or a father fights for his son. They are strong women, fighters who are very successful. They have helped me in everything'. This said, only a small proportion of the community used the services of such organisations (5 out of 50 randomly interviewed migrants in the second sample) linked with fear and general mistrust. Therefore, underlying the shallow nature of social networks and a general lack of cohesion were migrants trying to cope in a large city and competing more or less for the same resources.

Latin American identities were also bolstered and hybridised through the maintenance of very strong links with families and friends in their home countries. Although the transnational bonds maintained between London and Latin America did not involve fluid physical movement between countries as has been noted in the case of the US (Duany 2002), everyone interviewed made phone calls to parents, friends and other family members using cheap phone cards and mobile phones (Vertovec 2004b). Many people also used the internet, especially email and messaging services either through home computers or internet cafes.

Yet, while these fluid borders in terms of communication and cultural ties were strong and important, it was material linkages through sending remittances that dominated these connections. Again, this highlights the need for a combined a perspective that is cognisant of how identities and a transnational consciousness form but also how the underlying rationale revolves around material exigencies. Indeed, most people sent one average £100 per month to parents, children or spouses. This was viewed as both a necessity and an obligation, as Edgar, who sent between £200 and £250 per month to his parents pointed out: 'we have a noble heart, because everyone, the vast majority, 90 per cent of people help our families back home'. Generally this money was used for general living expenses, but it also paid for medical bills, education and the repayment of debts, with a minority also investing in land and housing back home (Datta *et al.* 2007a). Furthermore, it is also essential to recognise the precarious and exploitative conditions under which migrants live and work in London in order to be able to send this money, something that might routinely be over-looked in general, but especially from a postcolonial perspective (McEwan 2003).

However, this is not to argue that the creation of transnational identities is not important for Latin Americans. Indeed, the annual summer carnivals and the Latin American shopping centres that have emerged in London in the last few years have been crucial in how Latin Americans 'get-by' and maintain some sense of belonging through the development of an 'ethnic public' (Cock 2009; Román-Velazquez 2002, 2009). These diasporic or transnational identities were further strengthened by reading UK-based Latin American newspapers, sending children to Spanish-language Saturday schools or frequenting Latin American cafes and restaurants, as well as participating in Latin American football leagues. Yet it is telling that when questioned about the challenges of their lives, migrants constantly focused on their economic situation and the pressures of the immigration regime. This was especially notable among those who had arrived most recently, suggesting perhaps that a materialist postcolonial perspective is especially pertinent to 'new migrant groups' within relatively short migration trajectories.

What also emerges is that some practices mobilised by migrants are more successful than others, and that migrants make gains in some aspects of their lives and not in others. These changes were wound-up with negotiating identities and material circumstances from home in the context of the destination in challenging ways.

This was especially marked in the case of gender identities in that women migrants' lives had often improved in terms of experiencing greater levels of independence from men through employment or making claims on the state, but these gains had often been undermined in other spheres with some evidence of increased domestic conflicts (McIlwaine 2010).

Conclusions

This chapter has sought to explore the extent to which a postcolonial perspective can be useful for understanding international migration processes through an exploration of the experiences of Latin American migrants in London – a new migrant group with no direct colonial ties with the UK, yet who have moved from a colonised continent. Empirically, and in deliberately foregrounding the experiences and narratives of migrants, the chapter has shown that the realities of mobility and the nature of the quotidian lives of this population are underpinned by survival concerns that fundamentally revolve around material imperatives that are rooted in deep-seated inequalities inherent in national and global capitalist systems. As a result, the chapter suggests that only a materialised postcolonial perspective that accounts for these power imbalances and inequalities is relevant when examining international and transnational migration of people moving from the Global South to the Global North. Yet, as long as these material imperatives are taken on board, a postcolonial perspective can elucidate a range of processes that other approaches such as a cultural economy viewpoint cannot. Critical here is that a postcolonial gaze on transnational migration allows for the examination of the historically contingent nature of migration between the rich and poor parts of the world (Hall 1996). In turn, this can shed important light on why and how migrants can exercise their agency in subverting traditional flows of knowledge and power from North to South, even though their movement and their lives will always be constrained by wider and deeper structural constraints that facilitate their entry into countries as well as their experiences once they get there. A postcolonial geographical perspective can also illuminate and valorise the lived experiences of migrants in terms of how they negotiate across scales the wider global, national and local inequalities in their everyday lives in ways that vary according to their social positioning.

Acknowledgements

The research on which this paper draws was funded by the Leverhulme Trust (award no. RF/7/2006/0080) and the British Academy (award no. SG-37793) to whom I am extremely grateful. Many aspects of the research were facilitated by the Carila Latin American Welfare Group as well as the Indoamerican Refugee Migrant Organization (IRMO) and the now dissolved Colombian Refugee Association (CORAS). I would like to thank all the staff at these organisations, but especially Alba Arbelaez, for both access and support. I would also like to thank Carolina Velásquez, Flor Alba Robayo and Emilia Girardo for facilitating and transcribing interviews. I would also like to thank Alex Hughes, Cheryl McEwan and Jane Pollard for their helpful suggestions on an earlier draft of this chapter.

References

Ashcroft, B. (2001) *Post-Colonial Transformation*, Routledge, London.

Bailey, A. J. (2001) 'Turning transnational: Notes on the theorisation of international migration', *International Journal of Population Geography*, 7(6): 413–28.

Bailey A. J., Wright, R. A., Mountz, A. and Miyares, I. M. (2002) '(Re) producing Salvadoran transnational geographies', *Annals of the Association of American Geographers*, 92(1): 125–44.

Basch, L., Glick Schiller, N. and Szanton Blanc, C. (1994) *Nations Unbound: Transnational projects, postcolonial predicaments, and deterritorialized nation-states*, Gordon and Breach, Amsterdam.

Bermúdez Torres, A. (2003) *ICAR Navigation Guide. Refugee Populations in the UK: Colombians*, Information Centre for Asylum and Refugees, London.

— (2006) *Colombian Migration to Europe: Political transnationalism in the middle of conflict*, Working Paper Compas no. 39/06, Oxford.

Bhabha H. K. (1994) *The Location of Culture*, Routledge, London.

Blunt, A. (2007) 'Cultural geographies of migration: Mobility, transnationality and diaspora, *Progress in Human Geography*, 31(50): 684–94.

Blunt, A. and McEwan, C. (2002) 'Introducing postcolonial geographies', in A. Blunt and C. McEwan (eds), *Postcolonial Geographies*, Continuum, London, pp. 1–6.

Carlisle, F. (2006) 'Marginalisation and ideas of community among Latin American migrants to the UK', *Gender and Development*, 14(2): 235–45.

Catarino, C. and Oso, L. (2000) 'La inmigración femenina en Madrid y Lisboa: hacia una etnización del servicio domestico y de las empresas de limpieza', *Revista de Sociología*, 60, 183–207.

Cock, J. (2009) 'Colombian spaces of transnationality in London', Upgrade document from M Phil to PhD, Department of Geography, Queen Mary, University of London.

Datta, K., McIlwaine, C., Wills, J., Evans, Y., Herbert, J. and May, J. (2007a) 'The new development finance or exploiting migrant labour? Remittance sending among low-paid migrant workers in London', *International Development Planning Review*, 29(1): 43–67.

— (2007b) 'From coping strategies to tactics: London's low-pay economy and migrant labour', *British Journal of Industrial Relations*, 45(2): 409–38.

Duany, J. (2002) 'Mobile livelihoods: The socio-cultural practices of circular migrants between Puerto Rico and the United States', *International Migration Review*, 36(2): 355–88.

Duvell, F. (2003) 'Some reasons and conditions for a world without immigration restrictions', *ACME*, 2(2): 201–9.

Dyck, I. (2005) 'Feminist geography, the "everyday" and local-global relations: Hidden spaces of place-making', *The Canadian Geographer*, 49(3): 233–43.

Eade, J. (2000) *Placing London: From imperial capital to global city*, Berghahn Books, Oxford.

ECLAC (2006a) *Social Panorama of Latin America 2005*, ECLAC, Santiago.

— (2006b) *International Migration, Human Rights and Development in Latin America and the Caribbean; Summary and Conclusions*. Report no LC/G.2303(SES.31-11), ECLAC, Santiago.

Foreign and Commonwealth Office (FCO) (2007) *Latin America to 2020: A UK Public Strategy Paper*, FCO, London.

Glick Schiller, N., Basch, L. and Blanc-Szanton, C. (1995) 'From immigrant to transmigrant: Theorizing transnational migration, *Anthropological Quarterly*, 68(1): 48–63.

Guarnizo, L. E. (1997) 'The emergence of a transnational social formation and the mirage of return migration among Dominican transmigrants', *Identities* 4(2): 281–322.

Guarnizo, L. E. and Diaz, L. M. (1999) 'Transnational migration: A view from below', *Ethnic and Racial Studies*, 22(2): 397–421.

Guarnizo, L. E., Sánchez, A. I. and Roach, E. M. (1999) 'Mistrust, fragmented solidarity, and transnational migration: Colombians in New York City and Los Angeles', *Ethnic and Racial Studies*, 22(2): 367–96.

Hall, S. (1996) 'What was "the post-colonial"? Thinking at the limit', in I. Chambers and L. Curtis (eds), *The Post-Colonial Question: Common skies, divided horizons*, Routledge, London, pp. 242–60.

Henry, N., McEwan, C. and Pollard, J. (2002) 'Globalization from below: Birmingham – postcolonial workshop of the world? *Area*, 34(2): 117–27.

International Organization for Migration (2008) *World Migration 2008: Managing labour mobility in the evolving global economy*, IOM, Geneva.

Itzigsohn, J., Dore Cabral, C., Hernández Medina, E. and Vázquez, O. (1999) 'Mapping Dominican transnationalism: Narrow and broad transnational practices', *Ethnic and Racial Studies*, 22(2): 316–39.

Kelly, P. and Lusis, T. (2006) 'Migration and the transnational habitus: Evidence from Canada and the Philippines, *Environment and Planning A*, 38: 831–47.

Keown, M., Murphy, D. and Proctor, J. (eds) (2009) *Comparing Postcolonial Diasporas*, Palgrave Macmillan, London.

King, A. D. (1999) '(Post)colonial geographies: Material and symbolic', *Historical Geography*, 27: 99–118.

— (2003) 'Cultures and spaces of postcolonial knowledges', in K. Anderson, M. Domsh, S. Pile and N. Thrift (eds), *Handbook of Cultural Geography*, Sage, London, pp. 381–97.

Landolt, P. (2001) 'Salvadoran economic transnationalism: Embedded strategies for household maintenance, immigrant incorporation, and entrepreneurial expansion', *Global Networks*, 1(3): 217–42.

Lawson, V. A. (2000) 'Arguments within geographies of movement: The theoretical potential of migrants' stories', *Progress in Human Geography*, 24(2): 173–89.

Levitt, P. (2001) *The Transnational Villagers*, University of California Press, Berkeley.

Levitt, P. and Jaworsky, B. N. (2007) 'Transnational migration studies: Past developments and future trends', *Annual Review of Sociology*, 33: 129–56.

Li, W. and Teixeira, C. (2007) 'Introduction: Immigrants and transnational experiences in world cities', *GeoJournal*, 68(2/3): 93–102.

May, J., Wills, J., Datta, K., Evans, Y., Herbert, J. and McIlwaine, C. (2007) 'Keeping London working: Global cities, the British state, and London's new migrant division of labour', *Transactions of the Institute of British Geographers NS*, 32: 151–67.

McEwan, C. (2001) 'Postcolonialism, feminism and development: Intersections and dilemmas', *Progress in Development Studies*, 1(2): 93–111.

— (2002) 'Postcolonialism', in V. Desai and R. B. Potter (eds), *The Companion to Development Studies*, Arnold, London, pp. 127–31.

— (2003) 'Material geographies and postcolonialism', *Singapore Journal of Tropical Geography*, 24(3): 340–55.

McIlwaine, C. (2005) *Coping Practices among Colombian Migrants in London*,

Department of Geography, Queen Mary, University of London, available at: http://www.geog.qmul.ac.uk/docs/staff/4402.pdf.

— (2007) *Living in Latin London: How Latin American migrants survive in the city*, Department of Geography, Queen Mary, University of London, available at: http://www.geog.qmul.ac.uk/docs/staff/4400.pdf.

— (2009) *Webs of (Ir)regularity among Latin American Migrants in London*, Working Paper WP-09-0, ICMiC, School of Sociology and Social Policy, University of Nottingham.

— (2010) 'Migrant machismos: Exploring gender ideologies and practices among Latin American migrants in London from a multi-scalar perspective', *Gender, Place and Culture*, 17(3): 281–300.

Miller, R. (1998) 'Introduction', in P. Decho and C. Diamond (compilers), *Latin Americans in London: A Select List of Prominent Latin Americans in London c. 1800-1996*, Institute of Latin American Studies, London.

Mitchell, K. (2003) 'Cultural geographies of transnationality', in K. Anderson, M. Domosh, S. Pile and N. Thrift (eds), *Handbook of Cultural Geography*, Sage, London, pp. 74–87.

Nolin, C. (2001) 'Transnational ruptures and sutures: Questions of identity and social relations among Guatemalans in Canada', *GeoJournal* 55, 59–67.

Portes, A., Guarnizo, L. E. and Landolt, P. (1999) 'The study of transnationalism: Pitfalls and promise of an emergent research field', *Ethnic and Racial Studies*, 22(2): 217–37.

Raghuram, P. and Madge, C. (2006) 'Towards a method for postcolonial development geography? Possibilities and challenges', *Singapore Journal of Tropical Geography*, 27(3): 270–88.

Román-Velázquez, P. (2002) 'The making of a salsa music scene in London', in L. Waxer (ed.), *Situating Salsa: Global markets and local meaning in Latin popular music*, Routledge, New York, pp. 259–88.

— (2009) 'Latin Americans in London and the dynamics of diasporic identities', in M. Keown, J. Procter and D. Murphey (eds), *Comparing Postcolonial Diasporas*, Palgrave Macmillan, London.

Samers, M. (1997) 'The production of diaspora: Algerian emigration from colonialism to neo-colonialism (1840-1970)', *Antipode*, 29(1): 32–64.

— (1998) 'Immigration, "ethnic minorities", and "social exclusion" in the European Union: A critical perspective', *Geoforum*, 29(2): 123–44.

Sassen, S. (2001) *The Global City: New York, London, Tokyo*, 2nd edition, Princeton University Press, Princeton, NJ.

Sidaway, J. (2000) 'Postcolonial geographies: An exploratory essay', *Progress in Human Geography*, 24(4): 591–612.

Silvey, R. (2000) 'Diasporic subjects: Gender and mobility in south Sulawesi', *Women's Studies International Forum*, 23(4): 501–15.

— (2003) 'Spaces of rotest: Gendered migration, social networks, and labor protest in West Java, Indonesia', *Political Geography*, 22(2): 129–57.

— (2004) 'Power, difference and mobility: Feminist advances in migration studies', *Progress in Human Geography*, 28(4): 490–506.

Silvey, R. and Lawson, V. (1999) 'Placing the migrant', *Annals of the Association of American Geographers*, 89: 121–32

Simon, D. (2006) 'Separated by common ground? Bringing (post)development and (post)colonialism together', *The Geographical Journal*, 172(1): 10–21.

— (2007) 'Beyond antidevelopment: Discourses, convergences, practices', *Singapore Journal of Tropical Geography*, 28(2): 205–18.

Varsanyi, M. and Nevins, J. (2007) 'Introduction: Borderline contradictions: Neoliberalism, unauthorised migration, and intensifying immigration policing', *Geopolitics*, 12(2): 223–7.

Vertovec, S. (2004a) 'Migrant transnationalism and modes of transformation 1', *International Migration Review*, 38(3): 970–1001.

— (2004b) 'Cheap calls: The social glue of migrant transnationalism', *Global Networks*, 4(2): 219–24.

— (2007) 'Super-diversity and its implications', *Ethnic and Racial Studies*, 30(6): 1024–54.

Wills, J., Datta, K., Evans, Y., Herbert, J., May, J. and McIlwaine, C. (2010) *Global Cities at Work: New migrant divisions of labour*, Pluto, London.

Yeoh, B. S. A. (2001) 'Postcolonial cities', *Progress in Human Geography*, 25(3): 456–68.

— (2003) 'Postcolonial geographies of place and migration', in K. Anderson, M. Domosh, S. Pile and N. Thrift (eds), *Handbook of Cultural Geography*, Sage, London, pp. 369–80.

Section 3

Postcolonial economies: policy and practice

8

Development and postcolonial takes on biopolitics and economy

Christine Sylvester

There can be little doubt that development thinking cycles around in tight little bands of thought and practice that start and often end with economies. Orthodoxy once insisted that the economic drives development, and there are remnants of that insistence in some World Bank and IMF programmes and in national programmes of aid, even though it is apparent that the formal economic side of development has often been disappointing. For years, the only developing countries that could get onto a steady course of economic growth were those led by single-minded states driving economic agendas for non-landlocked countries with powerful political backers, e.g. Korea. Elsewhere, particularly in Africa, development became sacrificed to kleptocracy, social conflict and human rights travesties. For states sinking to the bottom of the global economic ranking system, decline, as Paul Collier (2008: x) points out, has not just been in relative terms; 'often it is absolute. Many of these countries are not just falling behind, they are falling apart'. They are caught in a conflict trap that can be impervious to UN efforts, say, to bring women within conflict zones to discussions of post-conflict development. NGOs may try to work with people in informal economic activities, only to face barriers to access by authoritarian or faltering states and warlords. Conflict and weak development hold hands – the one halting the other, weak development bringing on bouts of conflict or vice versus, or both producing situations requiring outside intervention to get a formal economy rolling and order restored, even if it requires donor states to sit with political leaders on a country's informal board of governors (Duffield 2007). Even mass publics in developed contexts increasingly get involved through fund-raising rock concerts and emergency relief appeals. To Dambisa Moyo, author of *Dead Aid* (2009, cited in *Guardian Culture*, 2/09), public solicitations and pop culture appeals indicate that something is very awry: 'despondent with their record of failure . . . western donors are increasingly looking to anyone for guidance on how best to tackle Africa's predicament'. And not just Africa.

Biopolitical components of the development dilemma contribute to the despondency on the ground. By biopolitics is meant the administration of lives and livelihoods via discursive 'rules' that establish and regulate normal processes of life by regulating bodily activities such as birth, death, gender, marriage, work, health, illness, sanity, rationality and so on. In developed and developing countries, and in the distinctions usually drawn between developed and underdeveloped countries, biopolitical elements intertwine with economic prescriptions (Duffield 2007: 5; Biccum 2005). It has been that way since the days of colonial administration, when efforts were made to govern and build economies by shaping native and coloniser bodies to fit the needs of empire. Minute aspects of life were moulded, from proper dress and hygiene to religion, education, labour, sport, residence and marriage (Sylvester 2006; Patel and McMichael 2004). At home, European citizens were similarly affected by race, class, gender and age discourses. Consider that UK football, although popular across all strata of the country, is characterised as a working class sport, while rugby is the posh (male) body's ball game. Or, consider that it took seventy years for the British Museum to allow bodies of working people, rather than aristocratic bodies only, to view the collection – and initially, only on holidays (Sylvester 2009).

Copied, codified and amplified across the empire, biopolitical policies moved the bodies of native farmers from fertile to less fertile lands, turned native bodies into slave or designated wage labourers, or had some bodies fighting other colonised bodies on behalf of the colonial state. As part of the decolonising project years later, colonial powers identified natives to manage self government and ongoing colonial economies in West-mimicking ways. Their bodies were stuffed with Western languages, foods and rules of etiquette, as well as force-fed Western histories and lessons on production and trade appropriate for capitalist intercourse. Biopolitical governance from the top affected everyone down and up the chain of bio-being, and it begat resistance through mirrored biopolitical–cultural actions targeted at white-settler bodies (Mau Mau in Kenya, guerrilla war in Rhodesia), mass protests against colonial policies from India to Latin America, and armed struggles where independence could be gained no other way.

The rise of development theory and practice, which ran parallel to decolonisation, solidified top–down understandings at the expense of resistance narratives or more mundane issues of life and living in newly independent countries (Parpart 1995). Early modernisation recipes, entirely macro in scale, focused on aggregate economic trends, not on people and their resistant and complicit actions. That miasma carried over to early dependencia and underdevelopment writings, where entire national economies were said to rise or made to fall on the basis of decisions, collaborations and finances effected by industrialists, state aid givers or compradors. People were what Foucault (1976, 1975) called humans-as-machines, albeit unnamed as such in development thinking, or they were problem-ridden populations suffering deficits of (proper) biopolitical health practice, education, housing, skills training and reproductive and infant-rearing knowledge. In the 1970s, those people popped up as subjects of development in basic needs thinking at the top, through development feminism (also from the top), and even to some degree through the social adjustment packages appended to World Bank structural adjustment plans.

But it would only be with the advent of postcolonial analysis that development would be seen through the eyes of local people making daily livelihood decisions in situations of conflict, hope, resistance, ambivalence despair and uncertainty, whether anyone concerned with development was noticing or not. Their situations are tricky and the choices they face are far harder than any hard figure of gross national product per capita can contain (Raghuram, Madge and Noxolo 2009). The strength of the postcolonial refocus on people rather than grand trends comes out in 'data sources' that development analysts would never use – novels, testimonials, drama and poetry. This chapter considers conflictual postcolonial biopolitics in contemporary Zimbabwe, 1960s Nigeria, and genocidal Rwanda of 1994 as depicted in novels and diaries rather than in economic or sociological statistics. Each case is about poor decisions taken by postcolonial governments and by international organisations involved in development. Yet, development *per se* is not the subject of the works. Life is – daily life under pressure. Ineffectual apparatuses of economic and political development are present only as a backdrop to the stories, but their errors are central to them. What emerges in these accounts is not discussed, and some of it is not even anticipated, in ever-cycling debates about effective or sustainable or empowering or modernising development.

A different biopolitics

Let us start with the body as it tends to be presented in development biopolitics. The body of the development expert is recognisable as you or me dressed for work – the body is fully formed, mobile, even athletic and is often pictured speaking. The subject of development biopolitics, by contrast, often appears thin, dull-eyed and sickly or thin, bright-eyed but deficient in something we have. He or she is the stick figure a young child draws, while the development expert is the mover and shaker. Stick figure women have curly hair, little mounds for breasts and triangle skirts. The men might have shoes at the end of leg sticks and eye glasses that make them look intelligent. Other than these few sex-based clues, the figure drawn has no obvious personality, talents or subjectivities. The man is the standard stick figure, the one to deal with in the main. The woman is the stick figure with breasts that feed too many children – she is all bio and little else. If one looks through the projects and policy guidelines of many international development agencies, it is readily apparent that women are portrayed as bio-deficits. They are subordinated beings who need empowerment training and modern skills of literacy, maternity, political participation and money-making, to say nothing of social freedom to enter male-entitled fields or even step out of male-dominant households. To the development expert, stick figures with breasts are not well integrated into development, too integrated into development at its lowest levels, or victims of unequal power relations of gender. Either way one turns, women are problem, and a combination of genuine urgency and also bean-counting accountability to donors finds the development expert rushing forward on fully operational bodies to help. There are deficits to count and correct, interruptions to counter, and conflict to manage, all of which ensure ongoing roles for outside development experts who will be called upon to deliver an elusive future through aid of all kinds (Moyo 2009).

Being full of deficit, the ordinary 'women' of a developing country are rarely seen in development circles as self-reflexive and agentic all on their own. They are creatures of habit who can be taught what it means to be a modern woman engaged with the social and economic processes of her society. Participatory development facilitators can work to harness local knowledge to development by encouraging open community discussions of problems and solutions, with women participating as equal inter-locutors with men. Of course, people long 'nurtured' by donors can expertly perform development scripts of cooperation and critique in ways that smokescreen everyday community dynamics rather than operate to change them. People enacting empowering (biopolitical) 'voice' can say what seems to please the facilitator or the power wielders of society, thereby winning them assistance, they hope. As well, jealousies, resentments and power relations can fester behind a façade of community agreeability (Kapoor 2008; Mosse 1994). Crucially, the wrong questions can be asked: so focused on problem-solving, the facilitator can fail to ascertain whether the identities of the bodies assembled before him or her by asking: are you women (or men) and how do you know? And what does women or men mean here?

Against this tendency to read stable gender off of sexed bodies, I found in the 1980s that a wide range of women in Zimbabwe picked up the identity question immediately and offered counter-hegemonic images of themselves: 'women are just dogs with puppies'; 'men call us women but I'd like to drive the tractor' (Sylvester 2000). In the days when Zimbabwe was flooded with development help for women, projects usually failed nonetheless because the women they were designed for were not the women the experts thought they were. Their gender aspirations could not be read off their bodies. Nor could their thoughts and achievements be equated with too many 'puppies'. Some were very adept at telling me what they would do if they could be the president of Zimbabwe. Others recited poetry they composed and showed me the household furniture they had designed and built. I do not doubt that some of them were solving mathematical puzzles in their minds as they smiled wanly at experts sent from the World Bank.

There is some effort via participatory development and other such endeavours to include people in large issues of political economy. But it can be inclusion of the sort we associate with 'going through the motions'. It is participation without long-term engagement, and it is participation with always-already predefined subjectivities or identity issues. When we forget the key questions, we can end up believing that people in developing countries are less fit overall compared to ourselves – less complex emotionally, less articulate, less intellectual, less capable and less quick. They thereby would need less than we do. We need counselling, gyms, reading groups and vacations. They need to be hooked tightly into the aid industry, sucking in Western knowledge through long feeding tubes. Perhaps these unequal expectations are part of what Mark Duffield (2007: 192) calls the enduring liberal paradox: 'its ability to speak in the name of people, freedom and rights while at the same time accepting illiberal forms of rule as sufficient or even necessary for backward or underdeveloped societies and people'. Development practice is inspired by liberal values but takes to the field with illiberal, know-all biopolitical practice. It is deficient in being able to experience the texture of culturally different lives (Mehta 1999) and so keeps falling down; and then advocating 'for more "appropriate" or "sensitive" forms of trusteeship' (Duffield 2007: 228 from Cowen and Shenton 1996; Cooke and Kothari 2001).

So what to do? Tinkering with the development mentality produces one after another faulty model of stick figure biopolitical economy. That stick figure is static, unmoving, trapped by its frail gendered body and absent aspirational daily acts, to say nothing of existing in a power vacuum. Development turns such figures into concepts – the people, or the women, or the vulnerable parties relative to larger political and market forces. Psychology seems a taboo topic in the field of development studies, which means one has to interpret intricate statistics in order to figure out what decisions people are making, the lives that they carve out, the dangers they are fleeing and the incentives and disincentives that move them. Very remarkably, imaginative literatures are usually 'out' of the development picture and citations. As an applied social science, development is aloof from the humanities. The subaltern must eat and work, not read novels or write poetry. Women who sing collectively in the fields as they work can be appreciated for their good spirit, but the musical potential is beside the point – unless it can be monetised. Development's sights are fixed on commercial outcomes.

What if we think of bodies differently than we have in the constraining and prescribing biopolitics of development? What if we think, as Erin Manning (2009: 6) does in another context, of sensing bodies in movement, 'a body that resists predefinition in terms of subjectivity or identity, a body that is involved in a recip-rocal reaching-towards that in-gathers the world even as it worlds'. If we do this, we will be light years from the usual starting place of development biopolitics. We will be in a different economy, one of movement, of 'thought in motion'. Motion is something that many people in developing countries experience as a frantic or bustling constant in their lives, albeit if hungry enough, they can lack movement entirely. Some can seem to stand still within movement. That is, they move about without ever moving out of a village, or without moving up the imagined ladder of development. Yet they might be thoughts in motion – on long bus journeys to visit relatives or to get to jobs, carrying water jugs on their heads, gathering wood for heating and cooking, hitch-hiking by the side of every road, hanging out the windows of an over-packed train, bouncing along on mother's backs with legs splayed about her waist, sneaking stealthily or devising intricate movements that will take them over this or that border of identity and politics and into zones of safety or prosperity. These world travellers who do not necessarily leave home, or who take their homes with them as they go (Sylvester 1995), are thinkers. They are people who think, people who make decisions, people who laugh, people whose version of eBay might entail smuggling goods across a border to sell and importing the profits to the home country as money stuffed in pant pockets.

In a word, these moving people are like us. Like those of us in the West who work long hours, travel a lot for business, and move about the World Wide Web, they are moving thoughts and bodies. Yet their contexts are not usually ours. At many points of movement, they who are like us over there must face and face-down challenges we rarely see, among them dealing with the frantically busy, bustling, fly in and fly out development industry, which does not have time to discern and take on board their concerns. We know this by reading about development practices through the fictions from and about postcolonial situations of everyday life.

In the novel, *A Sunday at the Pool in Kigali* (2003), Gil Courtemanche, a Canadian, presents us with a character called Methode. He is a skilfully portrayed Tutsi character who, at thirty-two, is in the last stages of AIDS just as the 1994 genocide is starting in Rwanda. The progress of his illness has not been slowed by any cocktail of AIDS medicines: international biopolitics keeps the best AIDS drugs for itself. Yet, Methode insists that it will be a relief to die from AIDS instead of from a machete wielded by a genocidal neighbour. As the end looms closer and the Hutu cry of killing the cockroaches roars around him, Methode plans and executes his own end. He has sex, one of his greatest pleasures, with a partner his friends have summoned. He gets shot full of morphine by a Canadian development worker who is clearly outside the usual development script and has 'gone native'. He drains a bottle of whiskey and asks his friend to film his parting soliloquy.

Methode's mode of dying highlights the body as a vessel of pleasure, even in situations of what Giorgio Agamben (1998) would term bare life. In his context, Methode is doubly bare – as an AIDS victim and as a Tutsi. But even in his bare life circumstance, damned either way it seems, Methode resists the predefinitions of approaching death – misery, suffering and-then-you-die. He reciprocally reaches towards his trusted friends and in-gathers them and the world even as he worlds them to a rewritten performance of dying. Another biopolitics, one Methode authors, substitutes for the ones he is meant to enact. He also refuses to let the state kill him with its genocidal governance strategy, and, instead, embraces, in effect, the pernicious international epidemiology of AIDS. This is not anyone's idea of an ideal trade-off, but it is thought in motion. It moves to the startling suggestion that for some people in some circumstances, it can be preferable to die from the very things that the UN and other development agencies seek to eradicate – AIDS – than die at the hands of a developmental genocidal state and its racist supporters. Methode refuses to be surplus and expendable life in a crazy race war that is another holocaust, this one less monstrously sanitised and hidden than the European Holocaust. He predicts sagely that in Rwanda the holocaust will be open, 'dirty, ugly, lots of severed arms and legs, women with bellies ripped, children with feet cut off . . . (Courtemanche 2003: 41–420). He, however, will be spared that by death.

Methode's insistence on a different method of apprehending life and impending death shows a grey area of choice that is foreign both to development thinking – stick-figure-fall-over-and-die – and to medical biopolitical thinking. It is also foreign or tangential to post 9/11 fascination with the high tech biopolitics of surveillance, state torture, asylum seeking, and anti-terror war making that can preoccupy students of security studies. Methode's choice is a low-tech machete moving towards him or a big virus taking him over. His answer is a form of thought in motion that wilfully celebrates selected motions of life within bare life, reaches towards these, embraces them and does so in the company of others who help him move the relations of life into a death saved from ugliness. As another character in the book says to a westerner who is trying to help: 'Leave us to die peacefully alive' (p. 82). That is Methode's method.

It is also a postcolonial move. Novels about postcolonial situations people the arenas where development operates with stick figures in mind and with methods not remotely of the sort that Methode uses. Novels about postcolonial situations downplay the ego of colonial conquest, the buffoonery of the local Big Man, or idiot foreigners who come to help out and find themselves way over their heads and needing to be helped. People emerge as hybrid and hyphenated subjects with intriguing challenges and relationships. They have bio-dilemmas like ours – AIDS, perhaps – and not like ours – neighbours wielding machetes in an orchestrated genocide. Psychological issues abound where Frantz Fanon still stalks as one of postcolonial studies' key progenitors. Development is there, too, narrated through the perceptions and in the conversations of natives; that is to say, development is not there on its own terms – never. Subjectivity, identity politics and culture take precedence in postcolonial imagination over material well-being; indeed to the near exclusion of the economic. It is the problem I have described elsewhere as the subaltern being able to speak but not necessarily to eat (Sylvester 1999). Yet the postcolonial terrain is also peopled by individual bodies that defy assigned subjectivity and identity, bodies that reach towards and in-gather the world even while they world. Consider two other fictions about the arenas in which development works, one highly conflictual but not deemed genocidal and the other as calm as the breeze on a still morning in Zimbabwe.

Postcolonial moves I

Consider the case of a glorious war without relief, a war waged in part for the right to choose a political economy of one's own. Chimamanda Gnozi Adichie's *Half of a Yellow Sun* (2006) depicts the Biafra War of the 1960s from the perspective of those enraptured by the Igbo nation's audacious freedom break from Nigeria. It is full of deaths' rattles and yet it is mostly a tale of the enthusiasms and unflinching convictions that lead a group of people to believe their cause is so just that it will prevail despite blockades, air attacks, starvation tactics, mounting fear and increasing evidence of defeat engulfing them. The collective delusion that one region of Nigeria could, with some military equipment plus home-made rockets and grenades, defeat a nation-state backed and armed by Britain takes a long time in the novel to dissipate – way past the time the blockade reduces incoming food and petrochemical supplies to a minimum, past the time hospitals run out of drugs, and even after so many people's hair turns red from malnutrition, and their children's hair too, and falls out by the fistfuls.

It seems so easy in the beginning. Professor Ekwenugo entertains his friends with news of the weapons his Science Group is making for the war on the 'vandals', the Nigerians of the North:

> "We launched it this afternoon, this very afternoon," he said . . . "Our own home-made rocket. My people, we are on our way."
>
> "We are a country of geniuses!" Special Julius said to nobody in particular. "Biafra is the land of genius!"
>
> Ugwu [a thirteen year old house boy] sang along and wished, again, that he could join the Civil Defence League or the militia, who went combing for Nigerians hiding in the bush. The war reports had become the highlights of his day . . . the guests sang and shouted drunkenly about the might of Biafra, the stupidity of the Nigerians, the foolishness of those newscasters on BBC radio . . .
>
> "They are surprised because the arms Harold Wilson gave those cattle rearers have not killed us off as quickly as they had hoped!"
>
> (pp. 198–9)

In Adichie's close-up of Biafra, we can see that the grand delusion is maintained mostly by those of privilege and education, who are not actually fighting what starts out as the promising war and ends in tears. Although we do not get to know actual fighters on the ground for Biafra, we also learn that their experiences are so brutalising that many stumble back home with the delusions and traumas of mental illness – if they are not killed outright by aerial bombardments and maybe even by their fans:

> A small crowd from the refugee camp was beating and kicking a young man crouched on the ground, his hands placed on his head to shield some of the blows. His trousers were splattered with holes and his

collar was almost ripped off but the half of a yellow sun still clung
to his torn sleeve . . . The soldier had been stealing from the farm.
It happened everywhere now, farms raided at night, raided of corn
so tender they had not yet formed kernels and yams so young they
were barely the size of a cocoyam . . . The soldier got up and dusted
himself off.

"Have you come from the front?" Kainene asks.

He nodded. He looked about eighteen. There were two angry
bumps on either side of his forehead and blood trailed from his
nostrils . . .

"Come. Come and take some *garri* before you go," said Kainene.

Tears crawled down from his swollen left eye and he placed a palm
on it as he followed her.

(pp. 403–4)

In that increasingly hopeless military and economic situation, a
story of humanitarianism manqué emerges 30 years before the case
in Rwanda that will scandalise us and the international community.
Biafra's cause is not the one the wealthy donor states back. And
in this case, instead of standing back and fretting about events
on the ground, as the world did in Rwanda 1994, powerful states
participate in subduing Biafra militarily. It is the 1960s: a Cold
War is raging in international relations and Britain must grapple
with a part of Africa that only recently was in its famed empire,
under its guiding wing. It intervenes against Biafra.

What if you are not a soldier at the front but just a Biafran with
hope for the new soi-disant country? What happens to you in a
humanitarian emergency? Adichie skilfully portrays the ways a disaster sneaks up rather unlike a neighbour with a machete. Its first
sign is the relief agency, an arm of aid that neither development
experts nor relief experts think of as development. Development is
long-term and sustained economic, political and social well-being.
Relief is short term assistance geared to emergencies. Relief was
occasionally available in Biafra during the war, trying to operate
despite an embargo on the renegade country. In its early stuffed-
bag days there, it was easy to be critical. 'The Red Cross irritated
Ugwu; the least they could do was ask Biafrans their preferred
foods rather than sending so much bland flour' (p. 284). Queuing
for food also irritated, and you might have to hold yourself 'from

pushing back at the woman who tries to nudge her out' (p. 268). That first time, you leave the relief centre with very little, because you do not know the rules of emergencies and which queue to join. The next time, you see someone you know and he slips a tin of corned beef into your basket. You are so surprised and happy that you laugh at the sight and foolishly take the tin out to admire it: A 'shell-shocked soldier followed her out of the gate. She quickened her pace on the dusty stretch that led to the main road, but five of them, all in tattered army uniforms, soon surrounded her' (p. 272). This pushing is of a different sort:

> They babbled and gestured towards her basket, their movement disjointed, their tones raised, and Olanna made out some of the words. "Aunty!" "Sister!" "Bring am now!" "Hungry go kill all of us!" . . . They were bearing down on her. They could do anything; there was something desperately lawless about them and their noise-deadened brains. Olannna's fear came with rage, a fierce and emboldening rage, and she imagined fighting them, strangling them, killing them . . . In a flash, done so quickly that she did not realize it until afterwards, the one wearing a blue beret grasped her basket, took the tin of corned beef, and ran off.
>
> (p. 272)

You return to the relief centre the next time wearing a rosary around your neck 'because Mrs. Muokelu said the Caritas people were more generous to Catholics' (p. 283).

Others come to record your increasing misery:

> He walked over to the children and gave them some sweets and took photographs of them and they clamoured around him and begged for more. Once, he said, "That's a lovely smile!" and after he left them, the children went back to their roast rats' (p. 370). At the airport, ready to leave, Western journalists run into relief work unfolding before their eyes: "Men were hauling sacks from the planes. The lights went on and off. Pilots were screaming. "Hurry up, you lazy boys! Get them off! We're not going to be bombed here! Get a move on boys! Hurry up, damn it!" There was an American accent, an Afrikaans accent, an Irish accent. "The bastards could be a little more gracious," the plump [journalist] said. "They're fucking paid thousands of dollars to fly the relief in."
>
> (p. 373)

On it goes like that until the day when you return to the relief centre with another trick up your sleeve and find the gate bolted.

> "They said they have nothing and that our emphasis now is self-sufficiency and farming."
> "Farming with what? And how are we going to feed millions of people on the tiny territory we hold now?"
> Richard looked at her. Even the slightest hint of criticism of Biafra made him uncomfortable. Worries had lodged in the cracks in his mind since Umuahia fell, but he did not voice them.
>
> (p. 405)

Duffield (2007: 18) argues that self-reliance is always the main goal of development. Stick figure people do not need welfare safety nets or other forms of insurance. They need greater self-reliance –in the best of times and in days of emergency. He says: 'Rather than questioning the biopolitics involved . . . aid agencies usually infer that the emergency exists because communities and peoples are not self-reliant enough'. Yet here was Biafra trying to be self-reliant but running up against the sovereign state that had mistreated the Igbo, a state that was retaliating with its principal friends in ways designed to de-develop the dissident area. Consequently, Duffield goes on, 'each disaster initiates a fresh developmental attempt to return the population concerned to a new and more resilient condition of homeostatic self-reliance' (p. 18). Nearby, a 'nun cradled the smallest, a shriveled doll with stick legs and a pregnant belly' (Adichie 2006: 374). Dying peacefully already dead is the antithesis of a thought in motion, so is crawling into a situation of bare life as life, being beaten by the very people who needed you at the front fighting for them.

Postcolonial moves II

Sekai Nzenza-Shand is a Zimbabwean woman, and also an Australian citizen, who writes about life in a country undergoing postcolonial changes. Her *Songs to An African Sunset* (1997) predates by about three years the orchestrated fall of Zimbabwe from its impressive post-independence phase of postcolonialism.

Called the Pride of Africa in the 1980s, for its efforts at racial reconciliation, free primary education, and mixed economy, by 2000 the ruling Zanu-PF party of Robert Mugabe will start pulling out latent authoritarian tools to clamp onto power in the face of dwindling popular support. Today, it is wallowing around in failed state territory. That is, the country is suffering intense de-development as a governance strategy. The state has not even been trying until very recently to satisfy the fundamental needs of its citizens for security and survival. Indeed, Zimbabwe has the highest unemployment in the world, one of the highest inflation rates, malnutrition, low production, a destroyed agricultural sector, little Western aid and direct foreign investment, decayed infrastructure, ruined tourism and disease. Yet the state hangs on, bolstered by leaders of other African states who seem in awe of Mugabe, and by the jerry-rigged, but crucial addition of Morgan Tsvangarai to the executive of the country.

Nzenza-Shand tells of different experiences than this. Her mother is strategising to sell or exchange her old steer for a heifer. The maize in the fields is high and the sorghum and sunflowers are bursting. 'On either side of the path, the fields were full of a promising harvest. After three years of drought, the rains had come as a most valued blessing. No one would starve this year or be forced to line up for drought relief handouts from benevolent Western governments. It had been a good year' (p. 9). She has encounters with those benevolent government representatives in a number of places and presents them as strangely disconnected from the societies they seek to serve:

> "We will teach the Tonga how to farm," declared a zealous young aid worker in an air-conditioned office in Melbourne. "We will build schools for them," said his counterpart in Oslo. "They do not have cattle because of the tsetse flies, so let's give them tractors to plough the land," said a New Yorker. A group of English workers from the Save the Children Fund flew to Omay and began to teach the locals how to grow vegetables. UNICEF introduced feeding programmes for all children under five. And a women's church group sent the Tonga truckloads of secondhand clothes.
>
> (p. 202)

Clearly the thoughts are on the move, but the international development community is not seen here as keen to be gathered-in and worlded to Zimbabwe. Quite the contrary.

Meanwhile we remember Mazvita from the late Yvonne Vera's powerful novel, *Without A Voice* (1994). Back in the rural area, the kind of area Nzenza-Shand describes nostalgically, Mazvita 'felt a strong sense of her own power and authority, of her ability to influence and change definitions of her own reality, adjust boundaries to her vision, banish limits to her progress' (p. 34). But, like Methode in Rwanda that same year, Mazvita moves her thoughts away from dreams of power and strength and finds herself confronting a much uglier reality. Owing to the treachery of her partner and the harshness of life in Harare, she ends up living a bare life existence which she refuses to relinquish to death: 'She lost all capacity for dreams. She felt less burdened, less susceptible to injury . . . Empty and abandoned, she walked, leaning forward, past caring . . . The idea was to go forward, even those who had died in the streets knew that. They crawled towards the alleys. Death, properly executed, could be mistaken for progress' (pp. 35–6).

Ending it

Duffield (2007: 227–8) notes that 'while development studies and postcolonialism sit uncomfortably together, the one belonging to the immediate world of practice and the other to cultural analysis and reflection, when attempts have been made to bring the two together, it is often to argue that the insights of the latter can somehow help or enhance the former'. The result is that development becomes the standard realm of thought and practice and the novel or postcolonial theory is brought to bear on 'it'. That effort can be part of a larger experience of trying to find ways to soften the hard facades of development and render a powerful field more consistently concerned to theorise development from the position of postcolonial people and their daily dilemmas. Development studies are not likely to yield to that challenge. The real challenge is to keep up the pressure on it *and* simultaneously develop alternative paradigms and practices to pursue. To date, critical development thinking has fallen down on that last bit and critical practitioners have found themselves forced to play by the rules of whichever agency funds their work.

Meanwhile locals keep facing the prosaic challenges that escape notice, or that, in their numbers, overwhelm instances of development progress. They queue up for relief or development aid, waiting, so to speak, for their ship to arrive. Or if they are Mazvita, development feminism might pick her up and put her into a shelter for homeless women, en route perhaps to a literacy class. If they see her, that is: 'No one cast her a pitiful glance. She was not there at all' (Vera 1994: 46). One individual is not what development is all about –that is the realm of social work. Development is about life in the aggregate, in national collectivities, in markets of the globalised world. There is nothing inherently wrong with that large focus. And yet it is undeniable that development theory and practice have much mistaken progress to account for in their journeys to assist. So too does the international relations of favouritism and indifference: some people get aid and some, like the Biafrans, get aid only when they capitulate to the logic of the system. Today Zimbabwe is turned away both by Western states and by development agencies or funded covertly. Yesterday it was the international community turning away from Rwanda, mid-1990s.

Larger schemes of social protection, schemes that do not rely on states as the main administrators, are clearly needed, as Duffield (2007) cogently points out. We recall that this was, in part, what the call and plan for a New International Economic Order represented in the 1970s. Then the insistence on reorganising aid, trade and management of global resources, placing much of the work in the hands of the developing country-strong UN, was seen as radical – a militant and communist plot to replace the Bretton Woods principles with international welfare socialism. Solidarity around the plan was whittled away by aid offers, and the Organization of the Petroleum Exporting Countries (OPEC) turned out not to be the Third World-friendly organisation militants had expected. Today, that call for a new order might sound fresh and timely. But it would have to be accompanied by a shift in at least some development thinking and funding, away from preoccupations with national economies to individuals victimised by them. The obligation to protect is an international one, and gradually that fact is recognised, at least in the realm of military interventions. The World Bank, it seems, is also aware that individuals need to count more in development thinking; but it cannot get its many heads around the problematic of the individual as level analysis and subject of development. It would help her or him through better international risk management programmes, which throw us back, once again, on feeble states to administer.

We could do worse than advocate a campaign of reading postcolonial stories as part of development theory, training, and practice in the field. We learn from these that people in crisis are already faced with an extreme biopolitical self-reliance. They are making life and death decisions on a daily basis. We need to know the nature of the challenges they believe they face and the ways they reach conclusions as to what they, as individuals, should do. It is their thinking, I repeat, that we need to grasp, not the choices economists dream up for them in rational choice models. What better way to begin the process of insight into individual biopolitical choices than to read about these challenges in novels about postcolonial settings? Collier (2008: xi) wisely, and yet rather obviously, maintains that 'change in these societies at the bottom must come predominantly from within; we cannot impose it on them'. He urges on us a better use of statistical evidence to educate politicians in the West and their constituents about the problems, the tools available, and the importance of coordinating international efforts. He is worried that the conflict trap over there could become a security nightmare for us at some point too.

That is all fine and useful. But I argue as well that there is urgency in learning how to think "development and individuals" rather than development aggregates, and how to put the information gained to use, without giving burdened people even more opportunities for self-reliance than they already have in bare life situations. And the place to start is by taking postcolonial renderings of life and bare life as seriously as we take the statistics – not just as a way of bettering development thinking and practice, which, given the resources available to development agencies is always useful, but to shift a focus that has been overweeningly statistical, all along. If we need vacations, perhaps so do they. If we need gyms and parks, perhaps that is what individuals dream about there too. We in development studies do not really know. And it is time we did, by moving our relations of analysis and our practices, reaching towards writings and situations and people and their economies of movement.

References

Adichie, C. N. (2006) *Half of a Yellow Sun*, Harper Perennial, London.

Agamben, G. (1998) *Homo Sacer: Sovereign power and bare life*, D. Heller-Roazen (trans.), Stanford University Press, Stanford.

Biccum, A. R. (2005) 'Development and the "new" imperialism: A reinvention of colonial discourse in DFID promotional literature', *Third World Quarterly*, 26: 1005–20.

Collier, P. (2008) *The Bottom Billion: Why the poorest countries are failing and what can be done about it?*, Oxford University Press, Oxford.

Cooke, B. and Kothari, U. (eds) (2001) *Participation: The new tyranny?*, Zed Books, London.

Courtemanche, G. (2003) *A Sunday at the Pool in Kigali*, Canongate, London.

Cowen, M. P. and Shenton, R. W. (1996) *Doctrines of Development*, Routledge, London.

Duffield, M. (2007) *Development, Security and Unending War: Governing the world of peoples*, Polity, Cambridge.

Foucault, M. (1975) *Surveiller et Punir: Naissance de la prison*. Gallimard. Paris.

— (1976) *Histoire de la Sexualité. Vol. 1: La volonté de savoir*. Gallimard. Paris.

Kapoor, I. (2008) *The Postcolonial Politics of Development*, Routledge, New York.

Manning, E. (2009) *Relationscapes: Movement, art, philosophy*, MIT Press, Cambridge.

Mehta, U. S. (1999) *Liberalism and Empire*, University of Chicago Press, Chicago.

Mosse, D. (1994) 'Authority, gender, and knowledge: Theoretical reflections on the practice of participatory rural appraisal', *Development and Change*, 25(4): 497–526.

Moyo, D. (2009) *Dead Aid: Why aid is not working and how there is another way for Africa*, Allen Lane, London.

Nzenza-Shand, S. (1997) *Songs to an African Sunset: A Zimbabwean story*, Lonely Planet Publications, London.

Parpart, J. (1995) 'Deconstructing the development "expert": Gender, development and the "vulnerable groups"', in M. Marchand and J. Parpart (eds), *Feminism/Postmodernism/Development*, Routledge, London.

Patel, R. and McMichael, P. (2004) 'Third Worldism and the lineages of global fascism: The regrouping of the Global South in the neoliberal era', *Third World Quarterly*, 25: 231–54.

Raghuram, P., Madge, C. and Noxolo, P. (2009) 'Rethinking responsibility and care for a postcolonial world', *Geoforum*, 40(1): 5–13.

Sylvester, C. (1995) 'African and western feminisms: World-traveling the tendencies and possibilities', *Signs: Journal of Women in Culture and Society*, 20(4): 941–69.

— (1999) 'Development studies and postcolonial studies: Disparate tales of the "Third World"', *Third World Quarterly*, 20(4): 703–21.

— (2000) *Producing Women and Progress in Zimbabwe: Narratives of identity and work from the 1980s*, Heinemann, Portsmouth, NH.

— (2006) 'Bare life as a development/postcolonial problematic', *Geographical Journal*, 172(1): 66–77.

— (2009) *Art/Museums: International relations where we least expect it*, Paradigm Publishers, Boulder.

Vera, Y. (1994) *Without A Voice*, Baobab Books, Harare.

9

Postcolonial economies of development volunteering

Patricia Noxolo

Introduction

The central question of the following chapter is: what are the moral economies (Ray and Sayer 1999) of development 'volunteering' in a postcolonial world and how do they produce difference? More specifically, what are the political tensions inherent within the double location of development volunteering, within the moral economy of a postcolonial international development terrain *and* within the moral economy of a globalised transnational market of highly mobile professional workers?

Development volunteering, like development tourism, is generally understood as a popular practice of 'volunteering' and of 'development' (Simpson 2004; Noxolo forthcoming). As such, there have been a number of pieces of research about the impact of development volunteers on the places in which they are working (Howes 2001), as well as a flourishing subgenre of autobiographical travel writing on the personal and professional experience of development volunteering (Bailur and Rana 2003; Joy 2004). In recent years however, as a response to the increasingly complex demands of employers and volunteers alike, development volunteering is beginning to be evaluated as a transnational moment within an ongoing professional career (Unterhalter *et al.*

2002; Schultz and Kelly 2007), the more so as, in contrast to gap year initiatives (Simpson 2004), the development volunteer is typically a qualified and experienced practitioner, aged 30 years or above, who undertakes a two-year placement in the middle of an established career, and who, crucially, is usually paid at the same rate and from the same source as their local colleagues when they are overseas.[1]

Over a decade ago, Kendall and Knapp (1995) identified volunteering as a 'loose and baggy monster' in terms of the difficulty of actually defining what it is and where it fits in the global economy. Since then, its popular connotation of either unpaid or underpaid amateurism (in often unspoken contrast with commoditised, professionalised labour) has become increasingly difficult to sustain as the phenomenon of volunteering develops an increasingly ambivalent relationship with both the state and the market. The privatisation of welfare provision draws more and more on the delegation of state responsibilities to the 'shadow state' activities of the voluntary sector (Conradson and Milligan 2006). In this competitive environment, volunteers are becoming increasingly managed as professionalised workers through performance-based managerial mechanisms (skills auditing, accountability processes, etc.) drawn from business environments, as volunteering becomes increasingly established as a formalised route through to professional status (Fyfe and Milligan 2003; Noxolo forthcoming).

The globalised field of development practice, which has traditionally been strongly marked by voluntarism, has also become increasingly subject to managerialised professionalism. Both multilateral organisations and non-governmental organisations (NGOs) have become party to performance-based managerialist practices in relation to both paid and unpaid workers, as well as service users, and these practices arguably diffuse and legitimise neoliberal values from the global scale to the most intimate arenas of everyday practice (Lewis 2008; Murphy 2008).

---

1 Voluntary Service Overseas (VSO), the largest UK-based development volunteer sending organisation, mainly recruits volunteers with at least two years' professional experience for a range of placements that are usually two years long, but can be as short as six months. VSO also runs a pre-professional youth volunteer programme (see www.vso.org.uk).

Therefore the globalised discursive contexts within which development volunteering is located, both voluntarism and developmentalism, tend increasingly towards a managerialised, performance-based professionalism. At the same time, professionalism is also a discourse that is increasingly transnational in its spatiality, with an emphasis on the global circulation of skills and knowledge, rather than on the management of settled individuals. As Vertovec (2002) argues, the short-term and intermittent movement of skilled professionals within and between nation-states has led to an increasing emphasis on mobility rather than settlement, with a concomitant interest in transnational networks within which workers build up the contacts, skills and opportunities on which mobility relies. The emphasis on networks focuses attention on the ways in which professional knowledge and skills are built up through transnational interaction and circulation, creating flexible 'communities of practice' (Wenger 1998), so that knowledge is multiply sourced, rather than 'grown' in one place and 'transferred' to another. Development volunteering is increasingly being marketed to employers as an arena for this kind of transnational professional development, through which individuals expand their professional knowledge and skills through networking with other professionals and gaining experience within different environments (Unterhalter *et al.* 2002), ultimately 'enriching' the professional environments in the UK to which they return (Schultz and Kelly 2007).

So development volunteering continues to be seen as a popular practice of international development, but is also an aspect of global professional practice because it stands at the confluence between two waves: increased managerialised professionalism in development practice and the increasing transnationalism of global professionalism. Drawing throughout on research with returned development volunteers in the UK,[2] this chapter will argue that development volunteering holds this dual moral economy – international development and transnational professionalism – in

2 This paper is based on research carried out with funding from a Royal Geographical Society Small Research Grant, and involving focus groups with a total of 61 returned development volunteers in three locations across England.

tension, and that this tension is productive of a range of differentiations in terms of 'value'. The next section will explain what is meant by moral economy and the particular insights to be gained by linking it with postcolonial theorisations of development to ask how moral economies are productive of difference. The following section will explore the processes of differentiation within the moral economy of development volunteering as development practice, drawing on Ilan Kapoor's (2008) work on development aid as g(r)ift. Drawing on Parvati Raghuram's (2009) work on the postcolonial routing of the 'brain drain' discourse in relation to skilled migrants, the fourth section explores the alternative moral economy of transnational professional mobility and the differences it makes in relation to development volunteering as 'gifting', while the conclusion draws out some of the implications of this analysis.

Moral economy, postcolonial development

The notion of moral economy implies a willingness to pay attention to the salience of both the cultural *and* the economic. The question of how culture and economy interact is of course a vexed one, with many expressing concern that the widespread 'cultural turn' in the social sciences has led to a dangerous diminution in academic interest in the local and global economy (Thrift 1998; Ray and Sayer 1999). Postcolonial theory, with its emphasis on literary and linguistic strategies, has been seen by some commentators as very much part of this turn (Dirlik 2002). Despite widespread interest in the potential of postcolonial theory to make important political interventions in relation to development theory and practice (Noxolo 2006; Kapoor 2008; McEwan 2009), it has been criticised for offering 'more in the way of new-fangled language than food' (Sylvester 1999: 718; Radcliffe 2005).

It is certainly clear, however, that fruitful interaction between cultural and economic perspectives is possible, not least in terms of economic analysis of the material conditions within which cultural practices and goods circulate (Hall 1996; Hudson 2008), and in terms of viewing cultural distinctions as economically determined (Bourdieu 1979). The notion of moral economy focuses on the ways in which culturally-produced values and norms mediate economic transactions (Goodman 2004). This is not only to make a point about cultural difference, i.e. that consensus around the values and norms that lie behind any aspect of the global economy cannot be taken for granted. It is also to point out the importance of examining those values and norms, in all their multiplicity and contingency, in any critical agenda for change: 'The point of a focus on moral economy is to bring out what is so easily over-looked, that economies are strongly influenced by moral norms and that changing such norms is fundamental to any alternative organisation of economy' (Sayer 1999: 71).

Postcolonial theory is peculiarly attuned to the exploration of multiplicity and contingency, not only as they manifest in literary and linguistic strategies (Spivak 1992; Bhabha 1994), but in a range of political and economic practices (Mbembe 2001; Dominy 2002). As such, applying postcolonial theory to notions of moral economy gives a sharpened edge to the exploration of differential value in economic transactions. Moreover, as Ray and Sayer (1999: 9) note, culture and economy, though increasingly interlinked, 'remain different and often pull against each other'. From a postcolonial point of view, a focus on the moral economy of development volunteering can therefore highlight not only the cultural meanings of development volunteering as part of a global economy, but also the forces that, *in this particular instance*, often push towards the production of a gap between culture and economy.

In other words, a postcolonial analysis of moral economy permits a focus on the specificity of the 'ethico-political agenda that drives the differentiation' (Spivak 1999: 332) as well as the elision of morality and economy. This focus on differentiation highlights two peculiarly postcolonial routes for an analysis of moral economy. The first is the production of difference as part and parcel of the production of the historical present (Spivak 1999), i.e. the ways in which the depiction of certain features as representative of the contemporary global economy is selec-tive, relegating other simultaneous features to a troubling space outside the present time, the space of the 'discursive time-lag' (Bhabha 1994: 198). Linked to this is a second, the constant and ongoing erasure of the 'residual and emergent' trace of the radically different 'other' (Spivak 1999: 332) within the historical present.

Development volunteering as 'gifting'

In focus groups, development volunteers were asked to reflect on their motivations for volunteering and on the impact of the experience after they returned. The desire to change the world was often given as a primary motivation, albeit with a strong sense of self-criticism in expressing this: 'I wanted to change the world. I was very young, I was very naïve'; 'it sounds a bit pious, but I think I always thought I wanted to go out and help people'. Some were able to look back on their work with a sense of achievement, believing that they had initiated sustainable change: 'when I left I feel the school was in a better situation than when I started and would . . . continue to do so . . .' However, some highlighted their frustrations with the complexity and difficulty of development as a terrain, sometimes linking these with what they saw to be their own insufficiencies: 'I probably went in with the same kind of naïve view of the world that it will be easy to sort things out . . . and it wasn't'; 'it was all about power politics. It was not about people. It was not about improving people's lives'; '[Local colleagues] got fed up with me trotting out my rubbish [local language] sentences . . . I got bored with trying because I wasn't achieving anything . . .'.

Whether satisfied or frustrated, this broadly conceived desire to bring change was often linked with a broadly-conceived voluntarism, a desire to bring change for some person or some *value* other than money: 'I didn't want always just to work for money and for myself . . . I had done some voluntary things, but I'd never really done anything that was purely not for me, and I wanted to do something like that'; 'I wanted to maybe do a bit of a rain check and see, using the volunteering aspect, to see another set of values in, in a different light, as it were, to see how I could stack up against what I thought, certainly in the late 90s'.

The volunteers generally deployed this developmentalist voluntarism, this desire to give without financial return, to differentiate themselves from other expatriates and from wealthy elites, many of whom they perceived as living relatively wealthy, enclave lifestyles: 'They have their own shops, their own entertainment, their own houses, and the money . . .' In fact, many saw this differentiation from wealthy expatriates as giving volunteers a sort of contrastive validation in the eyes of local colleagues: 'that put you on a different sort of footing. They called us "the barefoot" apparently'. However there was a disturbing ambivalence for others, who found that they could not in practice entirely separate themselves from wealth – for example, because they came from the UK, some were invited to garden parties in places that looked 'like the pictures of Hello!'.[3] Moreover, the few who had travelled both as development volunteers and as workers with private organisations said that there was actually very little difference in practice between the two lifestyles: 'we were completely undistinguishable I would say, the sort of housing, in fact our local salary was the same as their local salary . . .' Furthermore, though many volunteers experienced the material privations that they were looking for, some development volunteers expressed some concern at the fact that they often find themselves in a better financial situation during their placement and after their return than they expected. As one volunteer commented: 'I came away from VSO the first time with money in the bank, which is not actually the experience that I had expected to have'.

This blurring of boundaries between developmentalism as altruistic 'gifting' and the various other economic and geopolitical enterprises that characterise bilateral and multilateral relationships between richer and poorer countries has of course been a seam running through developmentalism since its earliest colonial and postcolonial inception (Rodney 1972; Riddell 1987; Abrahamsen 2000). In recent years this ambivalence has become even more diffuse since, though they remain substantially independent, through funding arrangements and agreements using concepts like 'partnership', the non-governmental sector has become increasingly linked into governmental and inter-governmental aid initiatives (Wallace 2003; Haque 2004;

---

3 *Hello!* is a well-known glossy magazine reporting on celebrity news (see http://www. hellomagazine.com/).

Kamat 2004). Volunteer-sending organisations are not in general an exception to this trend – for example, the charity Voluntary Service Overseas has a Partnership Programme Arrangement with the UK government's Department for International Development, meaning that in 2007–8 the organisation received £28 million from the government, constituting well over half of its £43.1 million income for the year (Voluntary Service Overseas 2008: 37). Effectively then, the UK development volunteers' desire to give without remuneration, and their doubts around their capacity to do so, is linked, through funding and discursively, into the larger moral economy of British aid-giving.

Ilan Kapoor's (2008) critique of development aid as 'gifting' draws on Derrida's philosophical consideration of the gift as 'the very figure of the impossible' (Derrida 1991: 7). In a formulation that is of particular interest in relation to the moral economy of voluntarism, Derrida argues that economics is essentially a relation of exchange – crucial to it is the figure of the circle (giving to receive). The gift (giving without receiving) is therefore a figure of that which is impossible in economic terms, even though the very notion of gift relies on an economic context: 'If the figure of the circle is essential to economics, the gift must remain *aneconomic*. Not that it remains foreign to the circle, but it must *keep* a relation of foreignness to the circle, a relation without relation of familiar foreignness. It is perhaps in this sense that the gift is the impossible'. (Derrida 1991: 7; emphases in original).

Using discourse analysis of governmental statements about their aid programmes, Kapoor uses this notion of gifting as the impossible in an economic context to deconstruct international development aid in terms of the work that it does in constructing a moral drama, in which the donor nation is constructed as generous and principled. This discourse is supported by a range of nationalistic practices surrounding aid-giving – branding aid with national flags, publicising donations and pledges, imaging nationally marked 'humanitarian heroes' (Kapoor 2008: 86–90). At the same time, he argues, the recipient nation is constructed in a binary relation with the donor nation – for example, where the donor is kind, the recipient is needy, etc. (Kapoor 2008: 79). Kapoor is not simply reiterating the well-known critique that aid donations are often in practice tightly linked to short-term or long-term financial return for the donor nation, so that gift becomes grift (Bose and Burnell 1991; Slater and Bell 2002; Baaz 2005). He is making the broader point that entering into a relationship constructed around a moral economy of gifting sets up self other relationships that require constant negotiation and questioning of the self 'lest giving wholeheartedly turns into taking back' (Kapoor 2008: 78).

In the context of the voluntarism of development volunteering, this argument does not have the implication that volunteers should obsessively seek out a purity of motivation. The observation that altruistic motives are always contaminated is in many ways banal. Moreover, as we shall see in the section on transnational professionalism, in the focus groups volunteers themselves often clearly recognised that they have had a mixture of other-oriented and self-oriented motivations. So, in this context, a question that is more interesting than that of *whether* the moral economy of development volunteering is in some ways politically contaminated, is what *work of differentiation* is performed by the creation of an explicitly moral economy of voluntarism in the context of a highly unequal development space.

Development volunteers were noticeably reflective and self-critical in relation to the social and political construction of their own motivations for volunteering, locating their decisions to volunteer within the historical specificities of their upbringing: 'This was the Kennedy era and there was a feeling that . . . development in this era of decolonization was going to be fairly short term, and would achieve things promptly. And therefore, there was a legitimate, interesting job of work to do'; 'now I have to balance that with a Thatcher child story'. Equally, some placed their experience within the discursive context of cultures of British childhood in which institutions (media, church, youth organisations) have historically promoted interaction with a wider world (MacKenzie 1986; Said 1994): 'I personally blame it on an overdose of Blue Peter[4] . . . and particularly that one where

---

4 *Blue Peter* is a long-running BBC children's programme, well known for its charitable campaigns (see www.bbc.co.uk/cbbc/bluepeter/). Valerie Singleton is one of their earliest and most well-known presenters.

Princess Anne and Valerie Singleton went off and built a school in Africa'; 'my grandfather was a Baptist missionary . . .'; 'I went to World Camp at Windsor Great Park with Guides[5] from all over the world . . . so that started an interest'.

By identifying the construction of their motivations with particular eras, particular Western leaders (Kennedy, Thatcher) and particular institutions (Girl Guides, Blue Peter), the volunteers located themselves within a narrative of Western-centred development history. At each moment the difference of the non-Western 'other' is produced as 'time-lag' (see above) in historically contingent ways: as short-term recipient who will soon 'catch up', or as long-term charity case or exotic visitor who can never be fully assimilable into the historical narrative of Western progression.

It is worth reminding ourselves here of Johannes Fabian's (1983) classic argument about anthropological practice as 'the denial of coevalness'. This argument, which has been taken up extensively in relation to development practice (Escobar 1995; Raghuram: 2009), is that in their representation of people living in economically poorer countries, anthropologists and development practitioners/ researchers tend to adopt an 'allochronic' discourse, which places their research subjects into a past time outside the modern era in which the researcher/practitioner is writing. As some have pointed out (Sbert 1992; Watts 1995), this is exacerbated in development discourse by the differential temporalities created by timelines of national progress from 'developing' to 'developed'. There is no intention here to suggest that development volunteers themselves unreflexively adopted an allochronic discourse – the intention is to suggest that it is *within and against* this discursive context that development volunteers negotiate the moral economy of development as 'gifting', locating their own volunteering as response or resistance to wider Western constructions of self/ other relationship.

---

5 The Girl Guides are an international girls' youth organisation (www.girlguiding. org.uk/home.aspx), which, as part of the World Association of Girl Guides and Girl Scouts, has organised an annual World Camp since 1924 (www.wagggsworld.org/ en/about/About/History). Windsor Great Park is a large deer park, located on the border of Berkshire and Surrey, in the UK.

Development volunteering as transnational professionalism

For many development volunteers who attended the focus groups, the emphasis was as much on professional development as on international development. For some this took the form of direct self-management in relation to the development of specific skill-sets:

> I was working for an institute in the UK, an agricultural institute; I was working with one disease on cereal crops. And there was not really a big problem with production of cereals at that time in the UK or Europe, in fact we were over producing. So I wanted to do something a bit different"; "It wasn't so much the money, but in the late '80s and early '90s, the interesting IT work, a lot of it was going on in Eastern Europe . . . I wrote to VSO and a number of other agencies about working in Eastern Europe.

These comments point to development volunteering's role in an alternative moral economy: that of transnational professionalism. Rather than working to produce a differentiation between donor and recipient, transnational professionalism puts the spotlight on a productive transnational space, within which the nation-state is not erased, but in which professional knowledges, resources and skills are in part the effects of multiply-located, networked circulations and interactions, rather than emanating from a donating/sending West. As Raghuram (2009: 29) argues in relation to seeing doctors as transnational workers, rather than simply victims or perpetrators of 'brain drain': 'doctors are not only part of national collectivities, they are also part of socio-cognitive communities that share tacit knowledges about the nature of a medical career . . . Thus the brain drain migrants' mobility is embedded not only in narratives of mobility, but also crucially of the brain'. The moral economy of transnational professionalism redefines professional skills (the 'brain' in 'brain drain') *from* that which can be owned and 'gifted' by and to particular nations *to* the distributed product of diverse transnational interactions.

The implications of a focus on transnational professionalism are that the notion of development is transferred from a focus on international development (the 'development' of poorer countries through the 'transfer' of skills from 'developed' countries) to development of and at a range of scales, from the individual to the global through the transnational generation of a range of professional skills. Beyond the development of the careers of individual development volunteers, in many instances the overall economy of a range of cities and small nation-states, such as Singapore, is heavily reliant on the sustained mobilities of workers and knowledges (Beaverstock 2002), or of course their relative immobilities (McDowell 2004). More broadly, theories of 'soft capitalism' posit an increasingly reciprocal relationship between the production of mobile professional knowledges and the production of early twenty-first century global capitalism (Thrift 1998), so that the production and distribution of knowledge has become increasingly central to global wealth generation.

However, transnational professionalism is fraught with inequalities – not only between skilled and unskilled workers (Morrison 2001) but also between elite travellers and those workers on whose relative immobility they rely (Gogia 2006). Inequalities in professional mobility largely reflect and draw on existing social and geopolitical inequalities (International Organization for Migration 2008). Even among skilled workers, a range of inequalities means that the meanings and effects of mobility are hugely differentiated globally. For example work on skilled and elite women reveals their multiple sites and roles in social reproduction (Kofman and Raghuram 2006), both within and outside paid work (Yeoh and Willis 2005), while different professions have different opportunities for mobility, depending not only on their structures of knowledge, qualification and recruitment, but also on the differing policy frameworks arising from the labour demands of different nation-states (Clark 2006; Welbourne 2007; Allsop 2009).

Development volunteers confronted the differential value accorded to transnational professional development when they returned to continue their careers in the UK. For some UK employers the very fact of transnationality, of having experience of working in different national environments and of adapting to cultural difference, is a professional skill to be valued in and of itself, whereas for other employers, time away from the UK (or perhaps from other similar contexts, such as the US or other European countries) is time away from the specific culture and dynamics of the UK workplace. Some, particularly in explicitly people-oriented professions such as teaching, found that the 'soft' skills that they were able to demonstrate (such as adaptability, working cross-culturally) were valued by their employers in the UK on their return. Others though, experienced what they termed a 'reverse culture shock', in which the differences between the ways they and the rest of British society had developed while they were away left them feeling estranged and isolated. Some (most notably those working in industry or in construction) felt misunderstood and out of touch:

> "people told me I wasn't even speaking proper English, which I hadn't picked up at all so I think it took me about a year in the UK, when I came back, to really find . . . People had moved on you know."; "they kind of said you're nearly three years off the pace and it took me . . . and I don't think I actually ever recovered because I went straight onto the dole. Never been on the dole in my life."

To appear more consistent with their professional culture therefore, some development volunteers have been known to bury the experience: '[development volunteering] is not on my CV because it might, I might appear to be a bit altruistic'. The long-term economic value of development volunteering, as a form of transnational mobility that develops professional capacity to draw down higher salaries, is therefore by no means certain.

The question of differential value brings us back to the central postcolonial question of this paper: what differentiating work does the moral economy of development volunteering as transnational professionalism do? Moreover, how does the moral economy of development volunteering as transnational professionalism combine with the moral economy of development volunteering as 'gifting' to contribute to the creation of differential economic value in global professional labour markets?

One answer to the first question relates to the foreshortened historicity of many narratives of transnational professionalism. In formulating 'soft capitalism' as a global historical moment in which certain features of capitalism have definitively changed (most notably dominant conceptions of knowledge as partial and differentiated), Nigel Thrift (1998) identifies the circulation of ideas and knowledge within a shared transnational space as constitutive of the *modern* creative business professional. This mobility of ideas relies not only on communication technologies, but also to a surprising extent on the mobility of personnel, particularly the well-attended lecture circuits of the 'business guru' or highly paid management consultant. Chris Gibson and Natascha Klocker (2004) helpfully also note the unevenness of the global circulation of ideas in this transnational space, showing that particular ideas become influential largely because they emanate from gurus based in centres that are best positioned to deploy global networks to their own advantage.

However the high mobility of labour, both skilled and unskilled, during the long centuries of European imperialism, has led many to question the foreshortening of history involved in typifying transnational professionalism as a recent effect of globalisation (Kerr 2006). Indeed, many professions can trace both the roots and the specific *routings* of present-day patterns of transnational mobility to colonial movements and relationships (Allsop 2009). For example, Diana Solano and Anne Marie Rafferty (2007: 1063) have argued convincingly that the transnational recruitment structure of the UK's national health service was routed and institutionalised through the work of the Colonial Nursing Service (established in 1940, initially to supply the nursing needs of British people settled in the colonies), so that certain postcolonial countries (in this case specifically the UK and its former colonies) are still the nodes of particular networks of transnational activity: 'nurse migration reflects the global flow of resources along established historical or emerging networks of economic power'.

In the context of the concept of the 'migrant worker', the difficulties that transnational professionals may have in adapting their skills to Western contexts have been documented for some years in various forms (Braithwaite 1990; Forster 1992), and there remains some disquiet about potential difficulties that workers in specific professions may have (Welbourne 2007). However, placing transnational professionalism in the context of postcolonial relationships raises questions about the possibly racialised and hier-archised transnational relationships through which professional knowledges may have developed. The racialisation of development discourses is only just beginning to be explored (Goudge 2003; Duffield 2006), particularly from the point of view of those with whom development workers interact in the Global South (Pink 1998; Nyamnjoh and Page 2002), while the hugely dynamic and diverse impacts of different racialised understandings both of and by mobile professionals moving through transnational space, and their effects on professional practice, requires the carrying out, consolidation and constant updating of a large amount of highly context-specific research (Hagey 2001). It is in the specificity of the historically informed networks and relationships that make up the overall moral economy of transnational professionalism that differential value is largely generated.

An answer to the second question – how the moral economy of development volunteering as transnational professionalism combines with the moral economy of development volunteer-ing as gifting to produce differential value in the global labour market – moves by similar, and in significant ways parallel, routes to the work performed by the 'brain drain' discourse (Beine 2008; Raghuram 2009), in which much concern has been expressed about the migration of skilled medical professionals from poorer countries that are hard-pressed to replace them, to richer countries. Parvati Raghuram (2009: 29) argues that much of the academic discussion of 'brain drain' constructs the nation as the primary focus of analysis, with the 'brain drain' migrant being trained in one nation-state, then effectively carrying those skills as a package into another nation-state context. The moral economy of development volunteering as 'gifting' is very similar in its nation-state focus, but with a parallel movement, so that the skills that the volunteer has are constructed as the product of one relatively wealthy nation, and these, embodied by the volunteer, are 'transferred' to another relatively poorer nation. Thus the differentiation between wealthy and poor nation – those that 'have' sufficient skills and those that do not 'have' enough – is compounded both by 'brain drain' arguments and by the concept of 'development volunteering'.

Moreover the 'brain drain' discourse retains the largely economically oriented 'push–pull' logic reserved for international migration, in which skilled bodies are 'pushed' out of a national space in which there are few skilled people but even fewer opportunities to earn high wages, and 'pulled' into a national space in which there are more skilled people but more opportunities to earn high wages. By contrast, in a morally oriented movement, the development volunteer discourse constructs the *voluntary* movement of skilled bodies, not being 'pushed' or 'pulled' by economic forces but *choosing for moral reasons to move against the tide*, out of a skills-abundant space with the opportunity to earn high wages and into a skills-impoverished space in which s/he chooses (unlike other expatriates but like her/his local colleagues) to earn relatively low wages by Western standards. The development volunteer's 'gifting' therefore relies on this 'aneconomic' (see Derrida above) logic – the volunteer is 'free' – neither 'pushed' nor 'pulled' – to temporarily refuse to use her/his mobility in her/his own interests.

The condition of this freedom of (aneconomic) movement is the differential value of labour in the spaces between which volunteers move. As we have seen, though the moral economy of transnational professionalism seems to hold out the promise of a global 'level playing field', in which knowledge is generated and shared by all in transnational space, in terms of wages and opportunities for skilled professionals from different places this is still not the case (International Organization for Migration 2008). The comments of development volunteers reveal their painful awareness of the prevailing economic inequalities that underpin the global labour market, and of the ambivalent insertion of development volunteering into this inequality. In common with other forms of volunteering (Fyfe and Milligan 2003), development volunteering is linked to a certain *de facto* level of monied privilege, because voluntarism requires the relatively high levels of freedom of mobility that come with a combination of skills and money (Nyamnjoh and Page 2002). Aware of their shared professional status, some volunteers contrasted their own easy mobility with the relative immobility of their colleagues in the places where they volunteered, expressing at some length their dismay at their colleagues' often unsuccessful struggles to obtain exit or entry visas: 'I go back a lot . . . I've been doing this for ten years now and I have some really good colleagues there . . . who've got brilliant English, but have never been to England . . . . They cannot get a visa, even though they work in tourism, they've got home, family, a good job background, British authorities won't let them'.

While the moral economy of development volunteering as transnational professionalism allows volunteers to frame their mobility as professional development (making the differential value placed on professional skills hugely problematic), the moral economy of development volunteering as 'gifting' remains anchored in a zero sum game, in which the generous donor nation is contrasted with conspicuously needy recipients. This in turn contributes to the differential valuing of labour that underpins the highly uneven global economy in professional mobility.

Conclusions

This chapter has argued that development volunteering lies at the confluence of two different moral economies: development volunteering as 'gifting', and development volunteering as professional transnationalism. Both of these moral economies are productive of difference: differences in wealth and opportunity, between the development volunteer and her/his 'others' (the isolated wealthy expatriate; the immobile local colleague); and differences in economic value in an uneven global labour market, in which volunteers' mobility is more highly valued than the problematised mobility of the 'brain drain' migrant, but their transnational skills are less highly valued than the potent knowledge-creation capacities of networked transnational elites.

The tensions between these two moral economies have particular implications for many development volunteers. Though some are able to make immediate use of the skills they have developed when they return to the UK, others find that, though their mobility is highly valued as 'gifting' on the way out of the UK, the skills that they develop transnationally are devalued as 'third world' on the way back in. In this context, for many development volunteers perhaps the long-term value of the experience is less about specifically auditable professional skills, and more to do with learning to live with the uncomfortable, unsettled ambivalence and reflexivity that marked many of their comments and is perhaps the basis for a responsible attitude in a complex postcolonial world (see Noxolo 2009).

This point about postcolonial responsibility brings us to broader considerations about the need to interrogate the spatialities and temporalities of transnational professional practice, whether as development volunteering or more broadly. As Raghuram (2009) notes, recognising the transnationality of knowledge-creation among professionals implies a focus on transnational spaces and relationships, rather than treating knowledge and skills as produced within and 'transferred' between discrete national spaces. A positive politics in relation to the transnational spatiality of professional knowledges and careers is to focus on developing mechanisms to 'maximise and disperse the benefits of such mobility' (Raghuram 2009: 31). Equally, a longer view of the history of transnational professional relationships promotes an acceptance of the possibility of inequality between professionals. This changes the focus of a networked concept like 'communities of practice' (Wenger 1998), for professional practice is not always necessarily good practice. In fact, professional communities can be hierarchical and exclusionary (Cowman and Jackson 2005; Phillips 2007), confirming each other's prejudices and complacencies, and with disciplinary mechanisms that aim as much to maintain privilege as to promote best practice (Fournier 1999, 2000). Work on mobile professionals, including development volunteers, will need to engage with the exclusions and marginalisations of transnational professionalism, as well as to celebrate its creativity.

Finally, this chapter, through a postcolonial analysis that is a determined effort to focus on the production of differentiation between morality and economy, has shown the particular work done by their differentiation in this context. In terms of development volunteering as 'gifting', a focus solely on (the limits of) altruism potentially obscures the monied privilege that enables and supports volunteering as one among many development practices that are tied in to a wider postcolonial geopolitics; in terms of development volunteering as transnational professionalism, a focus solely on economic mobility obscures the differential cultural value placed on the knowledge and skills of differently located professionals in a highly uneven world.

References

Abrahamsen, R. (2000) *Disciplining Democracy: Development discourse and good governance in Africa*, Zed Books, London.

Allsop, J., Bourgeault, I. L., Evetts, J., Le Bianic, T., Jones, K. and Wrede, S. (2009) 'Encountering globalization: Professional groups in an international context', *Current Sociology*, 57(4): 487–510.

Baaz, M. E. (2005) *The Paternalism of Partnership: A postcolonial reading of identity in development aid*, Zed Books, London.

Bailur, S. and Rana, H. (eds) (2003) *Volunteer Tales: Experiences of working abroad*, Lutterworth Press, Cambridge.

Beaverstock, J. V. (2002) 'Transnational elites in global cities: British expatriates in Singapore's financial district', *Geoforum*, 33: 525–38.

Beine, M., Docquier, F. and Rapoport, H. (2008) 'Brain drain and human capital formation in developing countries: Winners and losers', *The Economic Journal*, 118(April): 631–52.

Bhabha, H. (1994) *The Location of Culture*, Routledge, London.

Bose, A. and Burnell, P. (eds) (1991) *Britain's Overseas Aid since 1979: Between Idealism and Self-Interest*, Manchester University Press, Manchester.

Bourdieu, P. (1979) *La Distinction: Critique Sociale du Jugement*, Les Editions de Minuit, Paris.

Braithwaite, E. R. (1990) *To Sir With Love*, Jove, London.

Clark, P. F., Stewart, J. B. and Clark, D. A. (2006) 'The globalization of the labour market for health-care professionals', *International Labour Review*, 145(1/2): 37–64.

Conradson, D. and Milligan, C. (2006) 'Reflections on landscapes of voluntarism', in C. Milligan and D. Conradson (eds), *Landscapes of Voluntarism: New spaces of health, welfare and governance*, Policy Press, Bristol, pp. 285–95.

Cowman, K. and Jackson, L. A. (2005) 'Middle-class women and professional identity', *Women's History Review*, 14(2): 165–80.

Derrida, J. (1991) *Given Time: 1. Counterfeit money*, University of Chicago Press, Chicago.

Dirlik, A. (2002) 'Whither history? Encounters with historicism, postmodernism, postcolonialism', *Futures*, 34: 75–90.

Dominy, M. D. (2002) 'Hearing grass, thinking grass: Postcolonialism and ecology in Aotearoa-New Zealand', *Cultural Geographies*, 9: 15–34.

Duffield, M. (2006) 'Racism, migration and development: The foundations of planetary order', *Progress in Development Studies*, 6(1): 1–12.

Escobar, A. (1995) *Encountering Development: The making and unmaking of the Third World*, Princeton University Press, Princeton, NJ.

Fabian, J. (1983) *Time and the Other: How anthropology makes its object*, Columbia University Press, New York.

Forster, N. (1992) 'International managers and mobile families: The professional and personal dynamics of trans-national career pathing and job mobility in the 1990s', *The International Journal of Human Resource Management*, 3(3): 605–24.

Fournier, V. (1999) 'The appeal to "professionalism" as a disciplinary mechanism', *The Sociological Review*, 47(2): 280–307.

— (2000) 'Boundary work and the (un)making of the professions', in N. Malin (ed.), *Professionalism, Boundaries and the Workplace*, Routledge, London, pp. 67–87.

Fyfe, N. and Milligan, C. (2003) 'Out of the shadows: Exploring contemporary geographies of voluntarism', *Progress in Human Geography*, 27(4): 397–413.

Gibson, C. and Klocker, N. (2004) 'Academic publishing as "creative" industry, and recent discourses of "creative economies": Some critical reflections', *Area*, 36(4): 423–34.

Gogia, N. (2006) 'Unpacking corporeal mobilities: The global voyages of labour and leisure', *Environment and Planning A*, 38: 359–75.

Goodman, M. K. (2004) 'Reading fair trade: Political ecological imaginary and the moral economy of fair trade foods', *Political Geography*, 23: 891–915.

Goudge, P. (2003) *The Whiteness of Power: Racism in Third World development and aid*, Lawrence and Wishart, London.

Hagey, R., Choudhry, U., Guruge, S., Turrittin, J., Collins, E. and Lee, R. (2001) 'Immigrant nurses' experience of racism', *Journal of Nursing Scholarship*, 33(4): 389–94.

Hall, S. (1996) 'When was the post-colonial? Thinking at the limit', in I. Chambers and L. Curti (eds), *The Post-Colonial Question: Common skies, divided horizons*, Routledge, London, 242–60.

Haque, M. S. (2004) 'Governance based on partnership with NGOs: Implications for development and empowerment in rural Bangladesh,' *International Review of Administrative Sciences*, 70(2): 271–90.

Howes, A. (2001) 'Learning, difference and development: Volunteer placements in Indonesia', unpublished thesis, University of Manchester, Manchester.

Hudson, R. (2008) 'Cultural political economy meets global production networks: A productive meeting?', *Journal of Economic Geography*, 8: 421–40.

International Organization for Migration (2008) *World Migration 2008: Managing labour mobility in the evolving global economy*, available at: http://

www.iom.int/jahia/Jahia/op/edit/cache/offonce/pid/1674?entryId=20275 (accessed 18 May 2010).

Joy, E. (2004) *Green Oranges on Lion Mountain*, Eye Books, London.

Kamat, S. (2004) 'The privatisation of public interest: Theorizing NGO discourse in a neoliberal era', *Review of International Political Economy*, 11(1): 155–76.

Kapoor, I. (2008) *The Postcolonial Politics of Development*, Routledge, Abingdon.

Kendall, J. and Knapp, M. (1995) 'A loose and baggy monster: Boundaries, definitions and typologies', J. D. Smith, C. Rochester and R. Hedley (eds), *An Introduction to the Voluntary Sector*, Routledge, London, pp. 66–95.

Kerr, I. J. (2006) 'On the Move: Circulating labor in pre-colonial, colonial, and post-colonial India', *International Review of Social History*, 51(14): 85–109.

Kofman, E. and Raghuram, P. (2006) 'Gender and global labour migrations: Incorporating skilled workers', *Antipode*, 38(2): 282–303.

Lewis, D. (2008) 'Nongovernmentalism and the reorganization of public action', in S. Dar and B. Cooke (eds),*The New Development Management*, Zed Books, London, pp. 41–55.

MacKenzie, J. M. (ed.) (1986) *Imperialism and Popular Culture*, Manchester University Press, Manchester.

Mbembe, A. (2001) *On the Postcolony*, University of California Press, Berkeley.

McDowell, L. (2004) 'Masculinity, identity and labour market change: Some reflections on the implications of thinking relationally about difference and the politics of inclusion', *Geografiska Annaler*, 86(B): 45–56.

McEwan, C. (2009) *Postcolonialism and Development*, Routledge, London.

Morrison, P. S. (2001) 'Labour market geography in a global context: Notes on the New Zealand', Third Joint Conference of the Institute of Australian Geographers and the New Zealand Geographical Society, University of Otago, Dunedin.

Murphy, J. (2008) 'The rise of the global managers', in S. Dar and B. Cooke (eds), *The New Development Management*, Zed Books, London, pp. 8–40.

Noxolo, P. (2006) 'Claims: A postcolonial critique of "partnership" in Britain's development discourse', *Singapore Journal of Tropical Geography*, 27(3): 254–69.

— (2009) '"My paper, my paper": Reflections on the embodied production of postcolonial geographical responsibility in academic writing', *Geoforum*, 40(1): 55–65.

— (forthcoming) '"Purely not for me": Development volunteering and the postcolonial negotiation of British professional identity', *Transactions of the Institute of British Geographers*.

Nyamnjoh, F. B. and Page, B. (2002) '"Whiteman Kontri" and the enduring allure of modernity among Cameroonian youth', *African Affairs*, 101(4): 607–34.

Phillips, C. (2007) 'The re-emergence of the "Black Spectre": Minority professional associations in the post-Macpherson era', *Ethnic and Racial Studies*, 30(3): 375–96.

Pink, S. (1998) 'The white "helpers": Anthropologists, development workers and local imaginations', *Anthropology Today*, 14(6): 9–14.

Radcliffe, S. A. (2005) 'Development and geography: Towards a postcolonial development geography?', *Progress in Human Geography*, 29(3): 291–8.

Raghuram, P. (2009) 'Caring about "brain drain" migration in a postcolonial world', *Geoforum*, 40(1): 25–33.

Raghuram, P., Madge, C. and Noxolo P. (2009) 'Rethinking responsibility and care for a postcolonial world', *Geoforum*, 40(1): 5–13.

Ray, L. and Sayer, A. (eds) (1999) *Culture and Economy after the Cultural Turn*, Sage, London.

Riddell, R. (1987) *Foreign Aid Reconsidered*, The Johns Hopkins University, Baltimore, MD.

Rodney, W. (1972) *How Europe Underdeveloped Africa*, Heinemann, London.

Said, E. (1994) *Culture and Imperialism*, Vintage, London.

Sayer, A. (1999) 'Valuing culture and economy', in L. Ray and A. Sayer (eds), *Culture and Economy after the Cultural Turn*, Sage, London, pp. 53–76.

Sbert, J. M. (1992) 'Progress', in W. Sachs (ed.), *The Development Dictionary*, Zed Books, London, pp. 192–206.

Schultz, J. and Kelly, A. (2007) *Enriching Education: An exploration of the benefits and outcomes of a VSO placement for teachers and schools in the United Kingdom*, VSO, London.

Simpson, K. (2004) '"Doing development": The gap year, volunteer-tourists and a popular practice of development', *Journal of International Development*, 16: 681–92.

Slater, D. and Bell, M. (2002) 'Aid and the geopolitics of the post-colonial: Critical reflections on New Labour's overseas development strategy', *Development and Change*, 33(2): 335–60.

Solano, D. and Rafferty, A. M. (2007) 'Can lessons be learned from history? The origins of the British imperial nurse labour market: A discussion paper', *International Journal of Nursing Studies*, 44(6): 1055–63.

Spivak, G. (1992) 'The politics of translation', in M. Barrett and A. Phillips (eds), *Destabilizing Theory: Contemporary feminist debates*, Polity Press, Cambridge, pp. 177–200.

—— (1999) *A Critique of Postcolonial Reason: A history of the vanishing present*, Harvard University Press, Cambridge, MA.

Sylvester, C. (1999) 'Development studies and postcolonial studies: Disparate tales of the "Third World"', *Third World Quarterly*, 20(4): 703–21.

Thrift, N. (1998) 'The rise of soft capitalism', in A. Herod, G. O'Tuathail and S. M. Roberts (eds), *Unruly World? Globalisation, governance and geography*, Routledge, London, pp. 25–71.

Unterhalter, E., McDonald, J., Swain, J., Mitchell, P. and Young, M. (2002) *Time In: The impact of a VSO placement on professional development, commitment and retention of UK teachers*, Voluntary Service Overseas, London.

Vertovec, S. (2002) 'Transnational networks and skilled labour migration', *Ladenburger Diskurs 'MIgration' Gottlieb Daimler - und Karl Benz-Stiftung*, Ladenburg.

Voluntary Service Overseas (2008) *Annual Review 2007/08*, Voluntary Service Overseas, London.

Wallace, T. (2003) 'Trends in UK NGOs: A research note', *Development in Practice*, 13(5): 564–69.

Watts, M. (1995) '"A new deal in emotions": Theory and practice and the crisis of development', in J. Crush (ed.), *Power of Development*, Routledge, London, pp. 44–63.

Welbourne, P., Harrison, G. and Ford, D. (2007) 'Social work in the UK and the global labour market: Recruitment, practice and ethical considerations', *International Social Work*, 50(1): 27–40.

Wenger, E. (1998) *Communities of Practice: Learning, meaning, and identity*, Cambridge University Press, Cambridge.

Yeoh, B. S. A. and Willis, K. (2005) 'Singaporeans in China: Transnational women elites and the negotiation of gendered identities', *Geoforum*, 36: 211–22.

Notes on contributors

Dipesh Chakrabarty is the Lawrence A. Kimpton Distinguished Service Professor of History, South Asian Languages and Civilizations and the College at the University of Chicago. He is a founding member of the editorial collective of *Subaltern Studies*, a co-editor of *Critical Inquiry* and a founding editor of *Postcolonial Studies*. Major works include *Rethinking Working-Class History: Bengal 1890-1940* (1989, 2000), *Provincializing Europe: Postcolonial thought and historical difference* (2000; second edition 2007) and *Habitations of Modernity: Essays in the wake of subaltern studies* (2000).

Nitasha Kaul (www.nitashakaul.com) is an economist, novelist, theorist and poet. She is currently a Visiting Fellow at the Centre for the Study of Democracy, University of Westminster in London and an Associate Professor in Creative Writing at the Royal Thimphu College in Bhutan. She has a joint doctorate in Economics and Philosophy and was previously a tenured Lecturer in the Economics Department at the Bristol Business School. She speaks within and outside academia and has published books, essays in edited volumes, journal articles and newspaper comments on the diverse themes of identity, economics, critical social theory, democracy, technology, gender, civic governmentality and politics of knowledge production. Her first book was *Imagining Economics Otherwise* (2007). Her next book is a scholarly monograph on the history and politics of Bhutan. Her novel *Residue* was shortlisted for the Man Asian Literary Prize in 2009.

Wendy Larner is Professor of Human Geography and Sociology at the University of Bristol. Her research interests include globalisation, governance and gender. She publishes across the social sciences, and has recently co-edited *Calculating the Social: Standards and the reconfiguration of governing* and *The Point is to Change: Geographies of hope and survival in an age of crisis*. She is also editor of *Antipode* and associate editor of *Social Politics*.

Roger Lee is Professor Emeritus of Geography at Queen Mary University of London and an academician of the Academy of Social Sciences. Set within critical political economy, his work explores the inherency of the socialities of economic geographies and spatialities of economies. Roger is the author and co-editor of numerous books, including *Geographies of Economies*, the *Sage Handbook of Economic Geography* and the forthcoming *Sage Handbook of Human Geography*, and has published widely in a range of journals, including *Antipode*, *Environment and Planning A*, *Journal of Economic Geography*, *Progress in Human Geography*, *Society and Space* and *Transactions of the Institute of British Geographers*.

Hilary Lim is a Principal Lecturer in the School of Law at the University of East London. Her research interests include feminist legal studies, equity and trusts, land law, children's rights and Islamic law and land rights. Major projects include consultancy for UN HABITAT on Islamic Land Law (with Siraj Sait), leading to the publication of *Land, Law and Islam: Property and Human Rights in the Muslim World* (2006).

Cathy McIlwaine is a Reader in Human Geography at Queen Mary University of London. She has a background in research on poverty, gender and urban violence in the Global South, especially Latin America. More recently she has been working on international migration in the UK in relation to low-paid migrant workers and Latin American migrants in London. As well as a wide range of journal articles, she has published eight co-authored and co-edited books, including most recently *Global Cities at Work: New migrant divisions of labour* (2010) (with Jane Wills, Kavita Datta, Yara Evans, Joanna Herbert and Jon May) and *Geographies of Development in the 21st Century: An introduction to the Global South* (2009) (with Sylvia Chant).

Patricia Noxolo is a Lecturer in Human Geography at Sheffield University. Her work stands at the intersection between post-colonial, development and cultural geography, and deals specifically with the inter-relations between literature, voluntarism and global inequality. Relevant publications include 'Claims: A postcolonial geographical critique of partnership in development discourse', *Singapore Journal of Tropical Geography*, 27(3): 254–69.

Christine Sylvester is Professor of International Relations and Development at Lancaster University and the Kerstin Hesselgren Chair for Sweden (based in Global Studies, University of Gothenburg, 2010–11). She has recently been a visiting professor at the University of Connecticut and a Leverhulme Professor at SOAS. Her books reflect on feminist international relations, Zimbabwean political economy and, most recently, art museums in international relations. She has published development-related work in *Third World Quarterly*, *Alternatives*, *Geographical Journal*, *Journal of Modern African Studies*, *Journal of Southern African Studies*, *Signs* and *Differences*. She sits on the editorial boards of ten journals.

Eiman O. Zein-Elabdin is a Professor of Economics at Franklin and Marshall College, Lancaster, Pennsylvania. Her teaching and research areas include economic development, political economy of Africa, postcolonial studies, and gender and feminist econom-ics. She is the co-editor of *Postcolonialism Meets Economics* (2004).

Her most recent publication is 'Economics, postcolonial theory, and the problem of culture: Institutional analysis and hybridity', in the *Cambridge Journal of Economics* (November 2009). She is currently working on the book manuscript *Economics, Culture and Development*.

Index

About Zed Books

Zed Books is a critical and dynamic publisher, committed to increasing awareness of important international issues and to promoting diversity, alternative voices and progressive social change. We publish on politics, development, gender, the environment and economics for a global audience of students, academics, activists and general readers. Run as a co-operative, Zed Books aims to operate in an ethical and environmentally sustainable way.

Find out more at:
www.zedbooks.co.uk

For up-to-date news, articles, reviews and events information visit:
http://zed-books.blogspot.com

To subscribe to the monthly Zed Books e-newsletter, send an email headed 'subscribe' to **marketing@zedbooks.net**

We can also be found on **Facebook, ZNet, Twitter** and **Library Thing.**